Ukraine and Russia
People, Politics, Propaganda and Perspectives

EDITED BY

AGNIESZKA PIKULICKA-WILCZEWSKA
& RICHARD SAKWA

E-INTERNATIONAL RELATIONS PUBLISHING

E-International Relations
www.E-IR.info
Bristol, England
First published 2015
New version 2016

ISBN 978-1-910814-14-7 (Paperback)
ISBN 978-1-910814-00-0 (e-book)

This book is published under a Creative Commons CC BY-NC 4.0 license. You are free to:

- **Share** — copy and redistribute the material in any medium or format
- **Adapt** — remix, transform, and build upon the material

Under the following terms:

- **Attribution** — You must give appropriate credit, provide a link to the license, and indicate if changes were made. You may do so in any reasonable manner, but not in any way that suggests the licensor endorses you or your use.
- **NonCommercial** — You may not use the material for commercial purposes.

Any of the above conditions can be waived if you get permission. Please contact info@e-ir.info for any such enquiries.

Other than the license terms noted above, there are no restrictions placed on the use and dissemination of this book for student learning materials / scholarly use.

Copy Editing: Emma Kast, Corey McCabe and Michael Pang
Production: Michael Tang
Cover Image: Paganelj via Depositphotos

A catalogue record for this book is available from the British Library.

E-IR Edited Collections

Series Editors: Stephen McGlinchey, Marianna Karakoulaki and Agnieszka Pikulicka-Wilczewska

E-IR's Edited Collections are open access scholarly books presented in a format that preferences brevity and accessibility while retaining academic conventions. Each book is available in print and e-book, and is published under a Creative Commons CC BY-NC 4.0 license. As E-International Relations is committed to open access in the fullest sense, free electronic versions of all of our books, including this one, are available on the E-International Relations website.

Find out more at: http://www.e-ir.info/publications

Recent titles

Environment, Climate Change and International Relations

System, Society and the World: Exploring the English School of International Relations (Second Edition)

Restoring Indigenous Self-Determination (new version)

Nations under God: The Geopolitics of Faith in the Twenty-first Century

Popular Culture and World Politics: Theories, Methods, Pedagogies

Caliphates and Islamic Global Politics (new version)

About the E-International Relations website

E-International Relations (www.E-IR.info) is the world's leading open access website for students and scholars of international politics. E-IR's daily publications feature expert articles, blogs, reviews and interviews – as well as a range of high quality student contributions. The website was established in November 2007 and now reaches over 200,000 unique visitors a month. E-IR is run by a registered non-profit organisation based in Bristol, England and staffed with an all-volunteer team of students and scholars.

Abstract

The intense and dangerous turmoil provoked by the breakdown in Russo-Ukrainian relations has escalated into a crisis that now afflicts both European and global affairs. Since the beginning of the confrontation, a lot has been written about its root causes, the motivations of the main actors, and possible scenarios for the future. However, few have looked at what came to be called the 'Ukraine crisis' from the point of view of Russo-Ukrainian relations, and grasped the perspectives of various groups involved, as well as the discursive processes that have contributed to the developments in and interpretations of the conflict.

Agnieszka Pikulicka-Wilczewska is Blogs Editor with E-International Relations, and a member of the website's Editorial board. She holds a double MA degree in International Relations from the University of Kent and the Higher School of Economics in Moscow. Since 2012, she has worked in the human rights sector with various non-profit organisations in Ireland and the UK, focusing on areas such as ethnic minority and refugee rights and migration.

Richard Sakwa is Professor of Russian and European Politics at the University of Kent, an Associate Fellow of the Russia and Eurasia programme at Chatham House, and a Fellow of the Academy of Social Sciences. His main research interests are Russian domestic and international politics, European international relations and comparative democratisation. Recent books include *The Crisis of Russian Democracy: The Dual State, Factionalism, and the Medvedev Succession* (Cambridge University Press, 2011), *Putin and the Oligarch: The Khodorkovsky - Yukos Affair* (I. B. Tauris, 2014), *Putin Redux: Power and Contradiction in Contemporary Russia* (Routledge, 2014) and *Frontline Ukraine: Crisis in the Borderlands* (I. B. Tauris, 2015).

Note on transliteration

The editors of this collection decided to use the more common, anglicised, version of Russian and Ukrainian words in order to make the publication readable for a diverse audience.

Please note that in the case of the word 'Donbas/Donbass' we left the choice of transliteration to authors' discretion.

Contents

INTRODUCTION
    Agnieszka Pikulicka-Wilczewska   1

PART ONE - PEOPLE

1. ETHNIC AND SOCIAL COMPOSITION OF UKRAINE'S REGIONS AND VOTING PATTERNS
   David Marples   8

2. UNDERSTANDING THE OTHER UKRAINE: IDENTITY AND ALLEGIANCE IN RUSSOPHONE UKRAINE
   Nicolai N. Petro   18

3. BROTHERS GRIMM OR BROTHERS KARAMAZOV: THE MYTH AND THE REALITY OF HOW RUSSIANS AND UKRAINIANS VIEW THE OTHER
   Olga Onuch   35

4. ROOTS AND FEATURES OF MODERN UKRAINIAN NATIONAL IDENTITY AND NATIONALISM
   Denys Kiryukhin   57

5. EVERYDAY LIFE AFTER ANNEXATION: THE AUTONOMOUS REPUBLIC OF CRIMEA
   Greta Uehling   66

6. CRIMEA: PEOPLE AND TERRITORY BEFORE AND AFTER ANNEXATION
   Ivan Katchanovski   76

7. RUSSIANS IN UKRAINE: BEFORE AND AFTER EUROMAIDAN
   Mikhail Pogrebinskiy   85

PART TWO - POLITICS

8. UKRAINIAN POLITICS SINCE INDEPENDENCE
   Andrew Wilson   96

9. THE ORIGINS OF PEACE, NON-VIOLENCE, AND CONFLICT IN UKRAINE
   Taras Kuzio   103

10. THE UKRAINIAN CRISIS AND ITS IMPACT ON TRANSFORMING
    RUSSIAN NATIONALISM LANDSCAPE
    Marlene Laruelle   117

11. AN UNNECESSARY WAR: THE GEOPOLITICAL ROOTS OF THE
    UKRAINE CRISIS
    Peter Rutland   122

12. BETWEEN EAST AND WEST: NATO ENLARGEMENT AND THE
    GEOPOLITICS OF THE UKRAINE CRISIS
    Edward W. Walker   134

PART THREE - PROPAGANDA

13. 'HYBRID WAR' AND 'LITTLE GREEN MEN': HOW IT WORKS, AND HOW
    IT DOESN'T
    Mark Galeotti   149

14. PUTIN'S NATIONALISM PROBLEM
    Paul Chaisty & Stephen Whitefield   157

15. VLADIMIR PUTIN: MAKING OF THE NATIONAL HERO
    Elena Chebankova   164

16. DOMINANT NARRATIVES IN RUSSIAN POLITICAL AND MEDIA
    DISCOURSE DURING THE UKRAINE CRISIS
    Stephen Hutchings & Joanna Szostek   173

17. THE UKRAINE STORY IN WESTERN MEDIA
    Marta Dyczok   186

18. RUSSIA AS UKRAINE'S 'OTHER': IDENTITY AND GEOPOLITICS
    Mikhail A. Molchanov   195

PART FOUR - PERSPECTIVES

19. WESTERN ECONOMIC SANCTIONS AND RUSSIA'S PLACE IN THE
    GLOBAL ECONOMY
    Richard Connolly   212

20. DEMOCRACY AND GEOPOLITICS: UNDERSTANDING UKRAINE'S
    THREAT TO RUSSIA
    Paul D'Anieri   221

21. PERSPECTIVES FOR RUSSIA'S FUTURE: THE CASE FOR NARRATIVE
    ANALYSIS
    Edwin Bacon   229

22. DIVERSITY POLICY IN UKRAINE AND ITS NEIGHBOURS: RUNNING ON
    THE SPOT AGAIN?
    Alexander Osipov   238

CONCLUSION
    Richard Sakwa   247

CONTRIBUTORS   258

NOTE ON INDEXING   266

Introduction

AGNIESZKA PIKULICKA-WILCZEWSKA
E-INTERNATIONAL RELATIONS

When, on 21 November 2013, former Ukrainian President Victor Yanukovych decided to postpone the EU Association Agreement, few would have predicted that this, in consequence, would lead to a prolonged inter-communal conflict in Europe's borderland. What started as a peaceful demonstration of support for Ukraine's pro-European course by thousands of people in Maidan Square in Kiev has developed into a vicious confrontation dividing families, communities and the Ukrainian nation. According to the UN Refugee Agency (UNHCR), since the beginning of the conflict, over 500,000 people have left their homes looking for a safe place elsewhere in the country, and hundreds of thousands have fled from Ukraine, mainly to Russia. By February 2015, over 5,000 have been killed and well over 10,000 seriously injured in the conflict in the Donbass. The scale of the human tragedy is immense and, at the time of writing, the conflict is getting increasingly intense and militarised, despite the official ceasefire imposed as a result of the Minsk Accords of 5 September 2014 and various subsequent agreements.

Since the beginning of the confrontation, a lot has been written about its root causes, the motivations of the main actors, and possible scenarios for the future. However, in spite of the large number of analyses produced, few have looked at what came to be called the 'Ukraine crisis' from the point of view of Russo-Ukrainian relations, and grasped the perspectives of various groups involved, as well as the discursive processes that have contributed to the developments in and interpretations of the conflict. With this in mind, the editors of this volume have invited twenty-three world-leading academics, specialising in different areas related to Russia and Ukraine, to contribute to the following collection. The studies are divided into four sections: People, Politics, Propaganda, and Perspectives.

People

The first section looks at the social make-up of Ukraine and focuses on its ethnic and linguistic diversity, as well as relations between the different ethnic groups. Due to the fact that the Ukrainian conflict has developed, at least partly, as a consequence of existing divisions that have exacerbated the differences between various groups, this section provides the basis for analysis of the conflict and helps to make sense of the underlying structure of the Ukrainian society. The section opens with an analysis by David Marples, which focuses on the ethnic and social composition of Ukraine's regions and the existing voting patterns. He argues that while regional voting is the most characteristic feature of Ukrainian elections, there are a number of additional factors that may affect voting preferences, such as the social position of the voter or initiatives of the candidate.

The second chapter, by Nicolai Petro, titled 'Understanding the Other Ukraine: Identity and Allegiance in Russophone Ukraine,' analyses the political and cultural differences of traditionally Russophone regions of southern and eastern parts of the country. Petro argues that, in the Russophone areas, political conflict arises when the legitimacy of Russian culture in Ukraine is challenged.

The third chapter, by Olga Onuch, presents the reader with an analysis of how Russians and Ukrainians view each other, the relations between the two countries, and the ongoing conflict. Her research suggests that Ukrainians and Russians do not generally view each other in a hostile manner: each side believes there should be friendly relations between the two countries; however, she notes that each side views the current relations between the two in a different way.

This is followed by Denys Kiryukhin, who concentrates on the roots and features of modern Ukrainian national consciousness, nationalism and their historical development. He argues that there have been three main narratives which have shaped the modern Ukrainian national discourse, which can be summarised, following Patrick Colm Hogan, as reflective of heroism, sacrifice, and romanticism.

Subsequently, Greta Uehling's chapter titled 'Everyday Life after Annexation: The Autonomous Republic of Crimea' presents the situation in the area annexed by Russia, focusing on the experience of Crimean Tatars (the indigenous ethnic group of the peninsula). It is fear and anxiety, she argues, that have altered the ability of ordinary citizens to act, while assaults on freedom have become an everyday form of social control.

Ivan Katchanovsky then analyses the history of Crimea and its turbulent present, the periods before and after the secession, as well as the possible future developments in the area. He concludes that while Crimea, in its current status, is likely to remain a point of conflict between Ukraine and Russia, and between the West and Russia, the return of the territory to the Ukrainian state is virtually impossible.

The last chapter of this section, by Mikhail Pogrebinskiy, concentrates on the experience of Russians in Ukraine historically and after the 2013 Euromaidan revolution. He argues that the crisis has reinforced negative attitudes to, and marginalisation of, Russians and the Russian-speaking population of Ukraine.

Politics

The second section focuses on the political processes in Ukraine, Russia, and the world that have preceded the crisis, as well as the developments that have contributed to or, arguably, caused the current conflict. In the opening chapter of this section, Andrew Wilson evaluates the state of Ukrainian politics since the collapse of the Soviet Union and the subsequent emergence of Ukraine as an independent entity. He explains the processes of post-Soviet elite formation, the rules and pathologies of the system, and the role of civil society in the 2013 revolution. Ukrainian politics will remain a struggle between old- and new-style politics, he concludes, although it remains to be seen how much of the old informal politics has changed.

This is followed by a piece titled 'The Origins of Peace, Non-Violence and Conflict in Ukraine' by Taras Kuzio that examines why, after two decades of peace, a violent conflict broke out on Ukrainian territory. He highlights four main factors that have contributed to the crisis: the rise of authoritarian and neo-Soviet political forces, the pattern of western-supported popular protests, NATO and EU enlargement, as well as nationalism and revisionism of Russian foreign policy.

In the third article of the section, Marlene Laruelle discusses how the Ukraine crisis has affected the different Russian nationalist movements, explaining the popular narratives of Eurasianism and the *Russkiy Mir*, then outlining the contradictions between the two paradigms. She claims that the Ukraine crisis has fragmented the 'national-democrat' scene and has strengthened aspirations for the recreation of Soviet power - Russia's imperial mission - and the Eurasian Union project.

The final two chapters of the section, by Peter Rutland and Edward W. Walker, look at the geopolitical roots of the crisis and the international developments since the collapse of the Soviet Union that have led to the current conflict. Rutland argues that it was Ukraine's geopolitical position, and the interventions of competing outside powers pursuing their own self-interest, which led to the continuing civil war in Ukraine. Walker, on the other hand, concludes that it was the post-Cold War security architecture and the enlargement of NATO that have played the main role in creating the conditions for and exacerbating the crisis.

Propaganda

The third section seeks to analyse the different types and sources of propaganda that have been in play during the crisis - both state and media generated. It explains the processes behind the formation of different interpretations of the events and presents what the contributors believe to be the dominant views and opinions of the public in Russia, Ukraine, and the West. First, Mark Galeotti reviews the tactics used by Russia in the Ukraine crisis, such as the 'hybrid war,' the roles the 'little green men,' the *Spetsnaz* and the intelligence community have played in operations in both Crimea and the Donbas. While Russia has so far won the 'military war' to create *Novorossiya* and the 'intelligence war' to support combat operations, Galeotti argues it has not achieved its desired aims and thus is losing the 'political war.'

Following this, Paul Chaisty and Stephen Whitefield, in their chapter titled 'Putin's Nationalism Problem,' examine the new official narratives of Vladimir Putin's leadership, the problems associated with them, and how the Ukraine crisis has influenced the support for Putin's rule. They maintain that although the Ukraine crisis has contributed to the increase of support, the Kremlin will most likely fail to satisfy the aspirations of such a diverse group of moderate patriots and radical nationalists.

The following chapter, by Elena Chebankova, seeks to understand the roots of Putin's popularity by analysing the political, structural, and discursive spheres of Russian political life. The secret of Putin's success, she argues, is his ability to recreate a narrative of the Russian structure in the new form and, in the context of the Ukraine crisis, embrace the long-established search for self-rediscovery of Russian society.

The fourth analysis, by Stephen Hutchings and Joanna Szostek, concentrates on the main media and political narratives in Russia during the Ukraine crisis. They contend that the Russian media response to the crisis cannot be attributed to 'cynical eclecticism' alone, in the sense of exploiting whichever currents serve the needs. While they agree that such an instrumental approach has been present, the efforts to present dominant narratives in a form of a coherent worldview have also been apparent.

In the next chapter, Marta Dyczok explores how the conflict has been portrayed by the main western media outlets and presents the dominant competing narratives. She concludes that while it is difficult to determine what impact international reporting on the crisis has had on public opinion worldwide, information has been used as a weapon, and thus the rules of objective reporting have worked against the goal of providing accurate coverage.

Finally, Mikhail Molchanov focuses on the representation of Russia, Russians, and the crisis in the Ukrainian political and media discourse and the historical process of 'othering.' He maintains that in order to heal the ethno-regional split in Ukraine, the authorities in Kiev need to change their attitude towards Russia and the Russians.

Perspectives

This final section concentrates on the possible future developments related to the various aspects of the conflict. In the first chapter, Richard Connolly focuses on the economic side of the crisis and seeks to answer the question of how the economic sanctions imposed on Russia by the West may affect the country's place in the global economy. He argues that by using the narrative of an external threat, the Russian leadership seeks to justify centralisation of political economy, which involves the suppression of economic competition, state control over strategic sectors of the economy (in particular finance, energy and defence), and the deterioration of the business environment in Russia.

The second article, by Paul D'Anieri, focuses on the dominant views on the motivations of Russia's actions in Ukraine, the sources of Putin's legitimacy, and how the current crisis has threatened it. He concludes that for Russia to feel secure with regards to Ukraine, Ukraine needs to be geopolitically neutralised, and if neutralisation is not a viable strategy, then renewed stability would depend either on the West accepting Russian control of Ukraine or on Russia – the loss of Ukraine.

Subsequently, Edwin Bacon makes a case for narrative analysis as the most adequate tool to predict developments in international politics, and explains its importance in the development of future scenarios for Russia and the world following the Ukraine crisis. He claims that in relation to Russia, the scenario of authoritarian stability and global power alongside economic decline and consumer dissatisfaction is possibly a pertinent one.

The penultimate chapter, by Alexander Osipov, focuses on the analysis of the state of diversity policies in Ukraine and its neighbours, including the Russian Federation, and the possible future developments in this area. He claims that diversity policy in Ukraine and Russia – but also in Moldova and Belarus – has similar features and focuses on recreating a narrative of multi-ethnicity, but with an ethnic or cultural core, and thus a hierarchy of ethnicities and languages.

Finally, Richard Sakwa, in the concluding chapter of the volume, comes back to the systemic root causes of the conflict and argues that the confrontation in Europe's borderland is a result of three separate crises: the turbulence in the system of European security, the internal conflict in Ukraine, and the crisis of the Russian developmental model.

The authors of this volume present different and often contradictory opinions, and therefore the views expressed in each of the chapters should be attributed to their authors only. They each present a facet of the intense and dangerous turmoil provoked by the breakdown in Russo-Ukrainian relations, and thus we hope will contribute to a deeper understanding of a crisis that now afflicts both European and global affairs.

Part One

PEOPLE

1

Ethnic and Social Composition of Ukraine's Regions and Voting Patterns

DAVID MARPLES
UNIVERSITY OF ALBERTA

This article looks at the ethnic and social makeup of Ukrainian regions and its impact on voting patterns over the past two decades. While sceptical of a simplistic division of the country through spoken language and ethnic affiliation, it maintains that there are particular patterns of voting that have been repeated in each presidential and parliamentary election, and that regional voting is the most characteristic feature of Ukrainian elections. At the same time, there are a number of other factors that may affect voting that are not dealt with here, such as the social and economic initiatives of the candidate or party, the social position of the voter, fluctuations in the standard of living, and incentives to vote a particular way (Kulyk, 2011; Colton, 2011).

Upon gaining its independence in 1991, Ukraine had several distinct regions and a number of significant ethnic minorities, most prominent of which were Russians. The only part of Ukraine with a Russian majority was the Autonomous Republic of Crimea, but Russians comprised significant communities in the far eastern oblasts of Donetsk and Luhansk, as well as in Dnipropetrovsk, Odessa, Kharkiv, and others. The far western region of Transcarpathia has a significant Hungarian population, and there are numerous smaller nationalities that have had homes in Ukraine for many generations, such as Poles, Belarusians, and Jews, as well as Bulgarians in the Odessa Oblast in the South.

One difficulty about making any sweeping assertions about the composition of the population is the lack of censuses in the independence period. To date, there has been a single census in 2001 (the first since 1989), and an anticipated new census in 2010 has been postponed until 2016. That census may also be in doubt, given enforced territorial changes in Ukraine, with the Russian annexation of Crimea, and separatist movements in Donetsk and Luhansk, with the establishment there of so-called People's Republics supported by the Russian Federation. The 2001 census indicated mainly the consolidation and growth of the Ukrainian population (77.8%, up from 72.7% in 1989), partly through assimilation and changes in self-identity, and partly through migration, of Russians in particular. The Russian population, correspondingly, declined from 22.1% to 17.3% (State Statistics Committee of Ukraine, 2001).[1]

There is a marked difference, however, between ethnic Russians and Russian-speakers, and the latter predominate in the East and South, and maintain a significant presence in all parts of Ukraine other than the far western regions. In 2006-07, research conducted by the Razumkov Center revealed that the percentage of Ukrainians who considered Russian to be their first language was 25.7%, and that 52% of the population considered Ukrainian to be their native language (Lenta.ru, 2007). A more recent study suggests that about 27.5 million people 'actively' use the Russian language at work and about 37 million (or 80% of the population) has fluency in it. Ten years earlier, the figure had been 42 million (Aref'ev, 2013).

Keith Darden has noted a tendency in Ukrainian elections to continue habits that were familiar in pre-Soviet times. Thus, the former Austrian-Polish territories of Ukraine behave quite differently: supporting pro-Western candidates, adopting strong pro-European Union positions, and fearing Russian influence above all else (Darden, 2013). These regions are Ukrainian-speaking, and have consistently supported pro-Western candidates in presidential elections: Leonid Kravchuk rather than Leonid Kuchma in 1994; but Kuchma rather than the Communist candidate Petro Symonenko in 1999; Yushchenko in 2004; and Tymoshenko in 2010. The main difference between the pre-Soviet period and today is that ethnic Ukrainians now comprise a majority in urban centres, whereas in the past they were rural, marginalised, and at times disaffected. Many Western Ukrainian cities have adopted a strong nationalistic position, and Western Ukrainians played a prominent role in the 2013-14 protests known as the 'Euromaidan' (Nuzhdin et al., 2013).

---

[1] Incidentally, the former Prime Minister, Nikolay Azarov, claimed in that there were over 20 million Russians in Ukraine! See: http://lb.ua/news/2012/06/26/158078_azarov_naschital_ukraine_20_mln.html

Western Ukraine remains the most rural region of Ukraine. Yet its history is the most turbulent and controversial. The integral nationalism of the 1930s, which saw the rise of the Organisation of Ukrainian Nationalists (OUN), with its dictum of 'Ukraine for Ukrainians,' and the formation of the Ukrainian Insurgent Army (UPA) during the war (traditionally declared to have taken place in October 1942, but in reality in the spring of 1943), has created many of the legends of current historical memory: a quest for independence and freedom from the Russian-led Soviet Union, and from the incursive Russian Federation today. The legacy of these formations is controversial. They are accused not only of being anti-Soviet, but pro-Nazi and anti-Semitic (Katchanovsky, 2010). Though right-wing nationalism has been notably unsuccessful in terms of winning seats in Parliament, many observers perceive significant influence of right extremism during Euromaidan, and in the current war in the eastern regions (Cohen, 2014).

Western Ukraine forms one part of an electoral magnet that has pulled the country in two different directions simultaneously. The other is eastern Ukraine, but more specifically the two far eastern oblasts of Donetsk and Luhansk. Before discussing the characteristics of this region, it should be noted that the term 'eastern Ukraine' was formerly much broader than it appears today. The area was the heartland of industrial development in the Russian Empire, and its traditions were transferred to the Soviet Union during the crucial phase of its industrial development. It embraced Stakhanovism in its coal mines in the mid-1930s – a work ethic largely based on 'shock troops' and over-fulfilment of state plans by artificial means. It was also the very centre of the Soviet Communist Party. Former leader Nikita Khrushchev (1964-71) made his career in the Donbas, nurtured by his mentor, the Stalinist henchman Lazar Kaganovich. Leonid Brezhnev (Soviet leader 1964-82) was born in Dniprodzherzhinsk, a city named after the first leader of the Soviet secret police (the Cheka), Feliks Dzerzhinsky.

Not surprisingly, therefore, between 1991 and 1999, the Communist Party of Ukraine remained the most powerful force in the region. But after independence, there was a growing entrepreneurial class that arose from the ashes of Communism, using links to the former Communist leadership to establish private businesses. Bitter competition took place between elites of the cities of Donetsk and Dnipropetrovsk. In the mid-1990s, the latter city was in the ascendancy: Kuchma, the president, had been manager of the rocket-manufacturing plant at Yuzhmash in the region; Pavlo Lazarenko, Prime Minister in 1996-97, had headed the 'agro-industrial complex' of Dnipropetrovsk in the early 1990s, and his Deputy Prime Minister, Yulia Tymoshenko, was born in the city. The current governor of Dnipropetrovsk, the billionaire Ihor Kolomoisky, was originally a supporter of Tymoshenko and her Tymoshenko Bloc in parliament. Today, however, Dnipropetrovsk under

Kolomoisky's leadership has taken a strong pro-Ukrainian and pro-Western stance, separating it firmly from the staunchly pro-Russian cities of Donetsk and Luhansk.[2]

Donetsk and its region, on the other hand, have been the centre of the rise of the Regions Party, financed by the oligarch Rinat Akhmetov and personalised by the figure of Viktor Yanukovych, the central figure in the disputed election that brought about the Orange Revolution and the eventual victory of Viktor Yushchenko. The party's tentacles extended well beyond Donetsk, but the city remained its central location, and the Yanukovych Cabinet formed in 2010 was dominated by Donetsk politicians. The Party of Regions expanded through financial support of businessmen who exploited the country's assets, manipulated the legal system, controlled banks and businesses, and used parliament as a forum to control the rest of the country (Kuzio, 2015; Riabchuk, 2012). The year 2010 represented the peak of the Regions' power. The party's rise appeared mercurial, but it was facilitated by disillusionment with Yushchenko's presidency that appeared initially to be about to set Ukraine on a new Western-oriented journey.

Between these two magnets of the West and 'Far East,' the rest of Ukraine has not exhibited particularly strong political directions. In 1999, most voters perceived Kuchma as the most viable alternative, although the Communist Symonenko won a respectable 37.8% of the votes. In 2004, in the initial election runoff of the two leading candidates on 21 November, Ukraine was divided almost equally between supporters of Yushchenko and Yanukovych (voting manipulations aside). The latter had been endorsed by Vladimir Putin and his election posters appeared in Moscow, as well as Ukraine. The Orange Revolution represented a protest against electoral manipulations and a movement towards Europe. Yet the most notable feature of the second runoff on 26 December 2004 was the lack of districts in which voting was relatively even, despite the fact that Yushchenko won overall with 52%, compared to his rival's 44% (Romanyuk et al., 2010). The points are worth elaborating.

In the twenty-seven regions of Ukraine (the cities of Sevastopol and Kiev each constituted one region), in only one – Kherson – was the voting close (43.4% for Yushchenko and 51.3% for Yanukovych). Elsewhere, voters opted for one candidate or the other by large margins, and particularly in the two

---

[2] On the other hand, Kolomoisky remains a controversial figure, and there are reports that a confrontation between him and Poroshenko is distinctly possible in the near future. See: http://rian.com.ua/analytics/20141129/360126913.html (Accessed: January 11, 2015).

polarised regions noted above: Western Ukrainians (Galicia and Volhynia) voted over 90% for Yushchenko; the far east over 90% for Yanukovych; Crimea 81.4% for Yanukovych, and Sevastopol 88.8%. The election demonstrated a fatal divide in Ukrainian society, a lack of middle ground, and heralded the uncertain developments of the future. One cannot examine the 2010 election in the same way because of the deep divisions within the pro-Western, pro-European camp: former president Yushchenko thus campaigned against his former Prime Minister Tymoshenko.

In 2014, on the other hand, electoral politics were simplified and altered fundamentally by the events of the Euromaidan. Two elections were held in this year: the May 25 presidential elections and the October 26 parliamentary elections. Both were affected by protests and the continuing conflict. Crimea did not participate and only about 20% of voters in Donetsk and Luhansk could take part because of restrictions imposed by separatist leaders. The former president, Yanukovych, had been expelled from the ranks of Regions, which was represented by the ineffectual Mykhailo Dobkin, and Symonenko once again headed the Communists. Petro Poroshenko, a compromise candidate for the pro-Euromaidan factions, won convincingly with 54% of votes in the first round. His nearest challenger was Yulia Tymoshenko, recently released from prison, with 12%. Dobkin received just over 3%; Symonenko 1.5%. Their votes, on the other hand, were well above those of far right candidates Oleh Tyahnybok (Svoboda) and Dmytro Yarosh (Right Sector) at 1.16% and 0.7%, respectively (Centralna Vyborcha Komisija, 2014).

The same pattern continued in the parliamentary elections, except that the Petro Poroshenko Bloc and the People's Front, the parties led by the President and Prime Minister (Arsenii Yatsenyuk), dominated the vote almost equally. Together with the third-placed party – the Self-Reliance group, led by former Lviv mayor Andrii Sadovyi – they controlled 244 seats out of 450 in the assembly. The Opposition Bloc, led by Yurii Boyko, won 29 seats with a popular vote of less than 1.5 million (Tvi.ua, 2014). Boyko is a native of Horlivka, one of the Donetsk regional mining towns at the very centre of the conflict in the East. The elections marked the formation of a new pro-Western coalition in Ukraine, indicating that the Donbas has ceased to play a pivotal role in Ukraine, for the first time in the history of the independent state. Moreover, of all the regions of Ukraine, it has suffered the most, economically and socially, as a result of the war and conflicts on its territory. A mass exodus of population occurred in the second half of 2014, with over 1 million people choosing or forced to migrate to other regions, mostly to the Russian Federation, though there has been a population decline since 2004 (Ridna Kraina, 2014; Sakwa, 2015).

There are a number of different ways to interpret the recent voting habits in Ukraine. On the one hand – the view adopted by many Western analysts – they appear to give Ukraine a green light to sever all ties with the Soviet period and start a new pro-Western and pro-democratic path that will take it, irrevocably, out of the Russian orbit (RRI, 2014). The main parties in the parliament may disagree on the attitude to be adopted towards the larger neighbour: whether one of compromise, as suggested by Poroshenko, or of confrontation, the attitude manifested during the elections last October by Yatsenyuk. There is little disagreement, however, on overall policy, which to some extent has been catalysed by the hostile attitude of Moscow, though Russian president Vladimir Putin did recognise the legitimacy of the presidential elections and the ascendancy of Poroshenko.

A second way to view events, and one adopted by a minority of Western analysts as well as Russia and its spokespersons, is that Ukraine experienced a right-wing coup from February 2014 that removed a legally elected president and established a new regime – scornfully described as a 'junta' – and that Western agencies funded these events as a means to remove Ukraine from all Russian influence.[3] Further, there have been allegations that the 'coup' resulted in a general assault on Russian-language speakers in Ukraine, necessitating the Russian annexation of Crimea, which in any case simply righted a historical wrong perpetrated by the Soviet leadership in 1954. Russia has not recognised the new regimes in the east of Ukraine (DNR and LNR), but it has supported them with weapons and personnel, and essentially prevented their destruction, despite a variety of rifts within the respective leaderships and a manifest lack of policies and infrastructure. In this way, Russia is responding to Western aggression.

A third interpretation may be closer to the truth than either of the first two. It is that, in 1991, the issue of state formation had hardly been broached, and that Ukraine made progress in fits and starts, but without a clear conception of the nation, its past, and where it lay in the geopolitical space between Russia and the West. That space became more contested after the eastward expansion of the EU in 2004, which brought former Communist states and former Soviet republics into that entity for the first time. Ukraine at that time became the new frontier. The Russian side had attempted to create several integrationist formations and the Russian president took an active interest in Ukrainian elections. The differences became particularly acute under Yushchenko because of his overtly pro-Western stance, and also because of his efforts to

---

[3] The most obvious example here is the RT network, which has cited, inter alia, the comments of ousted president Yanukovych. See: http://rt.com/news/yanukovich-statement-ukraine-crimea-074/ (Accessed: January 11, 2015).

build a new nation on the exploits of anti-Soviet heroes such as OUN leader Stepan Bandera and UPA leader Roman Shukhevych, whom he made 'heroes of Ukraine' (Snyder, 2010).

For Russia, on the other hand, the danger appeared to be minimal for most of the post-Soviet period. Neither Kravchuk nor Kuchma could be described as anti-Russian; both presidents were primarily concerned with domestic issues and improving the economy. Though Yushchenko and the colour revolution caused great concern in the Kremlin, the victory of Yanukovych, an old ally, in the 2010 presidential elections brought hope that Ukraine might finally be a partner, alongside Russia, Belarus, and Kazakhstan, in the new Customs Union. Corruption in Ukraine was among the highest of any country in Europe, thus destabilising the country, and Ukraine was dependent on Russia for imports of oil and gas. Russia could anticipate the monopolisation of power by Yanukovych for years to come, somewhat along the lines of Aleksander Lukashenko in Belarus – at times unpredictable, but clearly an ally. That confidence was dispelled by the events that followed a meeting between Putin and Yanukovych in Moscow just prior to the EU summit in Vilnius in November 2013.

The elections of 2014 affirmed the success of Euromaidan, but also weakened Ukraine in a number of ways. They demonstrated that the multi-vectored foreign policy of Kuchma is no longer feasible. Ukraine has chosen its direction by removing its far eastern regions from the centre of power. Even without Russian intrusions, the Donbas would have been disaffected. From almost complete control over Ukraine, it is now isolated and alienated. And it is impossible to return to the past. Crimea may be lost for many years – no Ukrainian leader has come up with a strategy to facilitate its return. Thus, the elections mark the emergence of Ukraine as a truncated state, without key industrial regions. And while Euromaidan was popular among about half of the population, and especially those under 50, it has rendered the future more uncertain time than any before in the 23 years of the independent state. Moreover, the turnout in October 2014 was the lowest of any recent election at 52%, and an estimated 50% of those who had voted formerly for the Party of Regions or the Communist parties did not take part (The Economist, 2014).

Is Ukraine more united today than in the past? It is difficult to answer definitively. One can suggest that voters are prepared to give President Poroshenko an opportunity to lead the country. They are concerned about the conflict, but are preoccupied even more with the economic situation, job security, and standards of living (Esipova and Ray, 2014). The plethora of political parties has been a feature of Ukrainian elections since 1991. Other than the Party of Regions and formerly the Communists, none has wielded massive political or economic influence. Yatsenyuk's Popular Front, for example, which gained the highest overall percentage of votes in 2014, was a completely new formation, as was, for that matter, the Petro Poroshenko Bloc (Tvi.ua, 2014). Voters in Ukraine do not have firm alliances or party identities. They are concerned more with individual leaders and the list of candidates that is supplied by each party prior to each election. There has also been uncertainty concerning the division of powers between the president and the parliament, though most presidents – and particularly Yanukovych – easily circumvented constitutional issues to wield more power. Today, as in Russia, it is the president's own party that has most seats in Parliament, despite finishing only second in terms of percentages of the vote.

The future of Ukraine remains uncertain because of the precarious state of the economy and the relative fragility of the new ruling coalition. Control over elections by a corrupt leader and his minions ended violently and contentiously. Ukraine appears to have embraced democracy, however, and its elections have always been more open and honest than those of its former Soviet neighbours, like Belarus and Russia. The most pro-Russian regions have either been added to Russia or else remain in conflict. The Soviet legacy that affected and influenced earlier elections is now, like the statues of Lenin, consigned to memory, but the new leaders will need to make broader appeals to the electorate than has been the case hitherto. Ultimately, even without the full return of the Donbas to Ukraine, the electorate is centrist rather than rightist; and prefers compromise to confrontation. It remains fearful, justifiably, of further Russian encroachment, but is wary of the impact of closer association with an EU that appears, likewise, uncertain whether to fully embrace its new partner.

References

Aref'ev, A.L. (2013) 'Russliy yazyk v Ukrainskoy respublike,' *Demoskop Weekly*, 14-31 October. Available at: http://demoscope.ru/weekly/2013/0571/analit03.php (Accessed: 11 January 2015).

Centralna Vyborcha Komisija (2014) *Pozacherhovi Vybory Prezydenta Ukrainy 25 travnya 2014 roku*. Available at: http://www.cvk.gov.ua/info/protokol_cvk_25052014.pdf (Accessed: 18 January 2015).

Cohen, S. F. (2014) 'The Silence of American Hawks About Kiev's Atrocities,' *The Nation*, 7 and 17 July. Available at: http://www.thenation.com/article/180466/silence-american-hawks-about-kievs-atrocities# (Accessed: 18 January 2015).

Colton, T. J. (2011) 'An Aligning Election and the Ukrainian Political Community,' *East European Politics and Society*, 25(1), pp. 4-27.

Darden, K. (2013) 'Colonial Legacies, Party Machines and Enduring Regional Voting Patterns,' Paper prepared for the Post-Communist Workshop, The George Washington University, Washington D.C., 7 October.

Esipova, N. and Julie R. (2014) 'Ukrainians Ratings of Their Lives, Country, Hit New Low,' *Gallup,* 19 December. Available at: http://www.gallup.com/poll/180269/ukrainians-ratings-lives-country-hit-new-low.aspx (Accessed: 18 January 2015).

Katchanovski, I. (2010) 'Terrorists or National Heroes? Politics of the OUN and UPA in Ukraine,' Paper prepared for presentation at the Annual Conference of the Canadian Political Science Association, 1-3 June. Available at: http://www.cpsa-acsp.ca/papers-2010/katchanovski.pdf (Accessed: January 12 2015).

Kulyk, V. (2011) 'Language Identity, Linguistic Diversity, and Political Cleavages: Evidence from Ukraine,' *Nations and Nationalism*, 17(3), pp. 627-648.

Kuzio, T. (2015 forthcoming) 'Vigilantes, Organized Crime, and Russian and Eurasian Nationalisms: The Case of Ukraine,' in Marples D.R. and Mills F.V (eds) *Ukraine's Euromaidan: Analyses of a Civil Revolution*. Stuttgart: Ibidem-Verlag, pp. 57-76.

Lenta.ru (2007) 'Kolichestvo russkojazychnyh Ukrain ukraincev za poslednij god sokratilos.' Available at: http://lenta.ru/news/2007/12/17/language (Accessed: 11 January 2015).

Nuzhdin, S., Yetenko, M. and Halenda I. (2013) 'Evromaidan-2013: khto ta za shchto protestuvav?' *Academia.edu,* Available at: https://www.academia.edu/8955785/ЄВРОМАЙДАН-2013_хто_та_за_що_протестував (Accessed: 11 January 2015)

Radio România Internațional (2014) 'Ukraine Chooses Democracy,' 29 October. Available at: http://www.rri.ro/en_gb/ukraine_chooses_democracy-24358 (Accessed: 11 January 2015).

Riabchuk, M. (2012) *Gleichschaltung: Authoritarian Consolidation in Ukraine.* Kiev: K.I.S.

Ridna kraina (2014) 'Viina na Skhodi mozhe dokorinno zminyty demohrafichnu kartu Ukrainy,' 25 June. Available at: http://ridna.ua/2014/06/vijna-na-shodi-mozhe-dokorinno-zminyty-demohrafichnu-kartu-ukrajiny/ (Accessed: 18 January 2015).

Romanyuk, A.S., Skochylyas, L.S., et al. (2010) 'Elektoral'na karta L'vivshchyny u mizhrehional'nomu zrizi.' L'viv, TsPD. Available at: http://www.lnu.edu.ua/faculty/Phil/El_karta_knyzka/el_hystory_ukraine-2004.htm (Accessed: 18 January 2015).

Sakwa, R. (2015) 'Ukraine's forgotten city destroyed by war,' *The Guardian*, 7 January.

Snyder, T. (2010) 'A Fascist Hero in Democratic Kiev,' *The New York Review of Books*, 24 February. Available at: http://www.nybooks.com/blogs/nyrblog/2010/feb/24/a-fascist-hero-in-democratic-kiev/ (Accessed: 18 January 2015).

State Statistics Committee of Ukraine (2001) *National Composition of Population.* Kyiv. Available at: http://2001.ukrcensus.gov.ua/eng/results/general/nationality/ (Accessed 11 January 2015).

The Economist (2014) 'Good voters, not such good guys,' *The Economist,* 1 November. Available at: http://www.economist.com/news/europe/21629375-poll-results-were-promising-future-ukraine-dauntingly-difficult-good-voters (Accessed: 18 January 2015).

Tvi.ua (2014) 'Vybory do Rady-2014: povni spysyky kandidativ vid usikh partii,' 30 September 2014. Available at: http://tvi.ua/new/2014/09/30/vybory_do_rady_2014_povni_spysky_kandydativ_vid_vsikh_partiy (Accessed: 18 January 2015).

2

Understanding the Other Ukraine: Identity and Allegiance in Russophone Ukraine

NICOLAI N. PETRO
UNIVERSITY OF RHODE ISLAND

The cultural and political differences besetting Ukraine are the product of very different patterns of regional settlement. Among these, the settlement of eastern and southern Ukraine stands out, for in these traditionally Russophone regions, political conflict has arisen whenever the legitimacy of Russian culture in Ukraine has been challenged.

A Very Brief History of Russian Settlement

After the destruction of Kiev by Batu Khan in 1240, the land 'beyond the rapids' [za porog] of the Dnieper River became a no man's land disputed by the Kingdom of Muscovy, the Tatar Khanate, and the Polish-Lithuanian Kingdom. It is in this region (shown in Figure 1 in yellow) that the political life of the Ukrainian people begins, as the settlers known to history as Cossacks sought to preserve their independence, while defending their traditional Orthodox Christian faith.

One of the earliest distinctions that arose among them is the geographic distinction between those who settled west of the Dnieper River, known as the Right Bank as the river flows, and those who settled east of the river, known as the Left Bank.

Figure 1: Simplified historical map of Ukrainian borders: 1654-2014.[4]

The Left Bank, which includes the current regions of Crimea, Dnipropetrovsk, Donetsk, Kharkov, Kherson, Lugansk, Odessa, Nikolayevsk, and Zaporozhye, forms a relatively compact ethnic and cultural community that is distinguished by the strong influence of Russian culture, even where the majority of the population defines itself as Ukrainian.

In the eastern regions that supported Viktor Yanukovych in the 2004 elections, for example, the percentage of the population that considered itself 'Russian' was only 34.5 percent, but the percentage of those who considered themselves to be primarily 'Russian speakers' was 82.1 percent (see Table 1).

---

[4] http://en.wikipedia.org/wiki/File:Simplified_historical_map_of_Ukrainian_borders_1654-2014.jpg

Table 1. Percentage of Russians and Russian speakers in regions that supported V. Yanukovych.[5]

Region	% who consider themselves Russian	% of Russian speakers
Odessa	11%	85%
Dnipropetrovsk	16%	72%
Kharkov	24%	74%
Nikolaev	26%	66%
Zaporozhye	30%	81%
Donetsk	39%	93%
Lugansk	55%	89%
Crimea	75%	97%

The reasons for this heritage can be traced to the four distinct waves of Russian settlement east of the Dnieper River: Slobodskaya Ukraina, Novorossiya, Crimea, and Donbass.

Slobodskaya Ukraina

---

[5] http://www.analitik.org.ua/researches/archives/3dee44d0/41ecef0cad01e/

Slobodskaya Ukraina or slobozhanshchina, includes not only the Ukrainian regions of Kharkov and Sumy, but also the regions of Voronezh, Kursk and Belgorod, which are currently part of the Russian Federation.

The name derives from the sloboda, or fort settlements, that the Cossacks established on the left bank of the Dnieper. These were granted considerable local autonomy in exchange for service defending the borders of the Russian Empire. They also benefited from certain tax exemptions and trading privileges. Although their 'free' status ended in 1765, when Catherine the Great made the Cossacks into regular soldiers, many of these sloboda prospered and later developed into major Ukrainian cities.

Kharkov, Ukraine's second largest city and the capital of the Ukrainian SSR from 1919 to 1934, was the administrative and cultural capital of slobozhanshchina. Its university, the second oldest in the Russian Empire, made it a major Russian cultural centre, as well as a prominent centre for the study of the Ukrainian language.

Novorossiya

Novorossiya, a name that gained recent notoriety after it was used by Russian president Putin in April 2014, is actually the historical name of one of the youngest and most ethnically diverse regions of Ukraine.

Incorporated into the Russian Empire as a result of the Russo-Turkish wars of the 18th century, the settlement of this region followed a similar pattern of establishing military forts that eventually became cities, essentially an extension southward of Slobodskaya Ukraina. Since the conquest of Novorossiya added a new coastline to the Russian Empire, however, specific incentives were added to establish new ports and promote trade there.

This is how Odessa, now Ukraine's third largest city, became the region's cultural and commercial centre. Its early status as a free port, along with the appointment of foreign administrators, contributed to an aura of cosmopolitanism that attracted large numbers of Jews, Greeks, Armenians, and Italians. By the end of the nineteenth century, it was referred to colloquially as the 'Southern Capital of the Russian Empire'. Further inland from the coast, Russian rulers encouraged the settlement of Serbians, Bulgarians and Hungarians. Indeed, before the 1917 Revolution, Novorossiya's two largest administrative districts were known as New Serbia and Slavo-Serbia (ru.wikipedia.org, 2014a). Perceived as a region sympathetic to the Whites during the Russian Civil War, the use of the term Novorossiya was suppressed in Soviet times.

Crimea

Crimea, or Tauridia, is among the oldest recorded settlements along the Black Sea coast. Archaeological records reveal Greek colonies there as far back as the ninth century B.C. Later, the peninsula fell under Scythian, Gothic, and even Genovese control, until it was captured by Ottoman forces in 1475. It was finally taken by Russia in 1783.

Crimea was transferred administratively from the Russian Soviet Federated Socialist Republic (RSFSR) to the Ukrainian Soviet Socialist Republic (SSR) only in 1954, and is the only region of Ukraine whose population identifies itself as predominantly ethnic Russian. Along with the status of the indigenous Crimean Tatars, this has been a sore spot throughout the post-Soviet era. Given recent events there, it is worth summarising Crimea's tense history in independent Ukraine.

In January 1991, as the USSR disintegrated, the Crimean regional government decided to hold a referendum to 'restore' Crimean autonomy, abrogated in 1946, and have Crimea recognised as an independent participant of the new Union Treaty being proposed by Mikhail Gorbachev. This opened the door to separating Crimea from the USSR, of which Ukraine was then still a part. Nearly 84% of registered voters participated, and over 93% voted for autonomy (ru.wikipedia.org, 2014b). 12 February 1991 – the parliament of Soviet Ukraine acknowledged this referendum, and in June amended the Ukrainian SSR constitution. On 4 September 1991, the Supreme Soviet of the Autonomous Crimean Republic (ACR) proclaimed its sovereignty and declared its intent to create its own democratic state within Ukraine. On 1 December 1991, Crimean residents took part in the Ukrainian independence referendum and 54% voted for Ukraine's independence from the USSR - the lowest percentage of any region in Ukraine.

On 5 May 1992, the Supreme Soviet of the ACR adopted an 'Act Proclaiming the State Sovereignty of the Crimean Republic.' Under pressure from Kiev, it was revoked the next day, but the region nevertheless adopted a Crimean constitution that conflicted with the acting Ukrainian constitution in several key points. Meanwhile, the Russian parliament voted to rescind the 1954 decision transferring Crimea from the jurisdiction of the Russian SFSR to the Ukrainian SSR.

Over the course of the next several years, relations between the Crimean and Ukrainian governments remained tense. The situation, however, seemed to be resolved when Russia did not respond to Ukraine's decision in March 1995 unilaterally to revoke the 1992 Crimean constitution. Nevertheless, the situation reignited in early 2014 when street demonstrations in Kiev turned violent (newsru.com, 2014a). The day after President Yanukovych was removed from office, three thousand regional officials from eastern and southern Ukraine gathered in Kharkov, and voted to assume political control in their regions until 'constitutional order' was restored in Kiev.

In Crimea, the regional parliament, one of the instigators of this meeting, went even further. It called for a referendum on Crimean autonomy within Ukraine (Rada.crimea.ua, 2014). Kiev responded by putting the Ukrainian military under the direct command of then acting speaker/president Oleksandr Turchynov, who then tried to replace local military commanders and security forces in Crimea. The Crimean authorities then appealed to the resident Russian Black Sea Fleet for assistance in 'maintaining security.' On 1 March, citing the threat to Russian citizens, military personnel and compatriots in Crimea, Russian president Putin asked for and received authority to use Russian troops in Ukraine. A week later the Crimean referendum was moved up and the question changed from autonomy within Ukraine to secession with the intent of joining Russia. On 16 March, secession was approved by more than 80% of the population.

The Crimean leadership thus took advantage of the turmoil in Kiev to redress an old grievance – the abrogation of its 1992 Constitution. Russian intervention directly facilitated its ability to hold such referendum, which most international legal experts consider illegal. The Crimean government, however, noted that, in its advisory opinion on Kosovo's declaration of independence, the International Court of Justice found that 'there was no general rule – barring declarations of independence, or authorising them for that matter, that these were political acts.' Since Russia considered holding a referendum was just such a 'political act,' and the legitimacy of the government in Kiev was in dispute, it contended that the Crimean government was well within its rights to act (Newsru.com, 2014b).

Donbass

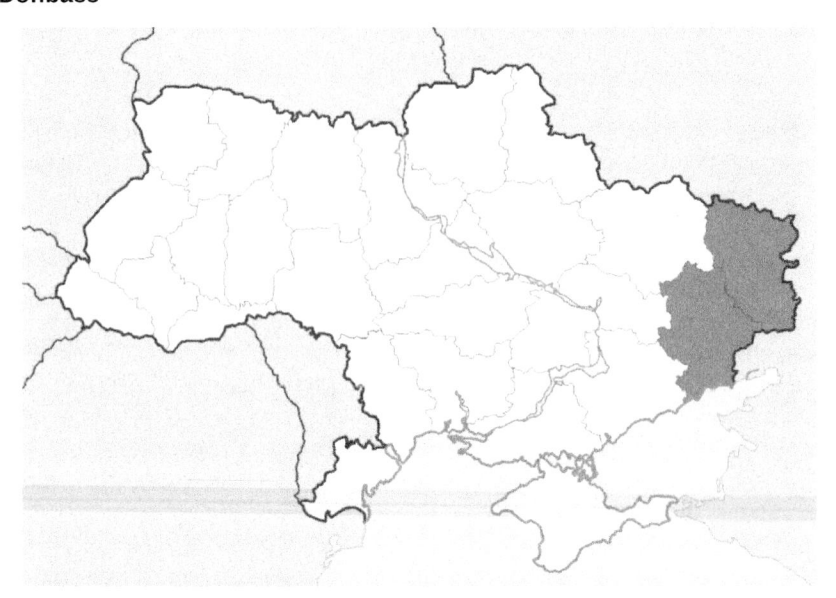

Donbass is in many ways typical of south central Russia. While other regions of Ukraine were settled due to territorial disputes and conquests, the growth of Donbass is linked to the discovery in 1720 of Europe's largest coal basin, and the rise of local industry. Until quite recently, the two regions of Donetsk and Lugansk contributed nearly 16% of Ukraine's GDP, and as much as a quarter of its industrial output (Poluneev, 2014).

Another specificity of this region is its periodic uprisings, fed in part by the half million Old Believers that settled in this region during the latter half of the 17th century. The descendants of this famously independent community would later form the backbone of anarchist Nestor Makhno's 'Black Army' (Gazeta. ru, 2014). At the end of the Soviet era, the political activism and initiative shown by the Donbass miners further added to the region's rebellious image (Kmet, 2014).

For Ukrainian nationalists, however, Donbass is also one of the most 'Soviet' and therefore 'alien' regions of Ukraine. Bohdan Chervak, the chairman of the Organisation of Ukrainian Nationalists, calls it 'not Ukrainian territory by content' (Chervak, 2014), and even former Ukrainian president Viktor Yushchenko recently referred to both Crimea and Donbass as regions 'where our language practically does not exist, where our memory is nonexistent, where our church is absent, where our culture is absent… utterly foreign lands [de chuzhina chuzhinoyu]' of which, he insists, 'not a single clump of earth' may ever be surrendered (Ukrainska pravda, 2014).

The solution most often proposed to this conundrum is to re-educate the local population into a proper appreciation of their ostensibly suppressed Ukrainian identity, a process that Donetsk University professor Elena Styazhkina euphemistically calls 'positive, peaceful colonisation' (Fakty.ua, 2014).

The Significance of the Past for the Present

These regions all rose to prominence as a direct result of the growth and expansion of the Russian Empire, and this fact has had a lasting impact on their identity.

First, the historical-cultural pattern of eastern Ukraine is bicultural. This Other Ukraine has developed a self-sustaining regional identity where both Russian and Ukrainian interact freely, and are interchangeable. It is interesting to note that, whereas in the Ukrainian constitution only the Ukrainian language is considered official, in the constitution proposed for the rebellious Donetsk People's Republic, both Russian and Ukrainian are declared official languages (Komsomolskaya pravda, 2014).

Second, this territory is a border region, distinct from both Moscow and Kiev. This can be seen in the Other Ukraine's version of Cossack mythology. While Ukrainian nationalists see the Cossacks as underscoring Ukraine's distinctiveness from Russia, the Other Ukraine emphasises a different aspect of this myth – the Cossack defence of the Russian Empire and traditional Orthodox religion (Hillis, 2013).

Finally, there is the remarkably stable voting pattern displayed by the Other Ukraine since 1994. Critics often attribute it to Soviet-era nostalgia, but it is better understood as a yearning for Soviet-era cosmopolitanism, which is more reflective of their identity. It manifests itself in the visceral rejection of the ethnic nationalism that is popular in regions of western Ukraine like Galicia, and in the affirmation of a Ukrainian identity that is inextricably linked to Russian culture, if not to Russian politics.

It is therefore no surprise that the country's political divisions have followed these historical patterns. Voting patterns in Donbass and Crimea stand out as being nearly the converse of those in Galicia (Kucheriva Fund, 2014). By contrast, voters in Slobozhanshchina and the inland parts of Novorossiya (Left Bank Ukraine) tend to be only marginally more pro-Russian, while the traditional areas of the Cossack hetmanate (Right Bank Ukraine) are marginally more supportive of integral Ukrainian nationalism (see Figure 2).

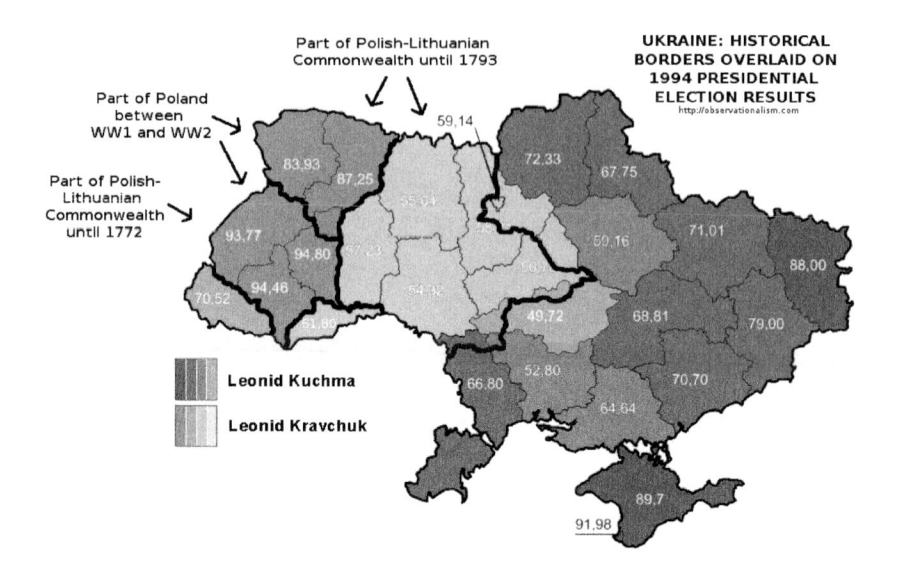

Figure 2: Historical borders overlaid on 1994 Presidential results.[6]

These patterns re-emerged in both the 2004 and 2014 Maidan movements. As Mark Beissinger notes, participants in the Orange Revolution of 2004 were eight times more likely to be from western Ukraine, and 92 percent claimed Ukrainian as their native language. By contrast, their opponents were overwhelmingly from the East, primarily from Donetsk, and three times more likely to speak Russian at home. 'Quite literally,' he concludes, 'Orange revolutionaries and opponents of the revolution "spoke different languages" in their everyday lives' (Beissinger, 2014).

The same pattern re-emerged in 2014. Surveys of the Euromaidan in late December and early February revealed that 81 percent and 88 percent of protestors, respectively, came from outside Kiev, a largely Russian-speaking city (Tyazhlov, 2014). Given that 82 percent of the protestors communicated in Ukrainian – it is very likely that they came overwhelmingly from the western regions, where support for the protests reached 80 percent, as opposed to only 30 percent in the East and 20 percent in the South (Andreyev, 2014).

---

[6] http://observationalism.com/2014/01/27/the-geographical-and-historical-divisions-underlying-ukraines-political-strife/

Sharply critical assessments of the Maidan movement persist in the Other Ukraine to this day. A survey of eight Russophone regions conducted 8-16 April 2014 (Zerkalo nedeli, 2014) by the Kiev International Institute of Sociology found that:

• Two-thirds of Donbass residents saw the Right Sector as 'a prominent military formation that is politically influential and poses a threat to the citizens and national unity';
• Most people in eastern and southern Ukraine (62 percent) blamed the loss of Crimea on the government in Kiev, rather than on Crimean separatists (24 percent) or on Russia (19 percent);
• 60 percent of those polled in Donetsk, and 52 percent in Lugansk, disagreed with the view that Russia is organising the rebels and guiding their actions;
• While 70 percent did not support secession, in April, only 25 percent wanted to join the EU, while 47 percent preferred the Russia-led Customs Union.

A follow up poll of all Ukrainian regions, conducted 12-21 September 2014 (Kucheriva Fund, 2014), confirmed the vast gulf that exists between popular attitudes in Donbass and western Ukraine. Thus, in answer to the question of whether Russia is responsible for the bloodshed and deaths of people in eastern Ukraine, only 19.1% of Donbass residents responded 'yes' (definitely or probably), while 62.8% said 'no' (definitely or probably). In western Ukraine, by contrast, 81.6% responded 'yes' (definitely or probably), while only 15.8% responded 'no' (definitely or probably).

A direct comparison of the same questions in both surveys provides some insight into the impact that six months of fighting (April to September) have had on local public opinion. Among the surprising conclusions:

• Fewer people in Donbass today believe this is a war between Russia and Ukraine than at the outset of hostilities (19.4% compared to 28.2%);
• More now feel that Russia is justified in defending the interests of Russophone citizens in eastern Ukraine (50.9% compared to 47% say 'yes'; 8.1% compared to 33.4% say 'no');
• The percentage favouring separation from Ukraine has jumped dramatically, from 27.5% to 42.1%, mainly at the expense of the undecided.

In sum, the military campaign has entrenched views on both sides. Western Ukrainians are now more convinced than ever that there is a Russian invasion, and that Ukraine ought to remain a unitary state, with Ukrainian as the only one official language. Eastern Ukrainians, by contrast, are now more convinced that the fault for this crisis lies in Kiev, that the Russian language ought to have equal status with Ukrainian (at least in their regions), and are now more receptive to the idea of separating from Ukraine.

A follow-up survey by the Kiev International Institute of Sociology, conducted 6-17 December 2014 (Zerkalo nedeli, 2014b), confirms the pattern. EU membership continues to be seen very differently, with only a quarter of residents of the portions of Donbass under Kievan control favouring EU membership, and nearly twice as many opposing it. In the Western regions of Ukraine, by contrast, 89.3% are in favour of EU membership and only 5.7% against.

In the Western regions of Ukraine, half (51.4%) have a positive view of the Ukrainian army's volunteer combatants. This figure falls to 24.1% in the South, 19.1% in the East, and 8.2% in the portions of Donbass now under Kievan control. Another telling indication of just how deeply regional differences are ingrained is a comparison of how the main events of 2014 are perceived in Donbass and the Western regions (Lviv, Ternopil, Ivano-Frankivsk, Volyn, Roven, Khmelnitsk, Transcarpathia, and Chernovtsy).

The following table shows the percentage within each district that named a given event the "most important of the passing year" (multiple answers were possible), followed by its rank within that district, and the percentage divergence between the two. The original wording used to describe the event was preserved.

Event	Western regions	Donbass	Divergence
Death of the Heavenly Hundred	71% (1)	15.1% (5)	55.9%
Self-proclamation of 'DNR and 'LNR'	2.7% (14)	30.5% (2)	27.8%
Russian troops invade Donbass	31.5% (4)	12.7% (6)	18.8%
Signing of the EU Association Agreement	18% (5)	1.5% (18)	16.5%
Russian occupation of Crimea	35.7% (3)	19.7% (4)	16%
The death of thousands of people in the war in Donbass	44.4% (2)	56.3% (1)	11.9%

We see that, while there is broad agreement that casualties in Donbass and Russian occupation of Crimea are key events, there is much less consensus about the significance of Russian troops in Donbass. This is no doubt due to the considerable uncertainty inside Donbass as to the precise nature of Russian involvement there. Meanwhile, the deaths of the Heavenly Hundred, the signing of the EU association agreement, and proclamation of the Donetsk and Lugansk Peoples' Republics are already being mythologised very differently in the different parts of Ukraine.

Conclusion

If these historical patterns have been stable for so long, why did fighting erupt only now? Because the peremptory removal of president Yanukovych violated the delicate balance of interests forged between Galicia and Donbass. It was thus seen as a direct threat to the core interest of Russophone Ukrainians. Only after Yanukovych's ouster do we begin to see a popular shift in the Other Ukraine from passive rejection of the Maidan, to outright rebellion in Crimea and Donbass. By mid-April, two-thirds of Donbass residents said they regard the Maidan as 'an armed overthrow of the government, organised by the opposition with the assistance of the West' (Zerkalo nedeli, 2014). Such sentiments have now been hardened by thousands of combat and civilian casualties.

But, as Ukraine's Minister of the Interior Arsen Avakov notes, war can have a salutary 'cleansing' effect (Avakov, 2014). There are now six million fewer Russophone Ukrainians under Ukrainian government control (not counting refugees). The previous balance of power among regions has thus been radically altered. This has encouraged some to argue that the centuries old cultural mixture that has characterised Ukraine now has a chance to be replaced by the triumph of western Ukrainian nationalism.

There are a few problems with this scenario, however:

- Overt discrimination against Russian culture is likely to lead to resentment among Russophone Ukrainians who, even with the loss of Crimea and possibly portions of Donbass, will constitute no less than a third of the population;
- Efforts to ban Russian cultural imports and curtail Russian cultural influence run into the problem that the Russian language is still widely preferred in daily usage, especially in large cities (Ukrainska pravda, 2014);
- President Putin stated in November that he will not allow 'all political opposition' to the current Ukrainian government to be eradicated (Govorit Moskva, 2014).

Most proposals for ending the current crisis have proved to be of limited value because they tend to overlook the deep historical and cultural roots of the conflict. Both the government in Kiev and opposition leaders in Donbass are pursuing a zero-sum game, when what is needed is a mutually respectful solution. One approach that might help is that of the Copenhagen School of Security Studies, which suggests that Ukraine's security can be enhanced by treating national identity as a shared security concern.

According to the Copenhagen School, the most profound security challenge that nations face today involves not sovereignty, but identity – specifically, the identity of the cultural subgroups that make up a society and whose cohesion and loyalty are essential for society's (and the state's) survival. State security could thus be significantly enhanced by satisfying, rather than suppressing, the cultural demands of minorities (Petro, 2009).

The fact that the Russian-speaking minority within Ukraine has a powerful external patron only makes this solution more attractive. Putin's only two demands for Ukraine, stated in his interview of 4 March 2014, are: (1) that the population in the East and the South be safe, and (2) that they be part of the political process (Petro, 2014).

By embracing the Russian language and culture as legitimate aspects of Ukrainian identity, Ukraine could thus allay Russia's concerns, while at the same time neutralising its popular support within the Other Ukraine. This would also have the salutary effect of shifting the discourse of Ukrainian patriotism away from its current obsession with "our language" and "our identity," toward the inclusive civic patriotism that is more common in western Europe and the United States.

Acknowledging the obvious reality that Ukraine is, at its heart, bilingual and bicultural, might finally allow Ukrainians to deal with domestic issues in ways that build loyalty to the state, rather than further divide the Ukrainian nation.

References

*Maps of Donbass, Crimea, Novorossiya and Slobodskaya Ukraina taken from http://reconsideringrussia.org/2014/05/15/historical-geography-of-ukraine/ (Accessed: 15 February 2015).

Andreyev, O. (2014) 'Power and money in Ukraine,' Open Democracy, 12 February. Available at: https://www.opendemocracy.net/od-russia/oleksander-andreyev/power-and-money-in-ukraine (Accessed: 12 December 2014).

Avakov, A. (2014) 'V eti paru dnei mnogo govoril s nashimi. . .,' Facebook, 22 June. Available at: https://www.facebook.com/arsen.avakov.1/posts/657281451028631 (Accessed: 25 June 2014).

Beissinger, M. (2014) 'Why We Should be Sober About the Long Term Prospects of Stable Democracy in Ukraine,' Washington Post, 11 March. Available at: http://www.washingtonpost.com/blogs/monkey-cage/wp/2014/03/11/why-we-should-be-sober-about-the-long-term-prospects-of-stable-democracy-in-ukraine/ (Accessed: 12 December 2014).

Chervak, B. (2014) 'Stanet li Donbas Ukrainskim?' Ukrainskaya pravda, 10 July. Available at: http://www.pravda.com.ua/rus/columns/2014/07/10/7031364/ (Accessed: 12 December 2014).

Fakty.ua (2014) 'Professor DonNU Elena Styazhkina: 'Donbas ne vernetsya v Ukrainy potomu chto Donbas ne sushchestvuyet',' 6 November. Available at: http://fakty.ua/190599-elena-styazhkina-Donbas-ne-vernetsya-v-ukrainu-potomu-chto-Donbasa-ne-sucshestvuet (Accessed: 12 December 2014).

Gazeta.ru (2014) 'O teorii i istorii anarkhizma rasskazyvaet doctor nauk Aleksandr Shubin,' 9 June. Available at: http://www.gazeta.ru/science/2014/06/09_a_6064065.shtml (Accessed:12 December 2014).

Govorit Moskva (2014) 'Mosksa ne pozvolit Kievu unichtozhit' svoikh opponentov v Donbase, zayavil Putin,' 15 November. Available at: http://govoritmoskva.ru/news/19114/ (Accessed: 12 December 2014).

Hillis, F. (2013) *Children of Rus': Right-Bank Ukraine and the Invention of a Russian Nation*. New York: Cornell University Press.

Kmet, S. (2014) 'Pravda Shaktera,' Ukrainskaya pravda, 11 December. Available at: http://www.pravda.com.ua/rus/articles/2014/12/11/7047109/view_print/ (Accessed: 12 December 2014).

Komsomolskaya pravda (2014), 'Konstitutsiia Donetskoi respubliki: Dva yazyka, federalism i pravoslavie,' 17 May. Available at: http://www.kp.ru/daily/26232.7/3114454/ (Accessed: 12 December 2014).

Kucheriva Fund (2014) 'Stavlennya naselennya do podii na Donbasi,' 21 September. Available at: http://www.dif.org.ua/ua/events/stavlennjcina-miru.htm (Accessed: 12 December 2014).

Newsru.com (2014a) 'Ne menee 85% krymchan namereny uchastvovat' v referendum,' 11 March. Available at: http://newsru.com/world/11mar2014/opros.html (Accessed: 12 December 2014).

Newsru.com (2014b) 'Na referendume zhiteli Kryma reshat, voidet li avtonomiya v RF,' 6 March. Available at: http://newsru.com/world/06mar2014/crimea.html#2 (Accessed: 12 December 2014).

Petro, N. N. (2009) 'The Cultural Basis of European Security: Analysis and Implication for Ukraine,' Sotsial'na ekonomika [published by the Kharkiv National University in Ukrainian, Russian, and English], No.1, pp. 35-41.

Petro, N. N. (2014) 'West Needs to Decide Which Is More Important: Punishing Russia or Preserving the Territorial Integrity of Ukraine,' Valdai Discussion Club, 11 March. Available at: http://valdaiclub.com/near_abroad/67320.html (Accessed: 12 December 2014).

Poluneev, Y. (2014) 'Desyat' shokiv Ukrainy (Part I)' Ekonomichna pravda, 12 December. Available at: http://www.epravda.com.ua/publications/2014/12/12/512627/view_print/&usg=ALkJrhizeiv1mTxjFgfZ3IW20aP_Wjjirw (Accessed: 15 December 2014).

Rada.crimea.ua (2014) 'Postanovlenie VR ARK, 'Ob organizatsii i provedenii respublikanskogo (mestnogo) referendum,' 27 February. Available at: http://www.rada.crimea.ua/act/11610 (Accessed: 12 December 2014).

Ru.wikipedia.org (2014a) 'Novorossiya.' Available at: https://ru.wikipedia.org/wiki/Новороссия (Accessed: 12 December 2014).

Ru.wikipedia.org (2014b) 'Istoriya Kryma.' Available at: https://ru.wikipedia.org/wiki/История_Крыма (Accessed: 12 December 2014).

Tyazhlov, I. (2014) 'Na tom i stoyat,' Dialog.ua, 7 February. Available at: http://dialogs.org.ua/ru/periodic/page32265.html (Accessed: 12 December 2014).

Ukrainska pravda (2012) 'Ukrainska mova vtrachae pozitsii v osviti ta knigovidanni, ale trimaet'sya v kinoprokati,' 9 November. Available at: http://life.pravda.com.ua/society/2012/11/9/115486/ (Accessed: 12 December 2014).

Ukrainska pravda (2014) 'Yushchenko pro Krym i Donbas: tam chuzhina chizhinoyu,' 26 December. Available at: http://www.pravda.com.ua/news/2014/12/26/7053324/ (Accessed: 26 December 2014).

Zerkalo nedeli (2014a) 'Mnenie i vzglyady zhitelei Yugo-Vostoka Ukrainy: Aprel' 2014,' 18 April. Available at: http://zn.ua/article/print/UKRAINE/mneniya-i-vzglyady-zhiteley-yugo-vostoka-ukrainy-aprel-2014-143598_.html (Accessed: 12 December 2014).

Zerkalo nedeli (2014b) 'Pesnya o rodina. Slova narodnye,' 27 December. Available at: http://opros2014.zn.ua/main (Accessed: December 2014).

3

Brothers Grimm or Brothers Karamazov: The Myth and the Reality of How Russians and Ukrainians View the Other

OLGA ONUCH
UNIVERSITY OF MANCHESTER

Since the fall of the Soviet Union in 1991, Ukrainians[7] and Russians[8] have been living peacefully in two separate and independent states for nearly a quarter of a century. Much has been said about the cultural and historical links between these two 'brotherly' countries, but also about the tensions between the two countries' different perspectives on nation building and democratisation processes (Jakubanecs, Supphellen, and Thorbjørnsen, 2005; Janmaat, 2000; Laba, 1996; Prizel, 1998; Puglisi, 2003; Shulman, 1998; Szporluk, 2000; Velychenko, 1992). Although Russian leaders, in the manner of an older brother, have consistently labelled Ukraine as the central element of Russia's 'near abroad' (Cameron and Orenstein, 2012; Rywkin, 2003; Trenin, 2006), the citizens and their foreign policies preferences have historically (i.e. on gas, on the Georgian War, on the EU and NATO) converged and diverged several times over the course of the last twenty-plus years.

Yet, even though there were sensitive moments during the last twenty-plus

---

[7] For the purpose of this article, all references to Ukrainians means citizens of Ukraine (residing in Ukraine).
[8] For the purpose of this article, all references to Russians means citizens of Russia (residing in Russia).

years of Ukraine-Russia relations (October 1996 crisis, 2004 Orange Revolution, gas crisis of January 2006, gas crisis of January 2009), the events of 2014 (the Euromaidan Protests, the annexation of Crimea, and the ongoing conflict in the Donbas[9]) are predicted by social scientists to not only sour formal relations between the two states, but also between 'ordinary' citizens. While there are many 'myths' about the way brother Russians and Ukrainians view the 'other' state and its people, the reality is much more complex, permeating with conflict, competition, and ideological disagreements, as in any other family. In such critical times, we must stop and ask: Do Russians and Ukrainians view the events of the last year differently? Or are there points of convergence? Do these events affect the way Russians see Ukraine and Ukrainians see Russia? If so, how? And can we identify any shifts in views overtime from before the 2014 crisis to today? Data on the topic is difficult to find and even more difficult to assess. This is specifically the case when so many contextual variables are in flux and when little, if any, of the available data consists of either a repeated and duplicated schedule of questions, or a panel (following citizens and their views) tracking preferences over time.

Thus, we must scour a variety of polls conducted at different times, by different institutions, to map out the views of Ukrainians and Russians. Employing a series of social surveys, this brief article aims to demonstrate that: a) most Russians and Ukrainians view the events of 2014 differently; b) on average, Ukrainians and Russians have very negative views of the other's state, military and political leaders; c) yet, concurrently, the majority of Ukrainians and Russians do not report having negative views of 'ordinary' citizens in the neighbouring country. But perhaps more importantly, it is necessary to keep in mind that the populations of each country are not homogeneous. And rather than focus on the more extreme minority views (which have unfortunately received much of our attention) it is interesting to look at the expanding Ukrainian and Russian middle classes, which seem to converge on policy preferences, peaceful external relations, and are not as easily susceptible to nationalist rhetoric.

Political science research on Ukrainian and Russian foreign policy (D'Anieri, 2012; Hagendoorn, Linssen, and Tumanov, 2013; Kravets, 2011; Taras, 2012), intergroup relations (Chinn and Kaiser, 1996; Hagendoorn, Linssen, and Tumanov, 2013; Sasse, 2007), and political behaviour and culture (Colton, 1996; Colton and Hale, 2009; Colton and McFaul, 2002; Frye, 2014; Hale, 2011; Meirowitz and Tucker, 2013; Pop-Eleches and Tucker, 2013;

---

[9] The Donetsk Basin: Donetsk and Luhansk oblasts of Ukraine, together commonly called the 'Donbas.'

Robertson, 2009; Sakwa, 2013) is vast, and it is impossible to do it justice in this short piece. But what is certain is that there has not been any consistent study of Russians' and Ukrainians' perceptions of the other that has traced these views systematically over time. The best way in which to do this at present is to provide an overview of relevant recent public opinion data, collected in both countries, and contrast and compare it over time where possible.[10]

In order to explore this topic further, I will organise the discussion in the following sections: Russians' and Ukrainians' views of the other countries, their views on the other country's political leaders, their views on the Donbas conflict and annexation of Crimea, and finally their preferences on cross-border relations and foreign policy more broadly. I will attempt to highlight areas of divergence, identifying the most concerning differences, and will flag up areas with potential for convergence and, thus, opportunities for conflict resolution. Finally, I will conclude the discussion by employing limited evidence based on a small sample of informal interviews conducted in December 2014 with thirteen Russian and Ukrainian NGO workers, drawing attention to areas of collaboration among Ukrainians and Russians in the cases of aid to Internally Displaced Persons (IDPs) and peace protest movements.

---

[10] There are several limitations to the data presented below, and the way in which we are currently able to analyse it. Due to the nature of the data presented below (not always available in full), and because it is derived from multiple sources, it is not possible at this time to conduct any meaningful statistical analysis.

Figure 1: How Ukrainians View Russians

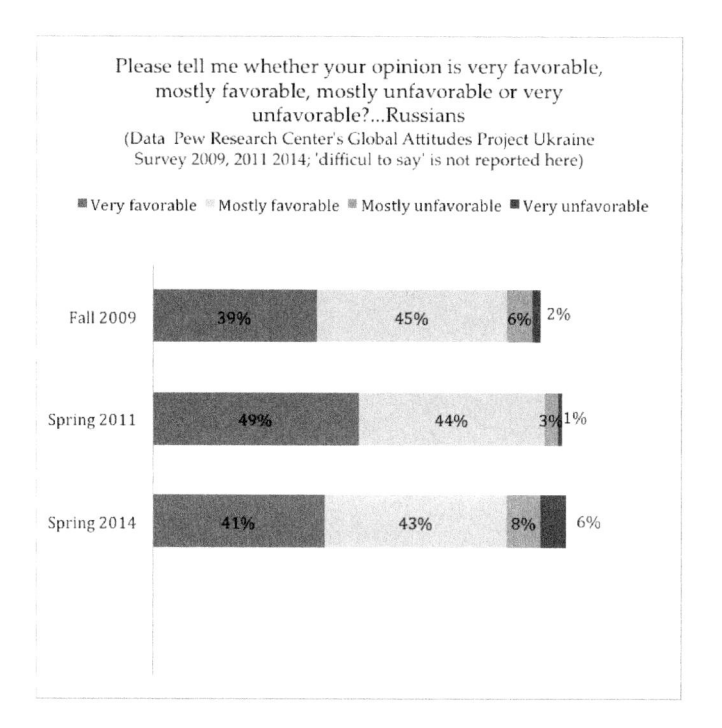

> Please tell me whether your opinion is very favorable, mostly favorable, mostly unfavorable or very unfavorable?...Russians
> (Data Pew Research Center's Global Attitudes Project Ukraine Survey 2009, 2011 2014; 'difficul to say' is not reported here)
>
> ■ Very favorable   Mostly favorable   ■ Mostly unfavorable   ■ Very unfavorable
>
> | | Very favorable | Mostly favorable | Mostly unfavorable | Very unfavorable |
> |---|---|---|---|---|
> | Fall 2009 | 39% | 45% | 6% | 2% |
> | Spring 2011 | 49% | 44% | 3% | 1% |
> | Spring 2014 | 41% | 43% | 8% | 6% |

Views of 'Ordinary' Citizens

Surprisingly, there is very little openly available data on how 'ordinary' Ukrainians view 'ordinary' Russians and *vice versa*. Anecdotal evidence (from past focus groups conducted by the author) points out that while 'ordinary' Ukrainians and 'ordinary' Russians equally believe that the other is under the influence of 'un-free' media or western/US propaganda or nationalists, 'ordinary' citizens seem to find the other as generally a brotherly and reasonable group. Several Razumkov surveys (1999-2013) show that the majority of Ukrainians do not trust Russian media and think it is biased. In focus groups, conducted for another purpose (protest participation in the region in the aftermath of the Orange Revolution), Ukrainian participants frequently explained the difference between the size and scope of protest participation in Ukraine and Russia as a product of the different information Ukrainians and Russians are exposed to, which, according to them, helps to shape different political cultures. They often say 'it's not their fault, they are normal [*zvychaini*] people just like us.' This anecdotal evidence can be used to underscore the fact that any difference that 'ordinary' Ukrainians see with 'ordinary' Russians is not hostile. As we can see from a recent survey conducted by Pew, Ukrainians' views of Russians have not changed dramatically since 2009 (see Figure 1). Yet, the number of Ukrainian respondents who saw Russians very favourably or mostly favourably has not altered much between fall 2009 and spring 2014 (84%); the number of respondents that viewed Russians unfavourably seems to have grown from 8% in fall 2009 to 14% in Spring 2014. It is thus a reasonable hypothesis that 'ordinary' citizens distinguish between the country, the state, the politicians, and *the people* they lead. As we will see below, there is a stark difference between the former three and the latter.

Figure 2: Ukrainians' View of Russia

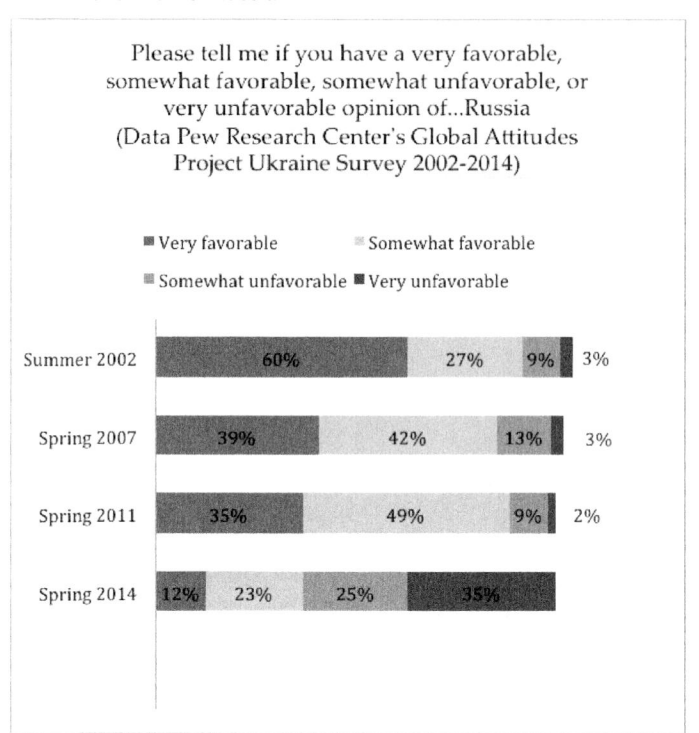

Please tell me if you have a very favorable, somewhat favorable, somewhat unfavorable, or very unfavorable opinion of...Russia
(Data Pew Research Center's Global Attitudes Project Ukraine Survey 2002-2014)

■ Very favorable   ■ Somewhat favorable
■ Somewhat unfavorable   ■ Very unfavorable

	Very favorable	Somewhat favorable	Somewhat unfavorable	Very unfavorable
Summer 2002	60%	27%	9%	3%
Spring 2007	39%	42%	13%	3%
Spring 2011	35%	49%	9%	2%
Spring 2014	12%	23%	25%	35%

To demonstrate this ability to differentiate between the 'state' and its people, we turn to how Ukrainians view Russia. Over the last decade of Pew surveying, in the period after the Orange Revolution, we can observe an exponential decline of respondents who saw Russia very favourably (see Figure 2). According to the Pew Survey, the total accumulative number of respondents who saw Russia very favourably or mostly favourably also declined overtime. This made up 87% of the respondents in Summer 2002, 81% in Spring 2007, and a record low of 35% in Spring 2014. The reported decline of 2014 (period when the survey was conducted) coincides with the fleeing of former president Yanukovych to Russia and the Russian annexation of Crimea. Moreover, what we see specifically in 2014 is a dramatic increase in the number of Ukrainian respondents who see Russia 'very unfavourably,' which went from a consistently low 3% or less of respondents in past surveys to more than a third of respondents reporting that they view Russia very unfavourably (see Figure 2).

Unfortunately, this survey does not allow us to check if the percentage of Russian respondents who view Ukraine unfavourably has equally risen in 2014, nor does the available survey data provide us with a regional breakdown within Ukraine. It is certainly possible that there is some regional variation in the distribution of the respondents who see Russia unfavourably. Yet, as we will see below, this also may not be the case, and region alone may not be the best predictor of a divergence in preferences. Data that can be used as proxy for viewing a country unfavourably could be Pew's question posed to Russians: 'Which country do you see a the greatest threat to Russia?' In each instance the question was posed (2009, 2010), Russians saw Ukraine as a significant threat only outnumbered by the United States and Georgia (Pew Research Center's Global Attitudes Project Russia Survey 2009 & 2010). While this data does not tell us much about the current trends in public opinion, if we take the rising rate of respondents who reported that Georgia was the greatest threat following the 2008 Georgia conflict as a predictor, we may hypothesise that this rate would also rise for Ukraine during the ongoing conflict in the Donbas. In 2014, Pew did ask Russian respondents: 'Do you think the government of Ukraine respects the personal freedoms of its people, or don't you think so?' And although this is a very different question, focusing on a different sentiment to a respondent's view of a state, it is worth noting that an overwhelming 73% of Russian respondents reported that the Ukrainian government 'does not respect the personal freedom of its people'. This can be interpreted pointing to a high level of unfavourability of the Ukrainian state among Russian respondents. Thus, similarly, we can hypothesise that Russians have positive views of 'ordinary' Ukrainians, but not of the Ukrainian State.

Views of Political Leaders

The next question to explore, given the lack of access to comparable data on the state, is what, exactly, about Russia and Ukraine do 'ordinary' Ukrainians and Russians disapprove of? First, we can look at how the respondents in each country view the political leadership in the 'other.' According to Russia's state-funded polling agency VTsIOM,[11] in the most recent poll of 1,600

---

[11] The state-owned and government-run institution reports to the Ministry of Labour and Social Affairs (also spelled wciom and vciom).

Russians, Ukrainian President Petro Poroshenko is viewed mostly negatively by Russians. According to the analysis of the agency, 43% of the respondents agree that Poroshenko is a puppet of the West, 37% believe he is controlled by oligarchs, and 21% believe he is highly influenced by nationalists (VTsIOM, 2014). Moreover, 55% of the survey's respondents believe that Poroshenko cannot be recognised as a legitimate head of state. Yet, while not so hostile, Ukrainians are not overwhelmingly supportive of the crisis President either. Although Poroshenko won the Presidential elections in the first round and is a rather popular politician, according to a poll conducted between 6-13 November 2014 by the Rating Group (n= 2500), only 49% of Ukrainians surveyed fully approve his track record since election. Thus, looking at this data, although Russians seem to view Poroshenko as illegitimate or, worse, view him as controlled by foreign agents or nationalists, it is not so clear that Ukrainians have a very high opinion of him, either. Alas, it should be noted that in all surveys conducted in Ukraine by Kyiv International Institute of Sociology (KIIS) and the Democratic Initiatives Foundation (DIF), Razumkov, and Rating Group, Poroshenko is seen as a legitimate leader by the broad majority of Ukrainian respondents, aside for in pockets of the Donbas. Thus, while 'ordinary' Russians and Ukrainians views of the Ukrainian leader are undoubtedly 'framed' by different public discourse of legitimacy and other propaganda, they do not diverge that dramatically on the whole.

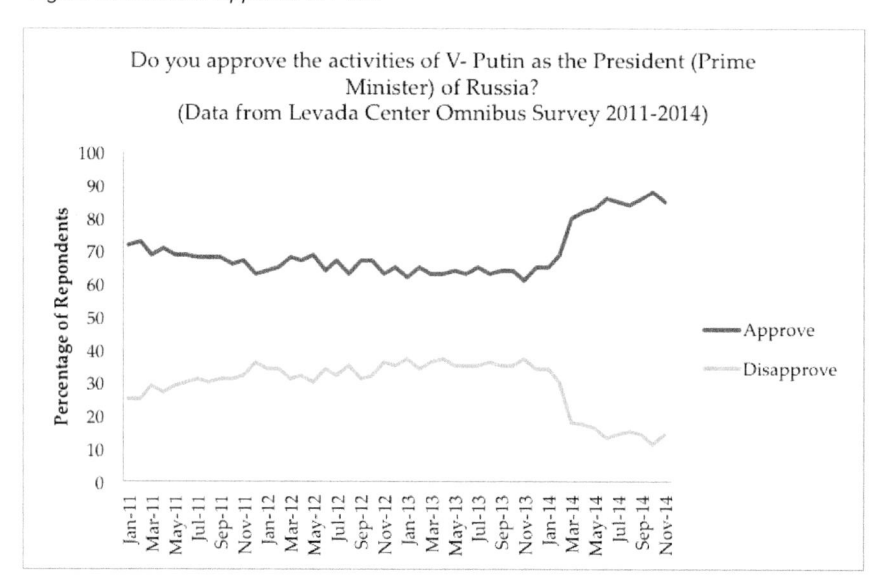

Figure 3: Russians' Approval of Putin

On the other hand, Putin's support among Russian respondents has grown exponentially this year, from 65% to 85% (a four year high, see Figure 3). Analysts working on the region have pointed out how positively the Ukrainian crisis (and Russia's involvement in it) has faired for Putin's popularity at home (Chandler, 2014; Greene and Robertson, 2014; Keating, 2014). Yet, this popularity has not extended beyond Russia's borders. Crucially, Ukrainians, who have historically viewed Putin as a strong and even impressive political leader, have changed their opinion of the politician dramatically. If we compare survey data collected by the Rating Group, 47% of the respondents had a 'positive view' of Putin in October 2013 and only 16% of Ukrainian respondents reported the same positive view in August 2014. Thus, we see that on the question of Russian leadership, Ukrainians' and Russians' views part significantly.

Figure 4: Ukrainians' View of Putin

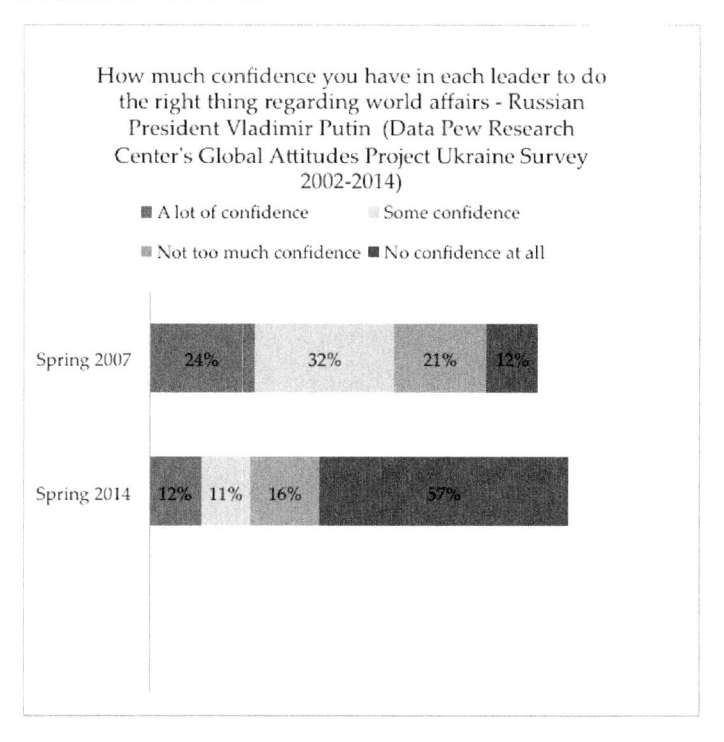

How much confidence you have in each leader to do the right thing regarding world affairs - Russian President Vladimir Putin (Data Pew Research Center's Global Attitudes Project Ukraine Survey 2002-2014)

- A lot of confidence
- Some confidence
- Not too much confidence
- No confidence at all

Spring 2007: 24% | 32% | 21% | 12%

Spring 2014: 12% | 11% | 16% | 57%

Moreover, Ukrainian respondents' 'confidence in Putin to do the right thing regarding world affairs' points again to a serious shift from 2007, when 56% had 'a lot or some confidence' in the Russian politician, to 2014, when a whopping 57% had 'no confidence at all' (Pew Research Center, 2014). Even if further survey and complementary qualitative work is required to fully unpack this significant shift, these survey results highlight the possibility that while Ukrainians do not blame 'ordinary' Russians for the crisis, they do seem to blame the state and the political elite of Russia, and Putin is the most significant focal point.

Figure 5: Russians' and Ukrainians' Views on the Crimean Referendum

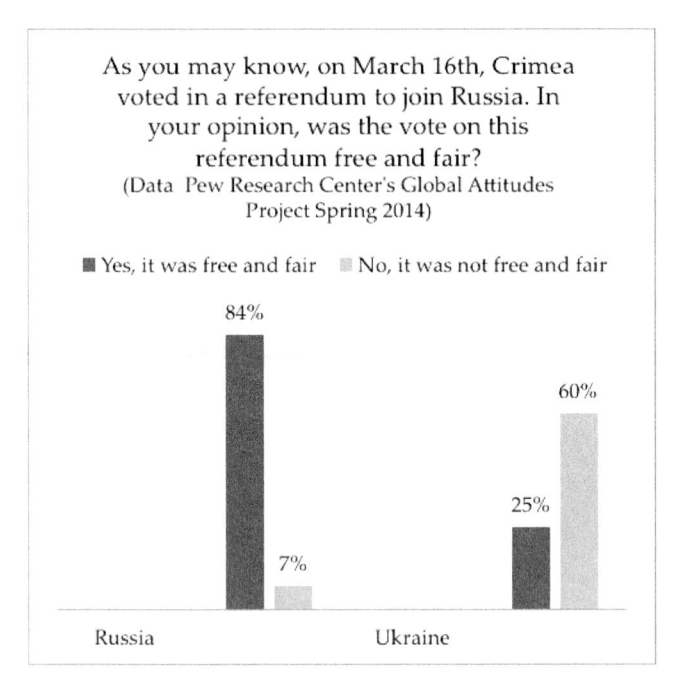

As you may know, on March 16th, Crimea voted in a referendum to join Russia. In your opinion, was the vote on this referendum free and fair?
(Data Pew Research Center's Global Attitudes Project Spring 2014)

■ Yes, it was free and fair   ■ No, it was not free and fair

	Yes	No
Russia	84%	7%
Ukraine	25%	60%

Figure 6: Russians' Views on Russian Presence in Donbas

What do you think about the fact that Russian volunteers are fighting in Ukraine with Militia? (Data Levada Center 2014)

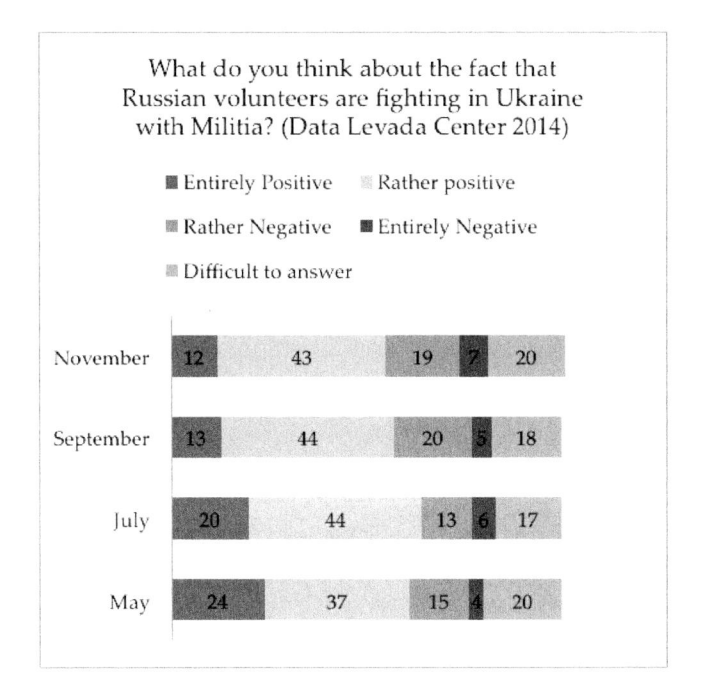

- ■ Entirely Positive
- ▫ Rather positive
- ▪ Rather Negative
- ■ Entirely Negative
- ▫ Difficult to answer

Month	Entirely Positive	Rather positive	Rather Negative	Entirely Negative	Difficult to answer
November	12	43	19	7	20
September	13	44	20	5	18
July	20	44	13	6	17
May	24	37	15	4	20

Figure 7: Views on Russia's Right to Defend Russian Speakers Abroad

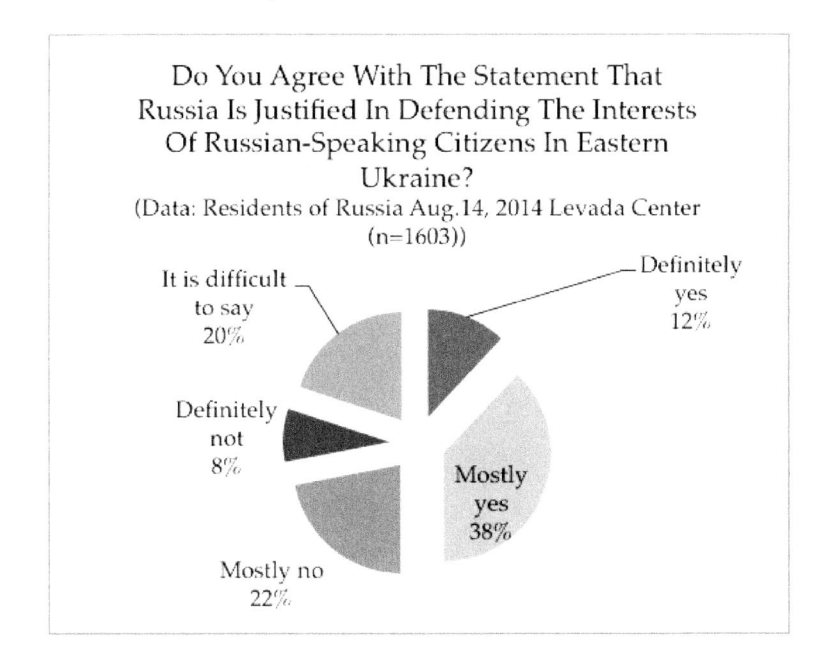

Do You Agree With The Statement That Russia Is Justified In Defending The Interests Of Russian-Speaking Citizens In Eastern Ukraine?
(Data: Residents of Russia Aug.14, 2014 Levada Center (n=1603))

- Definitely yes 12%
- Mostly yes 38%
- Mostly no 22%
- Definitely not 8%
- It is difficult to say 20%

Views on Current Relations between Ukraine and Russia

Thus, as we can see, the further we investigate, the more we can observe a growing distance between the way 'ordinary' Ukrainians and 'ordinary' Russians view each other's state, politicians, and politics. The next question requiring our exploration is how differently do Ukrainians and Russians view the conflict itself. According to the same VTsIOM study quoted above, 79% of Russian respondents believe that the guerrilla groups fighting in the Donbas are 'mainly made up of local residents', 20% believe that they are 'made up of hired mercenaries', and only 15% believe that the guerrilla groups are 'made up of Russian "volunteers".' In a more detailed study conducted by the Levada Centre, Russian respondents were asked repeatedly over the course of the last year: 'What do you think about the fact that Russian volunteers are fighting in Ukraine with militia?' The number of Russian respondents who view the role of Russian volunteers 'very positively' has decreased from 24% in May to 12% in November (see Figure 6). However, according to the Levada study, 50% of Russian respondents report that Russia is justified in defending the interests of Russian-speaking Ukrainian citizens residing within the borders of Ukraine (see Figure 7), and a significantly large portion (65%) do not believe that Russia is actively supporting the guerrillas in the Donbas (see Figure 8). Thus, while Russians feel Russia would be justified in supporting the guerrillas in the Donbas, the majority of respondents in Russia do not believe that their country has done so yet.

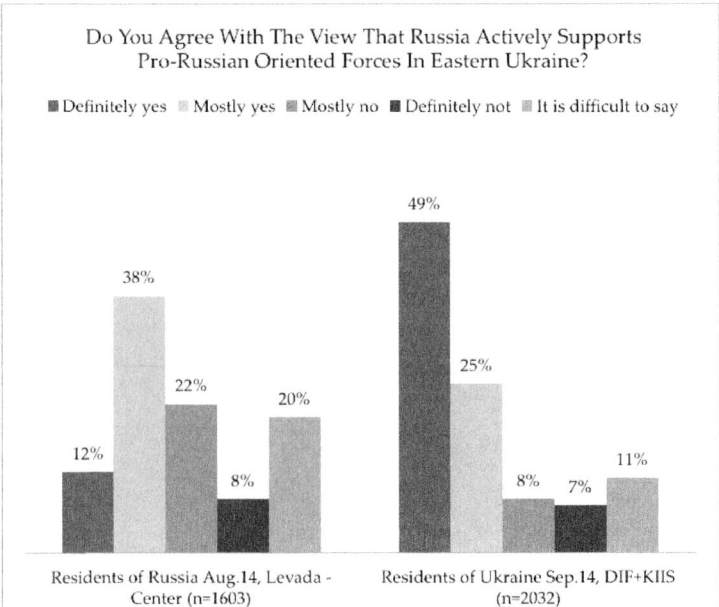

Figure 8: Views on Russia's Current Involvement in Ukrainian Crisis

The Levada Center worked actively with two Ukrainian sociological institutes, the Kyiv International Institute of Sociology (KIIS) and the Democratic Initiatives Foundation (DIF) on the execution of this survey, and many of the questions were also posed to Ukrainians (KIIS, 2014; Levada-Center, 2014), thus allowing us to compare the views more systematically. When asked: 'Do you agree with the view that Russia actively supports pro-Russian oriented forces in eastern Ukraine?' over half of the Ukrainian respondents agreed (see Figure 8). Thus, there is a substantial difference in the manner in which Ukrainians and Russians view the issue of Russia's involvement in the Donbas. Therefore, we can increasingly identify a growing divide among how 'ordinary' Ukrainians and Russians view the 'other,' specifically in terms of the on-going conflict.

But we must also note that there is some significant divergence among Ukrainians on the topic. A study conducted by Germany's largest market research institute GFK on behalf of Pact-Uniter (for USAID) polling residents of Ukraine, plus an (unrepresentative) sample of those residing in Crimea and a targeted sample of some IDPs currently residing in other parts of Ukraine, highlights some interesting trends among the survey respondents (Mikhanchuk and Volosevych, 2014). The study found that the majority of Ukrainians tend to blame Russia for the military operations in Crimea and the Donbas. A significantly large 65% of Ukrainian respondents believe that Russia 'provided both funds and weapons to local criminals', and 62% believe that 'the conflict was organised by the Russian special services'. The study found that IDPs agreed for the most part that Russia was involved with the financing and organising of the conflict in the Donbas. Yet, among the residents of Crimea surveyed, there is a general disagreement. The majority reported that they believe that Russia is not responsible for the conflict. Instead, 62% believe that the local citizens in Crimea and the Donbas have been forced to fight against the spread of nationalism. This being said, the study notes that even the residents of Crimea acknowledged the differential role of Russian TV propaganda. While there is no reliable data from the Donbas region, it is possible that this divergence will also be found among the residents of Luhansk and Donetsk oblasts.

What is most concerning in the way 'ordinary' Ukrainians and Russians view the 'other' is how they understand the boundaries of conflict itself. While Russians believe that the conflict is an internal Ukrainian problem caused by localised conflicts between Russian-speakers and Ukrainian-speakers, Ukrainians view the conflict as one that directly involves (and is fuelled by) a foreign state – Russia. Levada and KIIS/DIF asked their respondents whether they 'agree with the view that there is a war between Russia and Ukraine?' The divergence in responses is overwhelming, and should be a reason for concern.

The surveys find that 70% of Ukrainian respondents believe that their country is at war with Russia, while only a quarter of Russian respondents agree (see Figure 9). It is possible that the two surveys' divergent findings are caused by an event that took place between August, when the Russian survey was conducted, and September, when the Ukrainian survey was conducted. The only significant event that comes to mind is the confirmation (by EU, OSCE, and NATO) that up to 2,000 Russian troops entered into Ukrainian territory, which occurred in the second half of August 2014. It is possible that this temporal discrepancy could have affected Ukrainians views on the topic. Even so, this finding is still concerning for two reasons. First, looking at the divergent views on this question, as well as the other listed above, it is clear that the conflict is being reported on and framed very differently in the two countries. Second, and more importantly, there is a possibility that this differential view will not only shape broader attitudes of Ukrainians to Russians, but can also create opportunities for radical groups to promote acts of violence as justified by the 'de-facto war status.' Therefore, this divergence could make the further escalation and geographic contagion of the conflict more likely. While completely out of the scope of this brief article, it is necessary to further investigate the distinct way 'ordinary' Ukrainians and Russians view the conflict and, thus, also the 'other.'

Figure 9: Views on War Between Russia and Ukraine

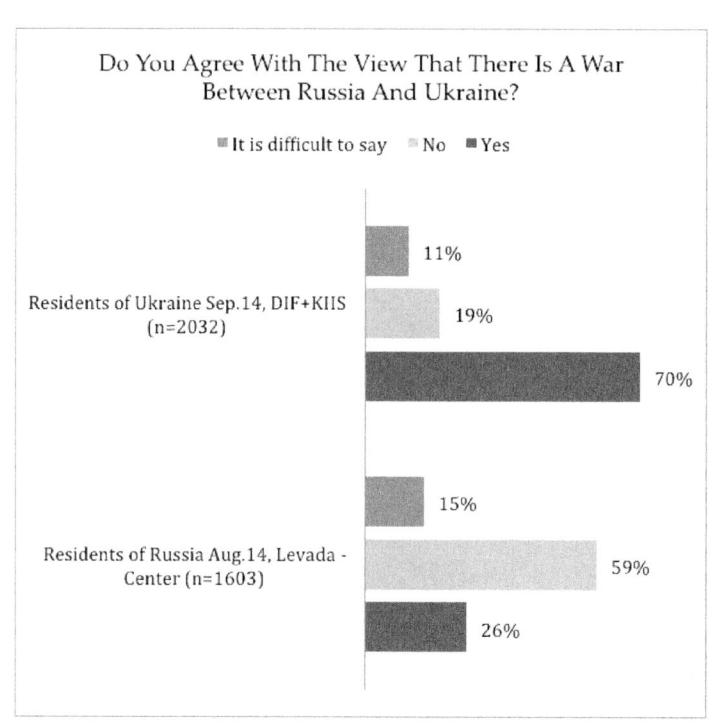

Do You Agree With The View That There Is A War Between Russia And Ukraine?

■ It is difficult to say ■ No ■ Yes

Residents of Ukraine Sep.14, DIF+KIIS (n=2032)
- It is difficult to say: 11%
- No: 19%
- Yes: 70%

Residents of Russia Aug.14, Levada - Center (n=1603)
- It is difficult to say: 15%
- No: 59%
- Yes: 26%

Views on How Relations between Ukraine and Russia Should Look Like

While there is already a clear distinction in the manner in which 'ordinary' Ukrainians and 'ordinary' Russians view each other, their states, their politicians, and their involvement in the ongoing conflict in the Donbas and Crimea, in order to better understand how these two populations view each other, it is useful also to inquire how they feel the relations between their two countries and their two peoples 'should be.' A recent survey conducted by KIIS along with DIF in 8-18 February 2014 (n=2032, representative random sample, all Ukraine including Crimea) asked respondents: 'What would you like to see the relationship between Ukraine and Russia look like?' The survey finds that 68% of all Ukrainians would like to see the two countries as 'independent but friendly states with open borders'. And whilst we would assume that respondents who have a negative attitude towards the Euromaidan protests would be much more likely to support border unification, only 21% out of such 'types' of respondents want to unite with Russia into a single state. When we look at the same question divided between the different macro regions of Ukraine, we see that most Ukrainians, regardless of region, agree. Even if in the centre, West, and South there was a slightly larger per cent of support for closed borders and visa regimes, and in the South and East there was slightly more support for the two countries uniting into one state (see Figure 10). What we can take away from this survey is that the overwhelming majority of Ukrainians want 'peaceful and friendly relations' with their neighbours to the East.

Figure 10: Ukrainians' External Policy Preferences

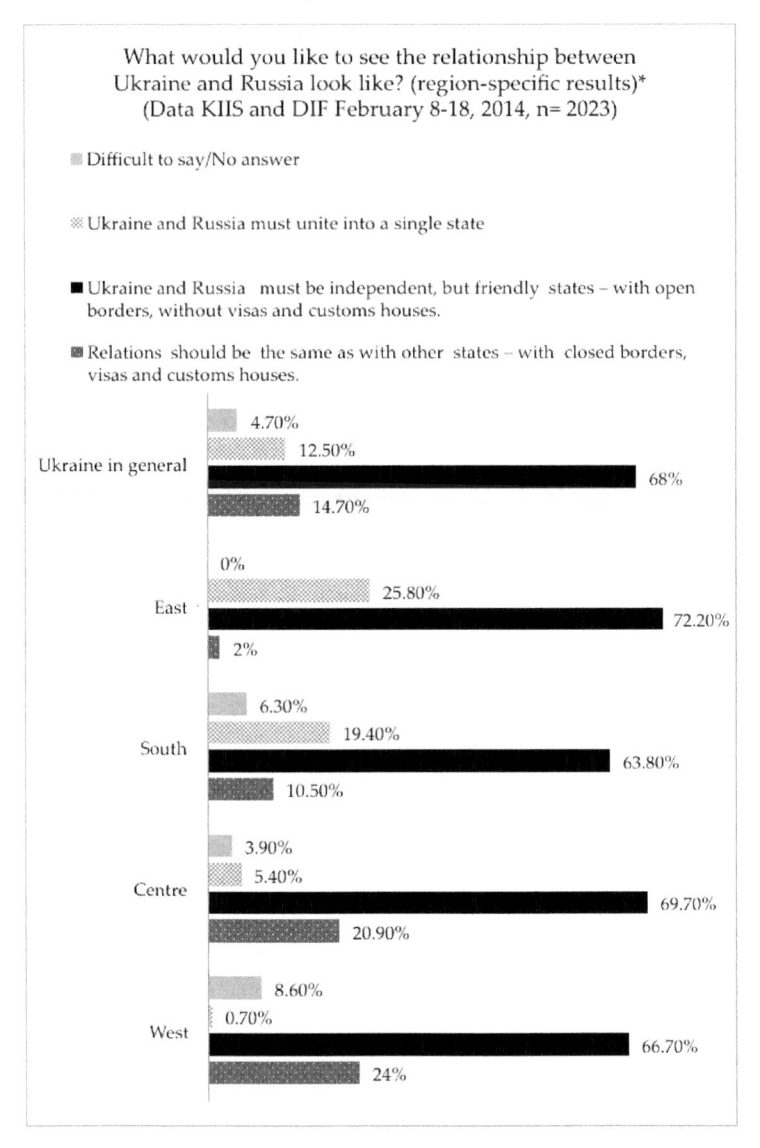

What would you like to see the relationship between Ukraine and Russia look like? (region-specific results)***
(Data KIIS and DIF February 8-18, 2014, n= 2023)

- Difficult to say/No answer
- Ukraine and Russia must unite into a single state
- Ukraine and Russia must be independent, but friendly states – with open borders, without visas and customs houses.
- Relations should be the same as with other states – with closed borders, visas and customs houses.

Ukraine in general
- 4.70%
- 12.50%
- 68%
- 14.70%

East
- 0%
- 25.80%
- 72.20%
- 2%

South
- 6.30%
- 19.40%
- 63.80%
- 10.50%

Centre
- 3.90%
- 5.40%
- 69.70%
- 20.90%

West
- 8.60%
- 0.70%
- 66.70%
- 24%

The Levada Centre also conducted a similar survey in 21-25 February 2014 (n=1603), and its data can be used for comparison. In Russia also, 63% of respondents want both countries 'to be independent, but friendly, with open borders, without visas and customs'. It is notable that since November 2013, the numbers of respondents who agree with this preference has increased by 4% in Russia and decreased in Ukraine by 5%. On the other hand, the unification of the two countries into one state is supported by 12% of Ukrainians and 32% of Russians. The survey's analysts also point out that those over the age of 40 are more likely to support the unification of the two countries (KIIS, 2014; Levada-Center, 2014). But again, we see that the broad majority of both countries' populations want to have 'friendly and open relations' between the two states. And although this number has diminished ever so slightly in Ukraine, we see that most Ukrainians and Russians want to maintain good ties with their neighbours.

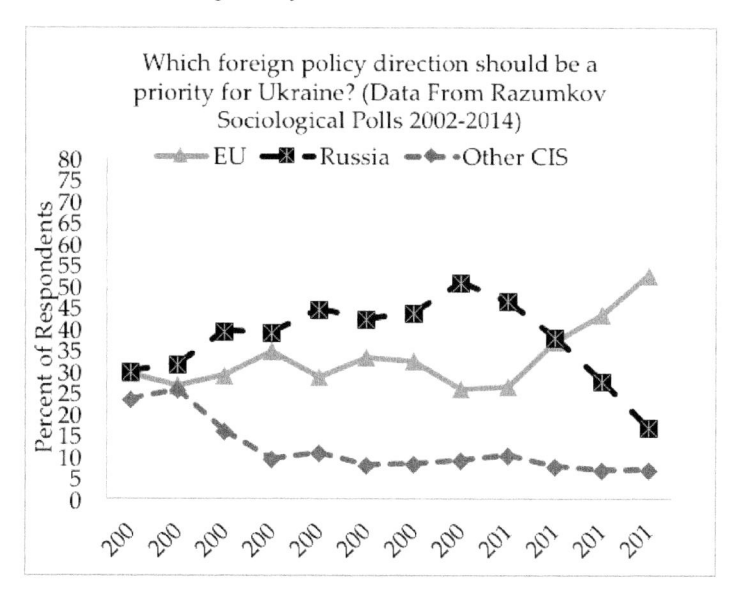

Figure 11: Ukrainians' Foreign Policy Preferences

The most significant shift is how Ukrainians view their foreign policy priorities. As reported by Razumkov, since 2011, there has been a trend whereby an increasing proportion of Ukrainians believe that the European Union – as opposed to Russia – should be their foreign policy priority (see Figure 11). In 2014, 52% of those surveyed believed that the country should focus on relations with the EU rather than Russia (16%) (Razumkov Sociological Poll, 2014). The 2014 Pew survey confirms this trend, but adds the level of complexity required in Ukraine by also asking if both should be equal policy priorities. Even in this case, the majority of respondents (43%) reported that it is more important to have strong ties with the EU, 27% reported that both are equally important, and even fewer reported that Russia should remain a priority focus (see Figure 12). Thus, once again, we see that Ukrainians have moved away from Russia and its leadership as a result of the crisis, even if wishing to maintain close ties with Russians.

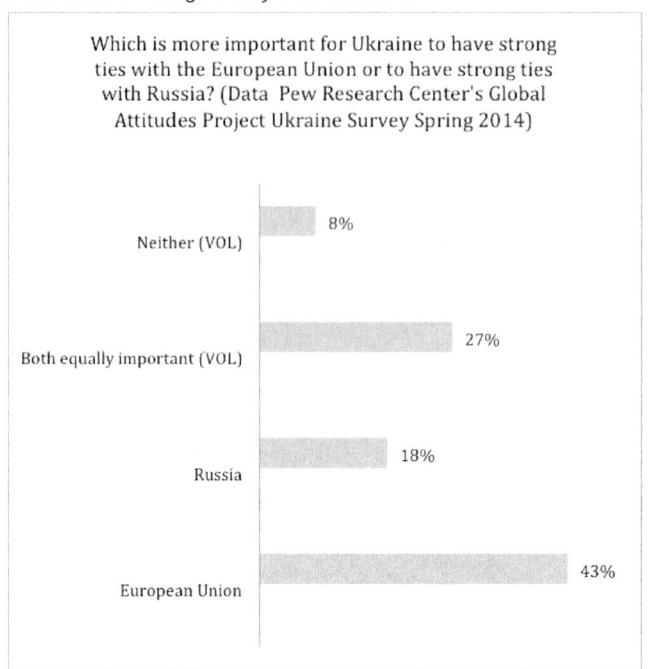

Figure 12: Ukrainians' Foreign Policy Preferences II

Which is more important for Ukraine to have strong ties with the European Union or to have strong ties with Russia? (Data Pew Research Center's Global Attitudes Project Ukraine Survey Spring 2014)

Preference	Percentage
Neither (VOL)	8%
Both equally important (VOL)	27%
Russia	18%
European Union	43%

Further Point of Convergence: The Growing Middle Class

The issue of electoral diversity within the two countries (regional, urban-rural, socio-economic, etc.), as well as the rise of the Russian (and Ukrainian) middle class, should not be overlooked. As I reported elsewhere (Onuch, 2014), the middle class was a significant supporter and participant of the Euromaidan protests across Ukraine. This is not insignificant and lends well to the often-studied role of the middle class median voter in achieving democratic stability. We see a similar type of Russian urban middle class in Moscow and St. Petersburg, who supported the Euromaidan and protested in 2014 against the annexation of Crimea and the involvement of Russia in the Donbas conflict. According to SONAR, an independent monitoring group that counts protesters passing through security checkpoints, more than 26,000 joined in the Moscow protests back in March 2014. While the protests died down over the summer, most recently on 21 September 2014, tens of thousands protested again across several cities 'against what they say is a covert Russian war in eastern Ukraine' (RFE/RL's Russian Service, 2014).

While these protesters represent, perhaps, a 'minority view' among Russians more generally, they do represent a group of Russians who not only see Ukrainians very positively, but also have collaborated with Ukrainian counterparts. Ukrainian NGO practitioners and activists interviewed by the author have explained that they have communicated with Russian organisers of the protests quite frequently – even though stressing that they were in no way part of the organisation and mobilisation process abroad (author's interview). They also have explained that Russian activists and NGOs have actively sought ways in which they can work with Ukrainian groups to provide basic care, food, and medicines to people living in the Donbas conflict zone and help with resettling IDPs (author's interview). While these are far from representing the majorities in each country, and for the most part this is only anecdotal evidence, it does point to a positive opportunity for reconciliation between the two populations. Specifically, the cooperation on humanitarian grounds and with the resettlement of IDPs, as it does not require similar ideologies, policy preferences, or agreement on the causes of the conflict – it only requires the willingness of these neighbours to remain friendly.

Conclusions

Thus, while Ukrainians and Russians do not generally view the 'other' in a hostile manner and both believe that there should be friendly relations between their countries, they do have very different views on where relations between their two countries actually stand. Russians and Ukrainians equally distrust the other's political leadership and view the other's country in an unfavourable light. Moreover, Ukrainians and Russians strongly disagree about Russia's involvement in the conflict in the Donbas. Namely, while most Ukrainians believe their country is at war with Russia, most Russians view this situation differently as an internal conflict caused by locals needing to defend themselves against the spread of nationalism. These harsh differences should be further analysed and systematically traced, as it is clear that these two populations are receiving very different information, which is framed in a very different manner. The most worrying aspect of this divergence is that it can create the opportunity for radical groups to escalate violence and further divide the two populations.

But lastly, there is a glimmer of hope. There have been a few instances of convergence in public opinion, but also in cooperation between activists, journalists, and NGO practitioners who wish to put political difference aside and cooperatively deal with the humanitarian crisis that has unfolded in the Donbas. These instances of cooperation may be few, but it would equally be worthy for political scientists to explore under what conditions (and which types of) 'ordinary' Russians and Ukrainians come together and cooperate.

References

Cameron, D. R., and Mitchell A. O. (2012) 'Post-Soviet Authoritarianism: The Influence of Russia in Its "Near Abroad,"' *Post-Soviet Affairs,* 28(1), pp. 1-44.

Chandler, A. (2014) 'Putin's Popularity Is Much Stronger Than the Ruble,' *The Atlantic*. Available at: http://www.theatlantic.com/international/archive/2014/12/putin-man-year-russia-ruble/383809/ (Accessed: 25 December 2014).

Chinn, J., and Kaiser R.J. (1996) *Russians as the new minority: Ethnicity and nationalism in the Soviet successor states*. Boulder, CO: Westview Press.

Colton, T. J. (1996) 'Economics and voting in Russia,' *Post-Soviet Affairs,* 12(4), pp. 289-317.

Colton, T. J. and Hale, H. E. (2009) 'The Putin vote: presidential electorates in a hybrid regime,' *Slavic Review*, pp. 473-503.

Colton, T. J. and McFaul, M. (2002) 'Are Russians Undemocratic?' *Post-Soviet Affairs,* 18(2), pp. 91-121.

D'Anieri, P. (2012) 'Ukrainian foreign policy from independence to inertia,' *Communist and Post-Communist Studies,* 45(3), pp. 447-456.

Frye, T. (2014) 'What Do Voters in Ukraine Want? A Survey Experiment on Candidate Ethnicity, Language, and Policy Orientation,' 7 August. Available at: https://papers.ssrn.com/sol3/Delivery.cfm/SSRN_ID2477440_code152639.pdf?abstractid=2477440&mirid=1 (Accessed: 25 December 2014).

Greene, S. and Robertson, G. (2014) 'Explaining Putin's popularity: Rallying round the Russian flag,' *The Washington Post,* 9 September. Available at: http://www.washingtonpost.com/blogs/monkey-cage/wp/2014/09/09/explaining-putins-popularity-rallying-round-the-russian-flag/ (Accessed: 25 December 2014).

Hagendoorn, L., Linssen, H. and Tumanov, S. (2013) Intergroup relations in states of the former Soviet Union: The perception of Russians. Hove: Psychology Press. Available at: https://books.google.co.uk/books?id=tMpqEkaQPXUC&lpg=PP1&dq=Russia%20Ukraine%20relations%20public%20opinion%20&lr&pg=PP1#v=onepage&q=Russia%20

Ukraine%20relations%20public%20opinion&f=false (Accessed: 19 December 2014).

Hale, H. E. (2011) 'The myth of mass Russian support for autocracy: The public opinion foundations of a hybrid regime,' *Europe-Asia Studies,* 63(8), pp. 1357-1375.

Jakubanecs, A., Supphellen, M. and Thorbjørnsen, H. (2005) 'Slavic brothers or rivals? Effects of consumer ethnocentrism on the trade between Ukraine and Russia,' *Journal of East-West Business,* 10(4), pp. 55-78.

Janmaat, J. G. (2000) *Nation-building in post-Soviet Ukraine: Educational policy and the response of the Russian-speaking population*. Utrecht: KNAG. Available at: http://dare.uva.nl/document/100270 (Accessed: 20 December 2014).

Keating, J. (2014) 'How Teflon Is Vladimir Putin's Popularity?' *Slate*, 17 September. Available at: http://www.slate.com/blogs/the_world_/2014/09/17/russia_s_economy_s_in_trouble_but_that_doesn_t_mean_russians_will_turn_on.html (Accessed: 25 December 2014).

KIIS (2014) *How Relations Between Ukraine And Russia Should Look Like? Public Opinion Polls' Results,* 4 March. Available at: http://www.kiis.com.ua/?lang=eng&cat=reports&id=236&page=8.

Kravets, N. (2011) 'Domestic sources of Ukraine's foreign policy: examining key cases of policy towards Russia, 1991-2009,' PhD Thesis, University of Oxford. Available at: http://ethos.bl.uk/OrderDetails.do?uin=uk.bl.ethos.568076 (Accessed: 25 December 2014).

Laba, R. (1996) 'How Yeltsin's Exploitation of Ethnic Nationalism Brought Down an Empire,' *Transition,* 2(1), pp. 5-13.

Levada-Center (2014) 'Levada - Center and KIIS about Crisis in Ukraine,' 11 May. Available at: http://www.levada.ru/eng/levada-center-and-kiis-about-crisis-ukraine (Accessed: 15 December 2014).

Meirowitz, A. and Tucker J. A. (2013) 'People Power or a One-Shot Deal? A Dynamic Model of Protest,' *American Journal of Political Science,* 57(2), pp. 478-490.

Mikhanchuk, D. and Volosevych I. (2014) *Sociological Poll For Uniter Project*. Available at: http://uniter.org.ua/data/block/uniter_gfk_poll_for_web_fall2014.pdf.

Onuch, O. (2014) 'Who Were the Protesters?' *Journal of Democracy*, 25(3), pp. 44-51.

Pew Research Center (2002) *Global Attitudes Project Ukraine Survey*.

Pew Research Center (2009) *Global Attitudes Project Russia Survey.*

Pew Research Center (2010) *Global Attitudes Project Russia Survey*.

Pew Research Center (2014) *Global Attitudes Project Ukraine Survey*.

Pop-Eleches, G. and Tucker, J. A. (2013) 'Communist socialization and post-communist economic and political attitudes,' *Electoral Studies,* Vol. 33, pp. 77-89. Available at: http://www.sciencedirect.com/science/article/pii/S0261379413000887 (Accessed: 27 December 27).

Prizel, I. (1998) *National identity and foreign policy: nationalism and leadership in Poland, Russia and Ukraine*. Cambridge: Cambridge University Press. Available at: https://books.google.co.uk/books?id=fE2quB852jcC&lpg=PR11&dq=cultural%20and%20historical%20links%20russian%20and%20ukraine%20brother&lr&pg=PR11#v=onepage&q=cultural%20and%20historical%20links%20russian%20and%20ukraine%20brother&f=false (Accessed: 20 December 2014).

Puglisi, R. (2003) 'Clashing agendas? Economic interests, elite coalitions and prospects for co-operation between Russia and Ukraine,' *Europe-Asia Studies,* 55(6), pp. 827-845.

Razumkov Centre (2014) 'Razumkov Sociological Poll.' Available at: http://www.razumkov.org.ua/eng/index.php (Accessed: April 23, 2010).

RFE/RL's Russian Service (2014) 'Thousands march against war in Moscow, St. Petersburg,' *RadioFreeEurope/RadioLiberty*, 24 January. Availanble at: http://www.rferl.org/content/russia-antiwar-marches-ukraine/26597971.html (Accessed: 19 December 2014).

Robertson, G. B. (2009) 'Managing society: protest, civil society, and regime in Putin's Russia,' *Slavic Review*, pp. 528-547.

Rywkin, M. (2003) 'Russia and the Near Abroad Under Putin,' *American Foreign Policy Interests,* 25(1), pp. 3-12.

Sakwa, R. (2013) 'The politics of protest in hybrid regimes: managing dissent in post-communist Russia,' *Nationalities Papers,* 41(1), pp. 220-222.

Sasse, G. (2007) *The Crimea question: identity, transition, and conflict*. Distributed by Harvard University Press for the Harvard Ukrainian Research Institute.

Shulman, S. (1998) 'Competing versus complementary identities: Ukrainian-Russian relations and the loyalties of Russians in Ukraine,' *Nationalities Papers,* 26(4), pp. 615-632.

Szporluk, R. (2000) *Russia, Ukraine and the Breakup of the Soviet Union*. Hoover Institution Press. Available at: https://books.google.co.uk/books?id=oLWeUoWEAGgC&lpg=PR9&dq=russia%20and%20ukraine%20brother%20countries&lr&pg=PR9#v=onepage&q=russia%20and%20ukraine%20brother%20countries&f=false (Accessed: 20 December 2014).

Taras, R. (2012) *Russia's Identity in International Relations: Images, Perceptions, Misperceptions*. New York: Routledge. Available at: https://books.google.co.uk/books?id=qYKSKDkqWzAC&lpg=PP2&dq=Russia%20Ukraine%20relations%20public%20opinion%20&lr&pg=PP2#v=onepage&q&f=false (Accessed: 19 December 2014).

Trenin, D. (2006) 'Russia leaves the West,' *Foreign Affairs*, July-August, pp. 87-96.

Velychenko, S. (1992) *National History as Cultural Process: A Survey of the Interpretations of Ukraine's Past in Polish, Russian, and Ukrainian Historical Writing from the Earliest Times to 1914*. Edmonton: CIUS Press.

VTsIOM (2014) *VTsIOM Survey of Russian Public Opinion.* Available at: http://www.wciom.com.

4

Roots and Features of Modern Ukrainian National Identity and Nationalism

DENYS KIRYUKHIN,
THE NATIONAL ACADEMY OF SCIENCES OF UKRAINE

Introduction

Ukrainian nationalism traces its origins back to the middle of the 19th century. It was developed after national movements had already appeared in the countries of Eastern Europe, and it owes much to their influence. Until the beginning of the 20th century, the history of Ukrainian national movement is mostly the history of the struggle of three projects of (Ukrainian) national identity, each of them in its own way determining the outlines and the principles of the relations between Ukraine and Russia.

Historically, the first project was one of Pan-Slavic identity. Within its scope, Ukraine and Russia were parts of the common Slavic world, i.e. special cultural, religious, and national commonality of the people of Eastern Europe, which was also considered, in the long term, as a potential political community. Shortly afterwards, the project of special Ukrainian ethno-cultural identity developed, different and opposed to Russian identity, with Ukraine and Russia seen as different national communities. Finally, in many ways as a reaction to the development of Ukrainian ethnic nationalism and under the impact of the development of Russian nationalism, a third project was formed – the project of the 'Little Russian' identity. Within its scope, Ukraine, on a par with Belorussia, was considered to be a part of the All-Russian national project based on the idea of common political history of Russia (Great Russia), Ukraine (Little Russia), including Galicia (Red Russia), and Belorussia (White Russia), all of them originating from the Middle Ages

Kievan Rus' and sharing common religion (Orthodox Christian) and language (Old Church Slavonic).

Due to several reasons, mostly of political nature, the Pan-Slavism project was never able to consolidate, and by the beginning of the 20th century, the two other major identity strategies were gradually formed. First, the Little Russian one, which had been long promoted by the government of the Russian Empire. It enjoyed the support of some part of the intelligentsia of both central and western Ukraine – the latter even formed religious and ideological movement of 'Russophiles' ('Moskophiles'), which lost its influence after World War I. Thus, in the long run, the propagation of the Little Russian identity proved to be ineffective – some investigators, like Russian historian Aleksey Miller, relate it to the weakness of the compulsory assimilation mechanisms that the Russian Empire had at its disposal in the 19th century.

The second identity project can be referred to as the 'Ukrainian proper'. Eventually it was ethno-cultural identity that became prevalent in the Ukrainian national project, and national politics conducted in the USSR played quite a role in its formation. Interestingly, for a long time (up to the 20th century), ideologists of the national movement hesitated to set out the project of an independent Ukrainian state. The necessity of Ukraine's independence was, for the first time, theoretically substantiated not on nationalist but on Marxist (or even national-Marxist) grounds by social-democrat Yulian Bachinski in his book *Ukraina Irredenta*, published in 1895.

Soviet National Politics

Contemporary Ukrainian nationalism is a heterogeneous phenomenon. As in the case of other national movements, it has both radical-extremist and liberal currents present in it. All of them were formed over a long period, including during the USSR times. On the surface, it might seem as if Ukrainian nationalism was developed during the seventy-year Soviet period only as an underground movement. It is worth recalling that, for many years after the end of World War II in western regions of the Soviet Union, Ukraine nationalists still waged guerrilla warfare against the Soviets. This constitutes a mythology that has played a large part in the formation of contemporary national identity. However, it was by no means the basis for the process of the formation of Ukrainian national self-consciousness during the Soviet period; rather, it was Soviet national politics that played the crucial part.

As Rogers Brubaker has aptly noted, 'although antinationalist, and of course brutally repressive in all kinds of ways, the Soviet regime was anything but antinational' (Brubaker, 2004, p. 53). It used to harshly crush all forms of unofficial class and ethno-political mobilisation of the population, as well as nationalism as political ideology (within the framework of the struggle with 'bourgeois nationalism'), but, at the same time, it still promoted practices of shaping the ethno-national identity of its citizens. Such a situation is explainable, as by the beginning of the 20th century, many national movements within the Russian Empire had developed, and the formation of the USSR republics just by national criteria was the response by the Soviet powers to the aspirations of those movements. In many cases, the USSR government had actively promoted the development of the national identity of its citizens, in particular when it was underdeveloped. The best example is the politics of compulsory Ukrainisation carried out in Ukraine in the 1920s.

A large part in the process of the development of national self-consciousness was played by population censuses. As Juliette Cadiot demonstrates in her book *Laboratory of Empire: Russia/USSR, 1860-1940* (Cadiot, 2007), the USSR government used the institutionalisation of ethnicity (nationality) as a tool for registering and monitoring the population, and for the spatial configuration of the power; and after much debate between Soviet ethnographers, it was 'native language' that was chosen as the major criterion for determining affiliation to a nation. The attention focused on language is in no way accidental. In contrast with Western Europe, where the formation of nations was either concurrent to the establishment of states or was related to their modernisation, the nations of Central and Eastern Europe were formed, as a rule, within empires (Austro-Hungarian or Russian), and thus at first they were defined mostly by cultural aspects: language, religion, and common history (Puhle, 2008, pp. 162-183). By the time of the formation of the USSR, national languages and national cultures were already parts of everyday practices and background knowledge, owing to which language was able to appear for the respondents of censuses as one of the most coherent criteria of their national self-identity.

We have to note that national politics in the USSR were fundamentally ambivalent. Practices of ethno-cultural identity were combined with the ideology of the formation of a special identity – the new 'Soviet person'. But in spite of all official declarations regarding the new communality of 'the Soviet people' having been formed in the USSR, the Soviet government was engaged in the systemic development of national cultures and national intelligentsia in the republics (together with promoting Russian national-cultural tradition as the principal representative of the Soviet culture).

Particularly, at the end of the 1950s, the training of national personnel for jobs in the system of state administration and economics was launched in Soviet republics: 'through a system of perks and "national recruitment" to colleges, local ethno-elite has been nurtured, its representatives earmarking in time managerial positions and prestigious social niches' (Nojenko, 2007, pp. 246). Thus, in many ways due to Soviet national politics, the political and geographical space we now call 'post-Soviet' experienced the formation and consolidation of the practice of dividing the people into social groups based on their ethno-national background. That also explains why, by the end of the 1980s, sociological studies in the USSR discovered tendencies to replace old socio-cultural identities (professional affiliation, social statuses, etc.) with ethnic identity. After the collapse of the Soviet Union, not only in the former Soviet republics, but in the countries of Central and Eastern Europe as well – for example, in Romania or in the republics of former Yugoslavia – the ideology of nationalism fashioned as ethnicity exerted significant (and in many cases crucial) influence on political practices.

After the dissolution of the Soviet Union, identity problems turned out to be more important than the problem of establishing democratic institutions. It is clearly evident from the discourse prevalent amongst the Ukrainian national intelligentsia since the proclamation of independence, which has been focused on debates about self-determination between the West and the East, national memory and history, religion, and culture – but not human rights. Describing the situation in Central and Eastern Europe after the fall of the Soviet Union, Timothy Garton Ash points out that in the 1990s it became almost a rule: the more ethnically diverse a post-Communist country, the higher the probability it would go the nationalist-authoritarian, and not liberal-democratic, way (Hnatiuk, 2005, pp. 277). The British author explains it by ethno-national homogeneity used to facilitate the carrying out of democratic transformations. However, the experience of many countries (Hungary, for example) testifies that ethno-cultural homogeneity is not a guarantee of democratic development. Rather, the degree of cultural homogeneity determines the degree of authoritarianism that will accompany the consolidation of nationalism – the more heterogeneous the society in its cultural aspect, the more force needs to be applied to realise a 'national project' – and, correspondingly, the more authoritarian the nationalism would be. Thus, Ash is obviously wrong on that, but what he grasps is precisely that many post-Soviet societies are oriented towards the realisation of nationalistic, and not necessarily democratic, projects.

Ukraine has been no exception. State politics since the proclamation of Ukraine's independence were, with a different degree of intensity, always aimed at the consolidation of the homogeneity in culture and language of the dominance of Ukrainian cultural traditions and, at the same time, at accentuating ethno-cultural differences between Ukraine and Russia. Russia served as 'the other' here, and contemporary Ukrainian national identity has been mostly constituted in opposition to it.

The Narratives of the Ukrainian Nationalistic Discourse

There are three major narratives that could be singled out of the contemporary Ukrainian nationalistic discourse (on the narrativism of nationalism, see, for example, Bhabha, 1990, pp. 1-7). Of course, it is often not possible to logically trace boundaries between them, especially as, over the years, proponents of one narrative could be seen to gradually drift toward another narrative (as a rule, such a transition takes place along the lines of radicalisation). Nevertheless, the proponents of national discourse themselves are aware of the differences between them. It is no accident that the version of the Ukrainian national project officially asserted just after the proclamation of independence – the first narrative legalised in the Soviet times – was very quickly apprehended by many intellectuals, especially of the younger generation, as inadequate.

We have already mentioned that the Ukrainian national project was developed and maintained by the institutions of the Soviet state within the scope of the politics of establishing ethnic elites in the republics of the Soviet Union. However, it would be false to claim that contemporary Ukrainian nationalism is the exclusive result of the Soviet national politics. It was those elites that came to power in the beginning of the 1990s that also played a role in the process of identity formation. The elite consisted not only of technocrat-managers and representatives of the Communist Party nomenklatura, who soon after the proclamation of independence took all leading positions, but also by scientists, journalists, and artists who defined the practices of symbolic self-representation and the rituals of the Ukrainian state, as well as its ideological policies. The latter, in particular, proceeded from romantic views on the history of the struggle for independence and on the necessity to spread Ukrainian language and culture as a means of saving Ukraine. Thus, the central idea of the first narrative has been the revival of Ukraine and social role of Ukrainian language that became possible after the collapse of the USSR. The first narrative was supported by the Soviet and post-Soviet state power system and has focused on national traditions, culture, and language. Within the framework of this narrative, Russia has been the 'other', but probably not the enemy.

However, this 'official state ideology' was, for various reasons, unacceptable for many proponents of the national idea. The essence of the complaints has been most accurately expressed by Ukrainian historian Mykola Riabchuk, who drew a parallel between the ideology of 'Little Russia' and the ideology of 'Kuchmism' (i.e. the state ideology of President Leonid Kuchma). The main accusation against the government from its right-wing ideological opponents was that it was unable to determine and to make the choice between the East and the West. This explains the critical attitude towards President Kuchma's policy of 'plural vectors' in the international arena. Meanwhile, for a number of 1990s intellectuals, that choice was obvious. They had their conception of 'Ukrainian national project' shaped by the templates of the notions widespread in many countries of Central and Eastern Europe, according to which Russia presents a threat to national and cultural identity of small European nations – one of the most erudite expressions of such notions being Milan Kundera's essay 'The Tragedy of Central Europe'. 'European choice' for this group has been a civilisational one, and the only way to save Ukrainian culture from the destructive influence of totalitarianism – a road back to the Western European humanitarian culture that Ukrainian culture used to belong to.

In many respects, under the influence of Eastern European intellectuals, the second narrative has come to predominate, with questions of civilisational choice and sacrifice stressed. If in the first case Ukraine used to appear as a breakaway part of Russia, then in the second it was an Eastern European country enslaved by Russia. Its people, culture, religion, and language were perceived primarily as victims of a totalitarian regime. That narrative obtained its political expression in the cult of victims of the artificial mass starvation of the 1930s (Holodomor), universally propagated at government level under President Viktor Yushchenko. Thus, the second narrative has been guided by the idea of opposition to Russia and identification with Europe. Moreover, this narrative is connected with the experience of collective tragedy that constitutes the basis for national integration and identity.

Finally, during the 2000s, a third narrative started to emerge, one related to the revival of the radical versions of Ukrainian national movement that first appeared on the historical scene in the course of World War II and a national discourse focused on fighting against the enemy. It is this third narrative that, today, with the armed confrontation taking place in Ukraine, gradually became the most common type of Ukrainian nationalism. At the end of the 1990s, representatives of the new wave of nationally-oriented Ukrainian intelligentsia were becoming more popular. These were primarily cultural figures, notably writers, who, among other things, began to experiment with literary styles and topics, including the question of sexual minorities, and were accused of post-modernism, an ideology that, in the judgement of radical nationalists, represents a threat to Ukrainian culture (Hnatiuk, 2005, p. 219). The radicals, in fact, equated post-modernism with democracy, and opposed both of them.

The issue of fighting against the enemy was related to the general disillusionment of the large part of nationally-oriented Ukrainian citizens within the elite, both political and cultural. This narrative reflects the social problems and social struggles in terms of nationalist ideology, hence the cult of national heroes and the idea of ethnocracy. It emphasises the fight for the political and social rights of ethnic Ukrainians against the corrupted government and the oligarchs, and, at the same time, the fight for extending the living space of ethnic Ukrainians who are 'constrained' in their own country. That narrative has recently been subject to certain transformations: the topic of ethnicity has receded into the background, with the topic of fighting the enemy becoming predominant, and because of that it is now not only ethnic Ukrainians who are drawn into that nationalist discourse. The third narrative is a radical expression of the national struggle for recognition and sovereignty against external and internal enemies.

While analysing the structure of nationalist thinking, Patrick Colm Hogan identifies its three narrative forms: heroism, sacrifice, and romanticism (Hogan, 2009, pp. 167-213). Those narrative forms are evident in Ukrainian nationalism as well: the first narrative we mentioned is clearly related to the prevalence of romanticism, the second is that of sacrifice, and the third is that of heroism. It is indicative that Hogan relates the prevalence of heroism to war and conflict.

Russian Language and the Conflict of Identities

The prevalence of nationalist discourse in Ukraine maintained by successive governments gave rise to a number of problems related to the formation of national identity. Although officially the Ukrainian nation is often described as a civil nation, nevertheless, school programmes, the system of state holidays and social rituals, and the symbolic self-representation of the Ukrainian state have invariably included an ethnic component. In most cases, that component is found to be dominant, determining everyday political practices as well. That is why it is no accident that Ukrainian national identity is mostly described as the identity being established on ethno-cultural ground. Neither is it accidental that Ukrainian citizens whose mother tongue is not Ukrainian (first of all, Russian-speaking people) face problems of self-identification and conflicts of identities.

Today in Ukraine, the question of Ukrainian/Russian language is not only and not so much a question related to the sphere of culture or the sphere of rights, but a question of politics, a question of the limits of the political community. It is language that has been historically established to serve as the principle marker of Ukrainian national identity. The language in the case of Ukraine is one of those obvious and self-explanatory agents that allow, within the scope of identity politics, to draw the line between 'us' and 'them' – in our case, this first means distinguishing between 'the Ukrainians' and 'the

Russians'. At the same time, a proportion of the ethnic Ukrainian population considers Russian to be their native language, and a number of Russian-speaking ethnic Ukrainians still count Ukrainian as their mother tongue. This curious phenomenon deserves some special attention.

The group of Russian-speaking people is heterogeneous, and there are two sub-groups that could be singled out among them (for more details, see Pogrebinskiy, 2010). The first one is the most numerous. It consists of those who treat the Ukrainisation policies of the government extremely negatively and who prefer Russian while watching TV and films, reading papers, and choosing the language of instruction in their children's schools. In other words, it is a group with clear cultural and linguistic identity, the latter having nothing to do with ethnic origins.

The second group is not as numerous; by a rough estimate, it constitutes up to 10% of all Russian-speaking citizens. These are people who are more loyal to the linguistic politics of the government and who are not against their children being enrolled in schools with Ukrainian as the language of instruction. That is to say, for a part of the Russian-speaking population of the country, it is not a problem to give up Russian – or, at least, to allow their children not to be primarily Russian-speaking like themselves. From this perspective, their preference to speak Russian does not coincide with their (ideological) image of a citizen of the Ukrainian state. In other words, they believe that national identity must be based on an ethnic foundation, and ethnicity is in turn considered by them to be related to language. Representatives of such a sub-group of Russian-speaking Ukrainian citizens highly value ethnic identity in their structure of identities, and they are aware of their own deficiency and inadequacy, compared to their representation of ethnic Ukrainians. They experience a conflict between linguistic and ethnic identities.

Conclusion

Today's crisis has significantly exacerbated all these internal contradictions, including those related to the problem of the formation of national Ukrainian identity. A common political project for Ukraine could be the establishment of a united civil political nation. But the elaboration and realisation of such a project is hindered by the resistance of the elites (both political and intellectual) who are not ready and, by and large, not capable of proposing and carrying out that project.

References

Bhabha, K. H. (ed.) (1990) *Nation and Narration*. New York: Routledge.

Brubaker, R. (2004) *Ethnicity without groups*. Cambridge, MA: Harvard University Press.

Cadiot, J. (2007) *Le laboratoire impérial : Russie-URSS, 1860-1940*. Paris: CNRS Editions.

Hnatiuk, O. (2005) *Proshchannia z imperieu: Ukrajinski dyskusii pro identychnist'*. Kyiv: Krytika.

Hogan, P.K. (2009) *Understanding Nationalism: On Narrative, Cognitive Science, and Identity*. Columbus: Ohio State University Press.

Nojenko, M. (2007) *Natsional'nye gosudarstva v Evrope*. Sankt-Petersburg: Norma.

Pogrebinskiy, M. (ed.) (2010) *Russkiy yazyk v Ukraine, Tom 2*. Kharkiv: HPMMS.

Puhle H.-J. (2008) 'Neue Nationalismen in Osteuropa – eine sechste Welle?' in Jahn E. (ed.) *Nationalismus im spät- und postkommunistischen Europa. Band 1: Der gescheiterte Nationalismus der multi- und teilnationalen Staaten*. Baden-Baden: Nomos.

5

Everyday Life after Annexation: The Autonomous Republic of Crimea

GRETA UEHLING
UNIVERSITY OF MICHIGAN

Imagine for a moment that tanks roll into your state. Armed and masked men without military insignia occupy your city streets. The airport is closed. Then, after a hasty vote, a new leader, someone you understood was part of the criminal underworld, is promoted to the top executive position. Suddenly, you must turn your clocks back two full hours to correspond with the new capital, some 1,400 kilometres away. Your ATM card stops working, and then your bank closes. Familiar foods, foods you have been eating your entire life, are banned and disappear from grocery store shelves to be replaced with foreign ones. Your medication becomes six times more expensive than before. Then your cell phone stops working, and you must find a new carrier to regain service. The television station you relied on for nightly news closes. You are told you have three months to turn in your passport for a new one, or you may not be able to renew your driver's license or return to your home after travel. This chaotic and liminal situation is not, of course, hypothetical. It is what happened to residents of Crimea following annexation by the Russian Federation.

The specific details are now clear: beginning in February 2014, convoys of Russian tanks and military personnel carriers rolled into the southern Ukrainian peninsula of Crimea. The men who jumped out toted the most modern of Russian weapons, took over the international airport in the capital city of Simferopol and, after a stand-off, gained control of the port at Sevastopol, where the Black Sea Fleet is stationed. They helped take over the Supreme Council of Crimea. Sergei Aksyonov, widely referred to as 'the

Goblin' from the 'Salem' criminal gang, was installed as Prime Minister at this time. The Supreme Council then held a much-disputed referendum. On March 17, after the official announcement of the referendum results, the Supreme Council of Crimea adopted a resolution 'On the Independence of Crimea.' Information later leaked from Russian intelligence services suggested that only about a third of the population, in contrast to 85% as officially reported, had voted, but the process was in motion for the Autonomous Republic of Crimea (ARC) to become a part of the Russian Federation. A Treaty of Accession of the Republic of Crimea was signed on March 18, 2014. Now, international maps are being re-labelled, new road signs are being mounted, and new passports are being distributed. In short, there has been a radical reconfiguration of quotidian life in Crimea.

Who Is Affected by the Recent Change in Power?

As of the last census (2001), the Ukrainian peninsula of Crimea was home to some 2,376,000 people. At that time, the peninsula was 58 percent Russian, 24 percent Ukrainian, and 12 percent Crimean Tatar. This is a unique mix: while Russians are a minority in Ukraine as a whole, they actually constitute a majority in the ARC. And while ethnic Ukrainians constituted a majority in Ukraine, they were a minority in the ARC. The Crimean Tatars consider themselves (together with the nearly vanished Karaims and Krimchaks), the indigenous people. With these demographics, all three primary ethnic groups considered themselves to be disadvantaged. Measures were taken to institutionalise respect for the rights of each group: Russian, Ukrainian, and Crimean Tatar were official state languages when Crimea was part of Ukraine. It should also be noted the three primary ethnic groups share the peninsula with many other ethnic groups, including formerly deported Armenians, Bulgarians, Germans, and Greeks.

The land they share is sometimes referred to as 'the Green Isle' because it is joined to the mainland by only a narrow isthmus to the north, the Isthmus of Perekop, and the fragile Strait of Kerch to the east. Deeper in history, this island ecosystem has been home to Greek City States and Mongol Hordes. Called the 'Pearl in the Czar's Crown' by Russians, the peninsula has been coveted for centuries because of its warm water port, fertile agricultural soils, and strategic location. Not surprisingly, the southern coast in particular was sought after since antiquity: Roman, Byzantine, Ottoman, Russian, British, French, Nazi German, and Soviet Empires have all set strategic sights on controlling this region.

While the annexation has been treated as a sudden turn of geopolitical events, it is more clearly understood as a predictable event that might have been foreseen if Crimea had been a focus of attention by international relations scholars. Based on my research for over two decades, the presence of a Russian separatist movement, as well as pro-Russian sentiments, have been a concern on and off for decades. This author's field notes from 1995 and 1996 contain statements to the effect that Crimea will sooner or later be part of Russia. The Spring 2014 annexation by the Russian Federation is therefore more accurately viewed as the most recent chapter in a much longer story.

A Contested Past

The current transition in power is fraught with tension in part because it takes place on the foundation of a highly contested past. The main ethnic groups – and here the focus is on Russians and Crimean Tatars – have orthogonal views of history, and consequently incommensurable ways of justifying their action on the peninsula they share. Few people realise the Crimean Tatars once had a thriving khanate or kingdom, called the Crimean Khanate, that extended far beyond the geographic boundaries of present day Crimea. Russians tend to deploy an idiom that legitimatises their presence by arguing the khanate was merely a vassal of the Ottoman Empire, and Crimea voluntarily acceded to become part of Russia, a status that lasted from Empress Catherine II in 1783 until the territory was ceded to Ukraine by Khrushchev in 1954. Crimean Tatars counter that the khanate was an independent state that was not only tolerant of diversity, but one of the strongest powers in Eastern Europe for some three centuries prior to the forced annexation.

There is a similar difference of perspectives on the period when Nazi forces occupied Crimean territory during the Great Patriotic War. Russians allege the Crimean Tatars committed treason, forming battalions to assist the Germans. While the battalions were real, Crimean Tatars counter by pointing to what the charges elide: all ethnic groups collaborated, and Crimean Tatars also fought valiantly as Soviet soldiers. Mustafa Djemilev, the former chairman of the Crimean Tatar political body, the Mejlis, pointed out that, at the time, Crimean Tatars were caught between two hegemons, neither of which respected their rightful place on the peninsula (personal communication). Djemilev is a member of the Ukrainian Parliament and a renowned defender of Crimean Tatars' minority rights.

Diametrically opposing views of the past also extend to the Crimean Tatar's 1944 deportation. Russians claim treason calls for capital punishment, and so the deportation that led to the death of an estimated 40% of the population was a 'humane' act that took them to warmer climates, eclipsing the fact they were interned in labour camps. Crimean Tatars see the deportation as genocide and point out that it was the women, children, and elderly that were carried away in cattle cars (not soldiers or combatants), while their husbands, fathers, and sons fought at the front. The people who were deported had not committed any crimes. Today, these deeply traumatic events, for which a unified national narrative is notably still lacking, complicate the transition in power because neither group sees the other very objectively. Russians continue to judge Crimean Tatars on the basis of the Nazi occupation.

It was only after the disintegration of the Soviet Union that the Crimean Tatars were able to repatriate on any significant scale. There had been state-approved programmes to resettle the Crimean Tatars announced in 1989. With the collapse of the Soviet Union, however, it was basically left to the Crimean Tatars to self-repatriate. Over 200,000 returned, in spite of challenging economic and political conditions. Local authorities were unprepared to handle this influx. Respecting and not wishing to displace the ordinary Russians and Ukrainians who had been given their property, Crimean Tatars developed a strategy of occupying former state property. Most of the settlements they formed (first called zakhvat or captures, and later renamed polyan protesta or fields of protest) remain without basic amenities like paved roads, plumbing, water, and gas.

Crimea as Part of Newly Independent Ukraine

The government of Ukraine made valiant attempts to reintegrate the Crimean Tatars and foster a tolerant society in Crimea. However, deep structural problems prevented success. For example, a law on the restoration of the formerly deported peoples' rights was drafted, but never passed the Ukrainian Verkhovna Rada. Crimean Tatars faced continuing obstacles to acquiring land, housing, and property throughout the 1990s. The government of Ukraine also refused to recognise the Mejlis as a legitimate organ of self-governance. While many Crimeans were in principle willing to integrate the formerly deported, Crimean Tatars remained underrepresented in organs of government, law enforcement, and many professions. These factors, combined with poverty, unemployment, and poor access to health and social services led many Crimean Tatars to feel like an underclass. The Slavic population contests this by pointing to Tatar entrepreneurialism and denies discrimination.

While little was accomplished to right the political wrongs, the cultural landscape blossomed. The truth about the deportation that had been silenced under Soviet rule re-emerged as the Crimean Tatars recovered mosques taken by the Soviets, opened a library of their own, and printed books and newspapers that would have been censored by Soviet authorities. They introduced Crimean Tatar as a language of instruction in the schools, and honoured their political and cultural heroes with monuments across the landscape. They began tending to graves of their ancestors, many of which had been desecrated by local Slavs. Crimean Tatars re-mapped the landscape with ancient toponyms erased by the Soviet regime. The central Ukrainian government was, for the most part, a partner in this process: for example, the 1944 deportation was written into Ukrainian history books, Crimean Tatars were elected to the Verkhovna Rada, and under President Kuchma there was a Presidential Council that created a direct channel of communication between Crimean Tatar political body, the Mejlis, and the central government in Kiev.

Russian Annexation of Crimea

Russia's annexation of Crimea in February and March 2014 has been referred to as one of Europe's greatest crises since the Cold War (Mankoff, 2014). The egregious disregard for Ukrainian sovereignty, followed by the failure of the Budapest Memorandum to protect a denuclearised Ukraine, has left many Crimeans feeling they have been abandoned by the international community and are now alone with their problems. While Ukraine failed to pass a law on rehabilitation when Crimea was part of its territory, Putin was quick to issue a decree to rehabilitate the group in April 2014. Whether it actually benefits the indigenous people is still a question.

What has annexation meant for the Crimean people? Articles in the Russian language press applaud changes like higher pensions, lower public transportation fares, and the very public 'battle' with corruption. Russians who long admired Russia's greater prosperity are now increasingly optimistic about their future. Business people are challenged by the new legal context, but overall, the area is being primed for growth: in October, Medvedev approved a free economic zone for Crimea to attract investors. The Russian government projects spending 15.6 billion dollars on development by 2020.

As in the past, however, barriers that are both structural and psychological remain. President Vladimir Putin assured Crimean Tatars and the international community that Russia will take measures to protect Crimean Tatars and make them feel they are 'full-fledged masters in their own land.' What has transpired since, however, could not be further from that description: forced disappearances, searches, and shrinking freedom of the press and speech have filled people of all ethnic backgrounds with fear and anxiety. An especially troubling development from a human rights perspective is that throughout summer and fall of 2014, searches of homes and schools became routine. Nightly news broadcasts showed personal belongings strewn from homes into courtyards and school libraries being searched by armed men. Families were often commanded to lay face down on the floor while possessions were ransacked and electronics taken. Those in possession of newspapers published by organisations banned after the annexation could be labelled 'extremist' and subject to further legal proceedings, regardless of their personal beliefs. The Federal List of Extremist Materials is growing, and there is a new centre for counteracting extremism attached to the Ministry of Internal Affairs.

What these experiences and more described below have in common is that they are being justified by local Crimean authorities with reference to law. Thus, rising fear and anxiety emerge not from lawlessness, but the ways in which the current authorities are using the laws of the Russian Federation, in a kind of 'lawfare,' to silence or eliminate potential dissent. Lawfare is used here in the anthropological sense (Comaroffs, 2006), as a means to accomplish the subordination or control of subaltern or less powerful groups. While authorities claim searches are in the interest of residents who will come under the laws of the Russian Federation in January 2015, it is clear to many that these laws are not applied equally to all.

A good example of this unevenness pertains to freedom of religion. Men in black balaclavas and camouflage gear have systematically searched mosques for literature that is banned under the laws of the Russian Federation. They break the law only by arriving unannounced. The manner in which these activities are being carried out is extreme. For example, 30 men in camouflage gear and bulletproof vests entered a mosque in the Yalta region without taking off their footwear, in blatant disrespect for Muslim ways (ATR, 2014). Subsequently, Prime Minister Aksyonov promised to correct this by working with religious leaders in identifying the banned literature (ATR, 2014).

The Ukrainian Orthodox Church faces uncertainty as well: its future depends on whether or not it is allowed to register in Russia. At this time, it is still unclear. The leader of the Ukrainian Church stated pressure from the authorities prompted him to close nearly one third of his congregations, and some of his priests have fled (Birnbaum, 2014). The church appears to be the last bastion of support for those identifying as Ukrainian in Crimea, because Ukrainian language has been eliminated from the school curriculum. Russian Orthodox churches have not been subject to similar searches.

The new legal framework is also being utilised to restrict freedom for the press. Security forces have, without warning, confiscated the computers, equipment, and other property of the major mass media outlet Chornomorsk, changed the staff at Kirim, and closed the Crimean Investigative Journalism Center. They sent a warning letter to the Crimean Tatar station ATR that they were implicitly inciting inter-ethnic hatred. These activities are being carried out in the name of the law: the authorities point out, for example, that all mass media outlets must now register with the authorities, and that the reason masked security forces suddenly confiscated the equipment of Chornomorsk was because of unpaid rent. Aspects of free speech have also become criminalised. In June 2014, the State Duma of Russia approved a bill that imposed prison sentences for spreading extremism on the Internet. The definition of 'extremism' here is broad, and responsibility extends to ordinary Internet users, even for 'liking' another person's post. In Yalta, for example, a resident is now facing a criminal case for his post on a social media site.

All of these changes are being reinforced through the election of cadres loyal to Prime Minister Aksyonov, and the removal of those perceived to be disloyal. The Crimean Tatar executive body, the Mejlis, was evicted, along with its newspaper, Avdet, from their premises. The past leader, Mustafa Djemilev, and current leader, Refat Chubarov, were not permitted to return to their homes on the peninsula and are now in exile in Kiev. They were served papers banning them for four years on the grounds that they were 'inciting ethnic hatred.' A scholar, Nadir Bekirov, was prevented from speaking at the UN Permanent Forum on Indigenous Peoples when men pulled up in an unmarked car, beat him, and took his passport.

Aksyonov's power appears to be expanding. The Autumn 2014 parliamentary elections were marked by complaints that candidates not belonging to Aksyonov's party were not allowed to run because of purported irregularities in the papers they submitted to support their candidacies. As regards the election of the head of the Parliament, Aksyonov's opponents in the election stood up and declared him the "only" alternative. The vote, as in Soviet days, was unanimous. Aksyonov now holds both top leadership positions in Crimea: he heads the executive as Prime Minister, and the legislature as head of the Supreme Council of Crimea (recently renamed State Council). The depth and the intensity of the incursions into the lives of ordinary Crimeans should now be clear. Many of these stories have escaped the mainstream international news, but they are important because they help us to understand the everyday realities on the Crimean peninsula today.

Crimeastan

It is perhaps unremarkable that events in Crimea somewhat resemble Agamben's description of a 'state of exception.' In Agamben's view, a 'state of exception' comes about when law is temporarily suspended, or when the only law that applies is that of the sovereign itself (Agamben, 2005, p.34). Sergey Aksyonov is a paradigmatic example of the sovereign as an exception: after his mercurial rise, he has been uniquely privileged to rule more or less by personal decree. With regard to the searches of homes, schools, and religious establishments, for example, Aksyonov justifies and reframes his activities in the name of law and order as 'protective.' But this defence is also marked by fractures and fault lines. According to some reports, he has suggested the Crimean Tatars be tried for WWII treason or be deported (Rayfield, 2014). A selective interpretation of history, almost melancholic in its conflations of past and present, impairs the ability to treat residents equally.

In this environment, we see discourses of legality – accompanied by a new rhetoric about rights, laws, and constitutions – multiplying. In a counterpoint to Agamben, John and Jean Comaroff (2006) have noted what they call a proliferation of parallel sovereignties that disorder post-colonies. While they base their work in Africa, Crimea, too, exhibits something akin to a spectacle of law. The new constitution, thrown together in a matter of days and filled with a multitude of typological errors, appeared on the Internet one night and then was just as rapidly taken down. Another example is provided by the Crimean Autonomous Republic government website. In what seems almost a parody, the government prides itself in hearing 13 draft laws in one day. As journalist Liliya Budjurova phrased it, 'We live in a time when the law has become a joke. Invoking the law is laughable when it is in the hands of anyone who holds an automatic.' The reference to the law being a 'joke' points to the sense that what is happening is not genuine law and order, but a spectacle.

We can better understand this situation following Wilson (2005) and Rigi (2012), who build on Agamben to explore the simulation and counterfeiting of law and order in the Russian Federation. In Crimea, the continuing use of 'self-defence' battalions with impunity to act as they see fit; the frequent references to Russian law without bothering to name any specific laws; and the rapid, sometimes mysterious, replacement of political cadres certainly point to a multi-layered network of organised chaos. On this confusing stage, the government has carried out a spectacle of law and order without actually protecting the most vulnerable citizens. Organisers of the Parliamentary elections suggested some candidates were marginalized because officials had to extemporize in creating and enforcing election rules: they were learning, implementing, and enforcing Russian Federation laws all at the same time. Thus, amidst charges of unfairness, Crimean authorities assert they did the best they could in a new legal environment.

Conclusion

A Crimean psychologist described the disorientation, fear, and anxiety accompanying the transition in power well when she likened it to waking up in a different country, without having moved from one's couch. The profound state of liminality and ambiguity described above reveal a time of contingency and uncertainty in which ideas and 'reality' were indeterminate. Thomassen argued that 'the modern world is inherently built of a series of revolutions' (2012, p. 702). They are the ground zero of history, dramatic moments of foundation. What we witnessed in Spring 2014 was a foundational moment for Ukraine and Crimea. However, a new order is solidifying that celebrates the reunion with Russia, even as the rights and the wellbeing of the indigenous people are eclipsed.

While the searches have stopped and life, on the surface, is calm, this is still a troubled region. The disjuncture between the authorities and the population has been well encapsulated by one young informant, who stated: 'Now the smart people keep quiet.' Will the next generation take law to be a joke and remain quiescent? Lawfare may be an inflammatory trope, but it encourages us to think carefully about the ways that both real and symbolic violence are impinging on the social imaginary. Fear and anxiety appear to be altering the ability of ordinary Crimeans to act and react. At the very least, we have an expanding state in which the relentless assault on freedoms has become an endemic form of social control. It is wise to mobilise a better response now because lawfare undermines the possibility of civil society in this fragile region. The changes we are witnessing are therefore more than a twist in power politics. The events explored here describe much deeper changes.

References

Agamben, G. (2005) *State of Exception*, translated by Attell, K. Chicago: University of Chicago Press.

ATR.ua (2014), video, 'Razgovor s prem'erom,' Talk-show Gravitacija, 17 October. Available at: http://atr.ua/video/2014-10-17-22-22-28-5867200 (Accessed: 20 December 2014).

Birnbaum, M. (2014) 'Eight months after Russia annexed Crimea from Ukraine, a complicated transition,' Washington Post, 27 November. Available at: http://www.washingtonpost.com/world/europe/eight-months-after-russia-annexed-crimea-from-ukraine-a-complicated-transition/2014/11/27/d42bcf82-69b3-11e4-bafd-6598192a448d_story.html. (Accessed: 20 December 2014).

Comarroff, Jo. and Je. (2006) 'Law and Disorder in the Postcolony: An Introduction' in Comaroff Jo. and Je. (eds) *Law and Disorder in the Postcolony*. Chicago: University of Chicago Press, pp. 1-56.

Rayfield, D. (2014) 'How the Crimean Tatars have Survived,' The Guardian, 21 June.

Rigi, J. (2012) 'The Corrupt State of Exception: Agamben in Light of Putin,' Social Analysis, 56(3), pp. 69-88.

Thomassen, B. (2012) 'Notes Toward and Anthropology of Political Revolutions,' *Comparative Studies in Society and History*, 54(3), pp. 679-706.

Wilson, A. (2005) *Virtual Politics: Faking Democracy in the Post-Soviet World*. New Haven, CT: Yale University Press.

For further reading:

The Moscow Times (2014) 'Medvedev Approves Special Economic Zone for Crimea,' 30 October. Available at: http://www.themoscowtimes.com/business/article/medvedev-approves-crimean-economic-zone/510383.html. (Accessed: 20 December 2014).

ATR.ua (2014), video, 'Parallel'nyj Kurultaj,' Talk-show Gravitacija, 25 September. Available at: http://atr.ua/video/2014-09-25-22-21-34-7616237. (Accessed: 20 December 2014).

Uehling, G. (2014), 'Crimeastan,' Cultural Anthropology, 28 October. Available at: http://www.culanth.org/fieldsights/617-crimeastan. (Accessed: 20 December 2014).

6

Crimea: People and Territory Before and After Annexation

IVAN KATCHANOVSKI
UNIVERSITY OF OTTAWA

Crimea before Secession and Russian Annexation

Crimea became a major flashpoint of a domestic conflict in Ukraine, and an international conflict involving Russia and the West, after the largely peaceful Euromaidan mass protests ended with a violent overthrow of the Viktor Yanukovych government in February 2014 (See Katchanovski, 2014 and Sakwa, 2015). Before its secession with direct Russian military support and its annexation by Russia in March 2014, Crimea already had a history of separatism in Ukraine. But this region avoided a violent conflict during the break-up of the Soviet Union, in contrast to Transnistria in Moldova, Abkhazia and South Ossetia in Georgia, Nagorno Karabakh in Azerbaijan, and Chechnya in Russia.

The Crimean Peninsula was historically populated by different people, and it was a place of many wars and conflicts. Its early inhabitants included the Cimmerians, the Scythians, and ancient Greeks, whose colonies were located on the Black Sea. The Goths, the Huns, Kievan Rus, Genoese and Venetian merchants, and the Mongol-led Golden Horde controlled various parts of the Crimean Peninsula over different historical periods in the end of the first millennium and the beginning of the second millennium. The Crimean Khanate emerged from the Golden Horde in the 15th century, and it later became a vassal state of the Ottoman Turkey. The Crimean Tatars often raided the Ukrainian, Polish, and Russian territories as a part of military campaigns and to capture large numbers of slaves. As a result of Russian-Turkish wars, Crimea was seized by the Russian Empire in 1783, and a significant part of the Crimean Tatar population resettled or was forced to move to the Ottoman Empire. The Crimean War in 1853-1856 brought a military defeat of Russia from an alliance led by Great Britain, France, and the Ottoman Empire, but the peninsula remained in the Russian Empire (Magocsi, 2014).

During and in the aftermath of World War I, the Bolshevik Revolution, the Civil War, and Ukraine's brief independence from the Russian Empire, control over Crimea was seized by the Ukrainian government, German military, the Russian White Armies, and then by the Bolshevik Red Army in 1920. In 1921, the Crimean Autonomous Soviet Socialist Republic was established as a Crimean Tatar autonomy in Soviet Russia and then as part of the Russian republic in the Soviet Union. However, the Soviet policy of Tatarisation was ended by Joseph Stalin. The artificial famine of 1932-1933 affected Crimea much less than neighbouring agricultural regions in Soviet Ukraine and Kuban in Russia. But mass political terror in the mid-1930s claimed large numbers of Crimean residents, arrested and executed or exiled to Gulag. Crimea became a major battlefield and a killing field during World War II and the German occupation in 1941-1944. In 1944, Stalin imposed a collective punishment on the Crimean Tatars, charging the entire ethnic group with collaboration with Nazi Germany. The Soviet government deported all of the Crimean Tatar population and other smaller ethnic minorities to Central Asia in 1944, and the formal Crimean autonomy was eliminated. A significant proportion of the Crimean Tatars perished during this ethnic cleansing and in its aftermath, primarily as a result of lack of food and medical care. A large number of migrants from Russia and Ukraine were settled in the region. In 1954, Nikita Khrushchev, the new Communist leader of the Soviet Union, transferred Crimea from Russia to the Ukrainian republic (Katchanovski, Kohut, Nebesio, and Yurkevich, 2013, pp. 115-116; Magocsi, 2014).

Separatism in Crimea started to manifest itself during the political liberalisation of perestroika and glasnost initiated by Mikhail Gorbachev, a reformist Communist leader of the Soviet Union. In January 1991, 93 per cent of the Crimean voters supported granting their region the status of the Crimean Autonomous Soviet Socialist Republic within the Soviet Union (Sasse, 2007, p. 138). At the same time, in the Ukrainian referendum on 1 December 1991, 54 per cent of the voters in Crimea backed the independence of Ukraine, much less than the national average of 91 per cent. However, the pro-Russian separatist movement grew popular during the first several years of independent Ukraine. The Russia Bloc, which favoured an independent Crimea or the region's reunification with Russia, received 67 per cent of the votes in the 1994 parliamentary election. Yury Meshkov, its candidate, won 73 per cent of the votes in the second round of the 1994 presidential election in Crimea.

Major differences along ethnic lines concerning support for separatism in Crimea became evident in the 1990s. Crimea was the only region of Ukraine with a majority ethnic Russian population. The 2001 census recorded 58 per cent of the population of Crimea, including Sevastopol, as ethnic Russian, and 24 per cent as ethnic Ukrainians. The Crimean Tatars constituted 10 per cent of the population (calculated from Vseukrainskyi, 2014). The 1996 USIA/SOCIS-Gallup survey showed that 59 per cent of ethnic Russians in Crimea supported their region joining Russia. A significant percentage of ethnic Ukrainians (41 per cent), and a much lower percentage of the Crimean Tatars (8 per cent), expressed the same preference. Conversely, 13 per cent of Russians and 29 per cent of Ukrainians in Crimea, and more than half of the Crimean Tatars (54 per cent), favoured their region remaining a part of Ukraine (USIA, 1996).

The absolute majority of the Crimean Tatars returned to Crimea in the end of the 1980s and the beginning of the 1990s (Allworth, 1998). They established and overwhelmingly supported their own ethnically-based political organisations, such as the Mejlis. Crimean Tatar leaders and organisations opposed pro-Russian separatism, and they allied with nationalist Ukrainian parties and politicians (Drohobycky, 1995; Katchanovski, 2005; Sasse, 2007).

Internal divisions and policies of the Ukrainian government led to the disintegration of the Russia Bloc in the middle of the 1990s. In 1995, the Ukrainian President Leonid Kuchma temporarily suspended the Crimean constitution and abolished its presidency. While Crimea retained its status as an autonomous republic in Ukraine, influence of the central Ukrainian government in the region increased significantly, both de jure and de facto. The Communist Party of Crimea and then the Party of Regions, which formed an electoral alliance with the Russian Bloc, became the most popular political forces in the region. However, overtly separatist pro-Russian organisations did not receive strong support in the regional elections since the mid-1990s (Sasse, 2007). Such developments led to conclusions that the pro-Russian secessionist movement in Crimea failed, that a potential conflict in Crimea was successfully prevented, and that this autonomous region became integrated into the Ukrainian polity (Kuzio, 2007; Sasse, 2007).

However, some other studies argued that separatism retained a significant popularity in Crimea and that its potential secession remained a possibility (Katchanovski, 2006). For example, the 2001 Razumkov Center survey showed that 50 per cent of the respondents in Crimea favoured their region becoming a part of Russia, and an additional 9 per cent preferred to see their region as an independent state (calculated from Krym, 2001). The separatist preferences in Crimea increased significantly after the 'Orange Revolution' in

2004 brought a pro-Western and nationalist president, Viktor Yushchenko, to power. Viktor Yanukovych, a relatively pro-Russian presidential candidate, failed to gain power in Ukraine through the falsification of the election results, but he received overwhelming backing in the region.

In the 2008 Razumkov Center survey, conducted soon after the Russian-Georgian war following an attempt by the Georgian government to seize the de-facto independent secessionist region of South Ossetia, 73 per cent of the Crimeans, who made their minds on this issue, backed the secession of Crimea from Ukraine with a goal of joining Russia (calculated from AR Krym, 2008). In this survey, 85 per cent of ethnic Russians, 65 per cent of ethnic Ukrainians, and 17 per cent of the Crimean Tatars wanted their region to secede from Ukraine (calculated from AR Krym, 2008). When asked separately in the same survey, 47 per cent of the respondents in Crimea, including 49 per cent of ethnic Russians, 45 per cent of ethnic Ukrainians, and 39 per cent of the Crimean Tatars, favoured the independence of Crimea. The 2008 Razumkov Center survey showed that 59 per cent of the Crimean Tatars supported Crimea becoming a Crimean Tatar national autonomy in Ukraine. Separately, 33 per cent of the Crimean Tatars backed the unification of Crimea with Turkey.

However, the outright secessionist preferences in Crimea declined afterwards, and they were expressed by 38 per cent of the respondents in the 2009 Razumkov Center poll. Thirty per cent voiced such views in the 2011 Razumkov Center poll after Yanukovych won the 2010 presidential election with promises of closer political and economic cooperation with Russia and making Russian the second state language in Ukraine (Iakist, 2011, p. 27). The 2011 Razumkov Centre survey showed that combined support for joining Russia and independence of Crimea decreased among ethnic Ukrainians to 25 per cent, from 35 per cent, in 2009. Attitudes of ethnic Russians demonstrated a similar decline of separatist preferences to 35 per cent from 43 per cent. Such separatist attitudes among the Crimean Tatars remained the same in 2011 (28 per cent), compared to 2009 (27 per cent), but their support for joining Turkey increased from 4 per cent in 2009 to 21 per cent in 2011 (Razumkov Center, 2011, p. 27).

Polls indicated that pro-Russian separatism in Crimea had significant but minority support during the Euromaidan. The absolute majority of Crimeans backed the Yanukovych government and opposed the Euromaidan, which started as a mass protest against backtracking by the Yanukovych government on the association and free trade agreement with the European Union, and then turned into the anti-government protest and a rebellion in western and a number of central regions.

Yanukovych, during his presidency, and his semi-oligarchic Party of Regions opposed separatism in Crimea, while receiving the support of the majority of voters in this region in various parliamentary and presidential elections. Yanukovych regarded Crimea as another source of enrichment for his personal network of family, politicians, and oligarchs, and he appointed a number of his associates from Donbas to senior positions in Crimea.

Top Russian leaders, such as President Boris Yeltsin in the 1990s and President Vladimir Putin prior to the overthrow of the Yanukovych government in February 2014, did not support separatism in Crimea. However, the Russian government declared that the NATO membership of Ukraine was an unacceptable threat to security of Russia. Putin stated during the NATO summit in Romania in April 2008 that such a move could result in a break-up of Ukraine along regional lines, and he reportedly claimed that Ukraine was an artificial country, which included historically Russian regions along with other regions (Dzerkalo tyzhnia, 2008).

Some other Russian leaders – such as Yury Luzhkov, the mayor of Moscow, and various nationalist and communist opposition politicians – publicly refused to recognise Crimea or Sevastopol City as parts of Ukraine, and they expressed their backing for reunification of entire Crimea or Sevastopol with Russia. In spite of differences and tensions, the Russian and Ukrainian governments managed peacefully to divide the Black Sea Fleet after the collapse of the Soviet Union, but Russia was able to maintain its navy presence in Sevastopol. In 1997, the two countries signed an agreement granting the Russian Black Sea Fleet a 20-year lease of the Sevastopol navy base. In 2010, President Yanukovych signed another agreement with Russia that extended the lease of the Sevastopol navy base by the Russian Black Sea Fleet for 25 years after the original lease was supposed to expire in 2017, in return for a discount for natural gas imported by Ukraine from Russia.

Crimea During and After Secession and Russian Annexation in 2014

The violent overthrow of the Yanukovych government in February 2014 gave a significant boost to separatism in Crimea. The Russian government used this overthrow to reverse its previous policy and to start backing both separatists and the annexation of Crimea. Yanukovych fled from eastern Ukraine to Crimea on 22 February, and the Russian military, there on instructions from the Russian government, helped him to escape to Russia.

The new government and the media in Ukraine, and their counterparts in Western countries, presented the change of the government as a result of peaceful mass protests during the Euromaidan. They maintained that Yanukovych abandoned his presidential position and fled from Ukraine because of his responsibility for the massacre of the Maidan protesters on 20 February 2014. Evidence, however, indicates that elements of the far right and oligarchic organisations were involved in the mass killing of both Maidan protesters and the police, and that this massacre played the decisive role in the overthrow of the Yanukovych government (Katchanovski, 2014).

The Russian leaders and the media often characterised the overthrow of Yanukovych as a fascist coup, and they justified support of separatism and annexation of Crimea by protection of ethnic Russians from the Ukrainian 'fascists' and by the Russian national security interests to prevent it from losing control of the main Black Sea naval base and its falling under control of NATO. Russian military forces without insignia, along with separatist 'self-defence' formations, seized control over the Crimean parliament building, other government buildings, and Ukrainian military installations in the peninsula. However, the Russian government initially denied its direct military intervention in Crimea, in spite of evidence that Russian military units ('little green men') were operating along with separatist armed units in Crimea beyond the Russian naval base in Sevastopol, and that they were seizing Ukrainian military units and government headquarters.

The Crimean Parliament, headed by Vladimir Konstantinov from the Party of Regions, refused to recognise the new government of Ukraine. The parliament at the end of February 2014 elected Serhii Aksyonov, a pro-separatist leader of the Russian Unity party, as the new Prime Minister of the Crimean autonomy (Aksyonov was reportedly involved in organised crime in the past). The parliament of the Crimean autonomy and the Sevastopol city council unilaterally declared their independence from Ukraine and set up a referendum on this issue. The official results of the referendum held on 16 March 2014 reported that 97 per cent of the voters in Crimea supported joining Russia.

The Ukrainian government and the media, and to a large extent their Western counterparts, characterised separatism in Crimea as having minority support and the referendum as illegal and falsified. The separatism in the region was attributed mostly to direct military intervention by Russia. However, the analysis of various survey data indicates that support for separatism in Crimea increased significantly after the Euromaidan that resulted in the overthrow of the relatively pro-Russian government. There is no directly comparable and publicly available reliable survey data concerning popular support for separatism and joining Russia in Crimea after the Euromaidan. However, in a Pew Center survey in April 2014, 91 per cent of the respondents in Crimea stated that the referendum was free and fair (Pew Center, 2014).

In contrast to Donbas, a separatist region in eastern Ukraine, Crimea avoided a violent conflict. Large sections of Ukrainian military, security service, and police forces on the peninsula switched their allegiance to the separatists and then to Russia, while others were blockaded and disarmed by the Russian military and the Crimean self-defence and returned to Ukraine. Major Crimean Tatar organisations, in particular the Mejlis, were the most vocal opponents of the secession and annexation of Crimea, and they boycotted the 16 March referendum. Over several days following this referendum, the former Crimean autonomous republic and the city of Sevastopol were formally incorporated into the Russian Federation. The Russian government justified its annexation of Crimea by humanitarian intervention and the precedent of Kosovo independence. However, the new Ukrainian government, the US and other Western governments, and most members of the United Nations, rejected the unilateral secession and annexation of Crimea as illegal under the international law.

The Ukrainian government's official stance, expressed, for example, by newly elected president Petro Poroshenko, is to reunite Crimea with Ukraine. The use of military force to take back control over Crimea was raised as a possibility by some Ukrainian officials, but such an option is very unlikely because it would lead to a war with the much more powerful Russia. By the end of 2014, the Ukrainian government moved to impose a limited blockade of Crimea by suspending train and bus links.

The Western governments rejected the possibility of using their military forces in Crimea. The US government, and governments of the European Union members and other Western countries, imposed economic and travel sanctions against separatist leaders of Crimea and Russian government officials for the annexation of the region. The sanctions also prohibited or severely restricted work of US and other Western businesses in Crimea. For example, following a new round of the US sanctions, Visa and MasterCard blocked the use of their credit cards in this region in December 2014.

However, the Russian government refused to reverse its annexation of Crimea and to negotiate any deal that would change the status of this region. In the September 2014 elections, the United Russia party of President Putin won 71 per cent of the votes in Crimea. Ukrainian and Crimean Tatar parties and organisations were generally limited or curtailed in their ability to continue functioning, and some of their local leaders and activists were subjected to violence, threats of violence, detention, or expulsion from Crimea.

The Future of Crimea

The secession of Crimea from Ukraine with help of the direct Russian military intervention, and the subsequent annexation of the region by Russia, represented a major turning point in the political history of the region, which experienced many conflicts in the past and was controlled by different powers during various historical periods. The significant rise in separatist orientations in Crimea after the Euromaidan, the direct Russian military intervention in support of pro-Russian separatists, and the Russian annexation of Crimea imply that a return of Crimea from Russia to Ukraine is virtually impossible. However, Crimea in its current status quo is likely in the foreseeable future to remain a point of conflict between Ukraine and Russia, and between the West and Russia.

References

Allworth, E. E. (1998) *The Tatars of Crimea: Return to the Homeland, 2nd ed.* Durham: Duke University Press.

'AR Krym: Liudy, problemy, perspektyvy' (2008), *Natsionalna bezpeka i oborona,* Vol. 10, pp. 2-72.

Derzhavnyi komitet statystyky Ukrainy (2014) 'Vseukrainskyi perepys naselennya 2001.' Available at: http://2001.ukrcensus.gov.ua. (Accessed: 20 December 2014).

Drohobycky, M. (ed.) (1995) *Crimea: Dynamics, Challenges, and Prospects.* Lanham, MD: Rowman & Littlefield.

Dzerkalo tyzhnia (2008) 'To shcho skazav Volodymyr Putin u Bukharesti,' 19 April.

Katchanovski, I. (2014) 'The "Snipers' Massacre" on the Maidan in Ukraine,' Paper presented at the Chair of Ukrainian Studies Seminar at the University of Ottawa, Ottawa, 1 October.

Katchanovski, I., Kohut, Z. E., Nebesio, B. Y., and Yurkevich, M. (2013) *Historical Dictionary of Ukraine, 2nd ed.* Lanham. MD: Scarecrow Press.

Katchanovski, I. (2006) *Cleft Countries: Regional Political Divisions and Cultures in Post-Soviet Ukraine and Moldova.* Stuttgart: Ibidem-Verlag.

Katchanovski, I. (2005) 'Small Nations but Great Differences: Political Orientations and Cultures of the Crimean Tatars and the Gagauz,' *Europe-Asia Studies*, 57(6), pp. 877-894.

'Krym na politychnii karti Ukrainy' (2001) Natsionalna bezpeka i oborona, Vol. 4, pp. 2-39.

Kuzio, T. (2007) *Ukraine - Crimea - Russia: Triangle of Conflict.* Stuttgart: Ibidem-Verlag.

Magocsi, P. R. (2014) *This Blessed Land: Crimea and the Crimean Tatars*. Toronto: University Of Toronto Press.

Pew Research Center's Global Attitudes Project (2014) 'Ukrainians Want Unity amid Worries about Political Leadership and Ethnic Conflict,' 8 May. Available at: http://www.pewglobal.org/2014/05/08/chapter-1-ukraine-desire-for-unity-amid-worries-about-political-leadership-ethnic-conflict.

Razumkov Center (2011) Iakist zhyttia zhyteliv Krymu ta perspektyvy ii pokrashchennia v konteksti stratehii realizatsii kontseptsii ekonomichnoho ta sotsialnoho rozvytku AR Krym na 2011-2020rr. Available at: http://www.uceps.org/upload/Prz_Krym_2011_Yakymenko.pdf. (Accessed: 20 December 2014).

Sakwa, R. (2015) *Frontline Ukraine: Crisis in the Borderlands*. London: I.B.Tauris.

Sasse, G. (2007) *The Crimea Question: Identity, Transition, and Conflict*. Cambridge: Harvard Ukrainian Research Institute.

USIA (1996) 'Crimean Views Differ Sharply from Ukrainian Opinion on Key Issues', Opinion Analysis, 15 March.

7

Russians in Ukraine: Before and After Euromaidan

MIKHAIL POGREBINSKIY
KIEV CENTER OF POLITICAL RESEARCH AND CONFLICT STUDIES

In the title of the article, I have reproduced the topic proposed by the editors of the collection, however, I consider the stylistic formula 'Russians in Ukraine' to be rather confusing and unable to grasp the essence of the problem. The idea of Russians in Ukraine being a national minority similar to, for instance, Hungarians in Romania or Slovakia, Swedes in Finland, or even Russians in Estonia, is in fact profoundly fallacious. And not because of the scope of inclusion – I will talk about that later. But it is this idea that underlies western policies towards Ukraine and the current crisis. According to that idea, the Ukrainians, with the moral support of the West, are trying to free themselves from the centuries-old Russian colonial oppression, while Moscow resists it in every way, and as soon as it 'lets Ukraine go', European values will triumph in Ukraine.

Before the crisis, the inadequacy of the European perception of the Ukrainian reality was more or less harmless. Except that it was gradually smoothing the way for 'inevitability' of the choice between Russia and Europe – naturally, in favour of 'the European choice'. During the crisis, such an approach has led to encouraging the inflexibility of the position of the Kiev government that came to power riding the wave of the Maidan, and that in turn has contributed to the loss of Crimea and to the civil war in the South-East.

Russians in Ukraine do not represent such a distinctive national group as other large minorities in other countries. The thing is that both contemporary Russians and Ukrainians (at least, inhabitants of the lands of the former Russian Empire, that is the majority of contemporary Ukraine) originate from the people of common (All-Russian, 'Orthodox') identity, where the differences between Great Russians ('Russians') and Little Russians ('Ukrainians') were rather of regional or sub-ethnic nature. I think that it would be more correct to consider Russians, alongside Ukrainians, to be a state-constituting nation of Ukraine within its 2013 borders, and not a national minority. It is worth noting that almost half of ethnic Ukrainians prefer to speak Russian in private life.

In order to provide an adequate description of the ethnic structure of the population of Ukraine, Ukrainian sociologist Valeriy Khmelko introduced the concept of 'bi-ethnors', i.e. people with 'double' Ukrainian-Russian identity (Khmelko, 2004). Representative surveys of the population of Ukraine carried out during the last 20 years are summarised in this table:

Identity	Years of Surveys				
	1994 – 1999	2001 – 2003	2012	2013	2014
mono-ethnical Ukrainians, %	59.8	62.9	65.6	66.6	73.8
Ukrainian-Russian bi-ethnors, %	24.4	22.5	22.9	21.8	20.0
mono-ethnic Russians, %	11.3	10.0	9.0	8.3	4.8
Others	4.5	4.6	3.2	1.4	2.4

As can be seen from the table, the share of mono-ethnic Ukrainians has increased by 10%, compared to the first survey, and the proportion of bi-ethnors has decreased, similarly to the number of mono-ethnical Russians, which is down by almost 30%. 2014 numbers are quite predictable due to the loss of Crimea, where the population is mostly Russian. Since Ukrainian civil identity has been shaped not only by ethnic Ukrainians, it is important to ask what has played a decisive role in the formation of Ukrainian civil identity. As Ukrainian researcher Aleksey Popov argues, it was the creation of the USSR with the quasi-statehood of its union republics. In the Ukrainian Soviet Socialist Republic, the Russian-speaking population started to identify themselves with Ukraine (Ukrainian SSR) – 'we live in Ukraine, so we are Ukrainian citizens, "Ukrainians."' It was particularly facilitated by the linguistic proximity of the Russian and Ukrainian languages, and had led to the fact that despite mixed population (Russian and Ukrainian speaking), there was no division into national communities, as was the case in the Baltic republics, in Transcaucasia, in Central Asia, and in the Russian autonomous republics of Caucasia. Partly because of the total absence of any conflicts between Russians and Ukrainians on the domestic level, the establishment of an independent Ukraine in 1991 was achieved practically seamlessly.

However, that lack of manifestation of the Russian element in Ukraine had its limits. Many Russians, and Ukrainians who identify with Russian culture and language, voted for Ukrainian independence from Russia, but did not support Ukraine's exit from Russia's sphere in favor of Western Europe. Similarly, support for independence did not mean support for a gradual ousting of Russian language – a tendency that at the time was only of a declarative sort. Moreover, the citizens clearly did not foresee that dramatic decline in the living standards. Russians and the Russian-speaking population above all have responded to the situation with a strong desire for closer ties with Russia and for the state status of Russian language, which found its expression during the presidential election of 1994. Ever since, practically every election has registered the splitting of the country into two Ukraines: the absolute majority of the Russian-speaking population voted for one presidential candidate, and the absolute majority of the Ukrainian-speaking population for their opponent.

At the same time, the Russian element in Ukraine does not represent a unified force. Russians do not have an influential party of their own, although the presence of such ethnic parties is an integral feature of other European countries. Belgium, for instance, is divided into parties by ethnic markers (Flemish and Walloon); Hungarians in Romania, Slovakia and Serbia; Albanians in Macedonia and Montenegro; Swedes in Finland; the peoples of Spain (the Basques, the Catalonians, the Galicians, etc.) – all of them have their own parliamentary parties. Therefore, one can often unmistakably count how many votes a national party would get – for the noted Hungarians, Swedes, and Albanians, that number corresponds to their share in the total number of voters in their country. In Spain or, for example, in Great Britain, with its Scottish and Welsh nationalists, such results fluctuate noticeably, thus apparently reflecting ethnic proximity as well.

In Ukraine, however, there have only been substitutes for Russian parties – such as the Communist Party (CPU) or the Party of Regions (PoR). Some of them, such as the CPU, reflected not so much the Russian but Soviet identity. Others – the PoR, tried to present themselves as representatives of industrial South-East, while forgetting their declarations after coming to power and ignoring the interests of their supporters.

The type of Ukrainian identity that has developed over years, and which has been shared by Russians and representatives of national minorities, can be referred to as a 'civil identity'. Importantly, the Ukrainian 'civil identity' was not anti-Russian and it presupposed sympathies toward Russia and Russian culture, therefore it was acceptable for Russians in Ukraine. Importantly, the devotion to this identity has been shared until recently by the absolute majority of the citizens of our country.

However, along with 'civil identity', another identity type has played a significant role in the events of the end of 2013 and 2014, namely 'political identity'. It presumes adherence to a certain assortment of political positions and it defines the community of people united by: a) the Ukrainian language, b) hatred for 'colonial' past in the USSR/Russia, c) memory of the 1932-1933 Holodomor seen as genocide of the Ukrainians, and d) reverence for OUN-UPA nationalist guerrillas and 'heroes of the nation' like Bandera, Shukhevych, and others. That is the community the third President of Ukraine, Viktor Yushchenko, used to call 'my nation'. Those who do not share that assortment of predicates are not considered by the proponents of this identity to be 'real Ukrainians' and, according to them, should be re-educated. This type of identity, until recently, was shared by an apparent minority of Ukrainian population, which, although constituting a majority in the West of the country and prevalent among some elite groups – people of letters, diplomats, etc. – still constituted less than 15% of the total population. The reservation 'until recently' is important here, as I would argue that the events of 2014, the loss of Crimea, and the war in the South-East, have essentially changed the balance between the two types of identity in favour of the 'political' one, with a considerable part of Russians and Russian-speaking Ukrainians now holding with it. However, it is difficult to say how large that group exactly is until corresponding research has been carried out.

Numerous surveys demonstrate that there are two issues causing the drastic polarisation of Ukrainian society: the status of the Russian language and the preferred integration vector (to the West or to the East). It is no accident that the pretext for the beginning of mass protests in the Autumn of 2013 was the decision by Yanukovych to delay the signing of the Association and Free Trade Agreement with the EU. The first issue on the agenda of the Ukrainian parliament on the day of Yanukovych's ousting on 22 February 2014 was the repeal of the liberal Kolesnichenko-Kivalov language law, which triggered the protests in the South-East that were later called 'the Russian Spring'. In addition, in the past year another topic has joined the two, which has contributed to the split in the Ukrainian society, namely the preferred form of power structure in Ukraine: unitary state or federation.

When it comes to the status of the Russian language, this topic had mostly served as an electoral 'friend-or-foe' marker used by presidential candidates and parties who relied on the support of the South-East (demanding the elevation of that status). However, after coming to power, those presidents (Kuchma, Yanukovych) and parties (Party of Regions) used to give up their promises wishing not to antagonise 'over trifles' the part of population and the elite, which may be lesser in numbers but is more active politically. Especially since before Yushchenko came to power (in 2005), the gradual ousting of Russian language went at a slow pace, although from 1991 to 2005, the number of pupils in schools with Russian as instruction language decreased by more than half, from 54% to 24%.

Since 2005, the frontal attack on the Russian language has commenced in all areas of social life, first of all in education and the media. The process continued but was slowed down after Yanukovych came to power in 2010. In 2012, as a preparation for another electoral cycle, the team of Yanukovych had backed the Kivalov-Kolesnichenko Language Law (K-K) that elevated the status of the Russian language in those regions where it has been used by the majority of population, however, without imposing it where the apparent region majority would oppose that elevation. That law was in full accordance with the norms of the European Charter for Regional or Minority Languages and, as surveys demonstrated, such a compromise was supported by the explicit majority of the society and had entirely met the recommendations by the Committee of Ministers of the Council of Europe from 7 July 2010 on providing languages with more rights, particularly in higher education, electronic media, and local government bodies (Council of Europe, 2010). Nevertheless, both public support (albeit unspoken) and recommendations by European experts did not hinder the opposition from launching a campaign against the K-K law. All opposition parties in the Verkhovna Rada soon had a common language bill advanced that, in fact, presupposed total Ukrainisation.

The K-K law had been repealed by Verkhovna Rada, but the repeal was never signed and the law is formally still in place. However, amendments to the law are being prepared to entirely emasculate the rights of the Russian language. There is little doubt that the current Verkhovna Rada elected in October 2014 will vote in favour of those amendments; there is limited representation of regions with high percentage of Russian-speaking population in that parliament, with 55 deputies from the South-East – Donetsk, Lugansk, Odessa, and Kharkov regions, 24 of whom represent 'Petro Poroshenko Block' and 'The Popular Front' party of Arseny Yatsenyuk – both openly anti-Russian. In contrast, Kiev and Western regions – Lviv, Ivano-

Frankivsk, Ternopil, and Chernivtsi – have 257 deputies. The large number of anti-Russian deputies from the South-East regions is due to two factors: the fact that they were included into nation-wide lists of pro-Maidan parties and the low attendance of voters in the South-East in general – and the voters of opposition parties in particular.

The events of the Autumn of 2013 and the Spring of 2014, referred to as a 'coup d'etat' by one part of the society (about one third) and a 'conscious struggle of citizens who get united to protect their rights' by another (a bit more than a third) (Mirror Weekly, 19 November 2014), were followed by the loss of Crimea and the war in the South-East. They also led to the marked aggravation of inter-civilian confrontation that, although not solely inter-ethnical (Ukrainians vs. Russians), does include such element.

Meanwhile, the information warfare against the militia of the South-East ('the Russian Spring') and Russia using all the resources of public and private (owned by oligarchs) mass media was in full swing, and, after the creation of a special Information Ministry by the new Ukrainian government, it will only increase. Total mopping-up of the information field from those who disagree with the mainstream narrative ('Russia is aggressor, there are terrorists and regular Russian army fighting against Ukraine in the South-East...') was effectively achieved by the end of 2014. The residents of the South-East and everyone in general who does not support the mainstream narrative are being labeled as 'Moskals', 'Little Russians', 'fifth column', and often are just dehumanised and designated by such terms as, for instance, 'Colorados'.

Patriotic hysteria leads to mass cases of conflicts on interpersonal level, with decades-old friendships wrecked and families disintegrated, and in those regions of the South-East where the protest against the government is strangled by repressions (Dnipropetrovsk, Odessa, Kharkiv), cases of 'guerrilla warfare' are being registered, luckily with no casualties.

In order to evaluate the degree of hatred cultivated by 'fighters of the information warfare', I would refer to a case of a recent charity fair organised by teachers and eight-formers in a high school in Nikolayev as fund-raising for the participants of the so-called 'anti-terrorist' operation on the East of the country. Among the products prepared by schoolchildren and advertised for sale there were, for example, 'tanks on Moscow' cookies and stewed fruit drink called 'the blood of Russian babies' (Korrespondent.net, 2014).

The government legitimises radical Russophobe organisations by co-opting its activists into power structures, including those of law-enforcement. Thus, the position of the chief of Kiev regional police was filled by a deputy commander of the 'Azov' battalion, known for their usage of Nazi symbols. The commander of that battalion, Andrey Biletskiy, with the support of the ruling 'Popular Front' party, has been elected to the Verkhovna Rada from one of Kiev's majority districts. Apart from him, a number of other nationalist-radicals known for their Russophobia have been elected to the parliament from majority parties' lists, including 'the Radical Party' of Oleh Lyashko. There were no cases registered of the country leaders – the President or the Prime Minister – distancing themselves from the actions and radical anti-Russian rhetoric of their coalition partners. Moreover, Prime Minister Yatsenyuk himself actively participates in the fomentation of that anti-Russian hysteria. All of this promotes the intensification of the degree of hatred towards Russia and, one way or another, towards Russians. Among other things, the fomentation of ethnic strife is furthered by torch-light processions of nationalists held on a regular basis (with the government's acquiescence) under the slogans 'Glory to the nation, death to enemies', 'Ukraine above all', and 'Moskals to the knife!' in many cities of the country, including Kiev and even Odessa.

The 2 May tragedy in Odessa was doubly horrifying: first of all, because of mass killings of the people, and second, because of the response of a considerable part of Ukrainian society to those events. The tragedy did not rally the society; on the contrary, it split it into those terrified by the events and those who directly or indirectly justified it by referring, inter alia, to the fact that there were 'Colorados' who were killed – not Ukrainians but enemies.

However, it cannot be claimed that it is Russians living in Ukraine who serve as enemies in the Ukrainian public discourse prevalent today. The enemy is mainly defined not in ethnic terms but ideologically – it is in the first place an opponent of the ideology universally propagated by the current government. Nevertheless, the civil confrontation in Ukraine is not entirely deprived of ethnic biases. The lack of commiseration, empathy, or compassion in relation to the death of 'Colorados' in Odessa, 'jokes' on the blood of Russian babies on a school charity fair, the openly Russophobe art exhibition titled 'Kill a Colorado' that took place in Kiev in December – those are not accidental events. They have been prepared by Ukrainian intelligentsia, just as the bloody civil war that led to the dissolution of Yugoslavia had been prepared by Serbian and Croatian scholars in arts and humanities.

One of the testimonial examples is a book published in Kiev in 2006, authored by a member of a Ukrainian Union of Writers and the former parliamentary deputy, Ivan Diak. The book is featured as a scientific edition: the academician of Ukraine National Academy of Sciences, Nikolai Zhulinskiy, was its supervisor and one of the reviewers was the head of the Ministry of

Education and Science in the current Ukrainian government, Sergey Kvit (in the past, the activist of a right-wing radical organisation '"Trizub" named after S. Bandera') (see: Diak, 2006). The book is a digest of xenophobic and chauvinistic views. It indicates, for example, that ethnic minorities (and particularly Russians in Ukraine) provided with the living space by the titular nation, are a potential 'fifth column' that could be used by Russia in its fight with Ukraine. There are several measures proposed to counteract that, specifically, an absolute isolation of minorities from their historical homeland, stimulation of political conflicts within minorities (the book directly refers to Ukrainian Russians), countrywide upbringing of children in the spirit of ethno-nationalist ideology, as well as compulsory Ukrainisation and introduction of ideological censorship of mass media.

If the tendencies we observe today persist, there is a high probability that the political conflict will develop into an ethnic one. With that in mind, room for the search for a break in the deadlock of a civil war is greatly narrowed, one of the reasons being the lack of any public discussion. Attempts to discuss some topics that would seem quite innocent for European discourse, for instance 'federalisation', are now elevated to the rank of crime on the whole.

Already, Ukraine President Viktor Yushchenko had set out against federalisation. In 2005, the head of Luhansk Oblast Administration Viktor Tikhonov and the former head of Kharkiv Oblast State Administration Yevhen Kushnaryov, who had publicly come out in favour of the federalisation of Ukraine, had criminal proceedings instituted against them for alleged separatism. And Yushchenko himself had openly admitted in 2006: 'I will never accept the topic of federalisation and separatism. It's a stab in our roots' (Fakty.ua, 2006). Today, the topic of federalism is treated with disregard just in the same way. While addressing the Parliament on 27 November 2014, Petro Poroshenko categorically declared: 'No federalisation!' (Lb.ua, 2014). The topic is identified with separatism and disintegration of the country, and thus it remains informally banned.

References

Council of Europe (2010). Available at: http://www.coe.int/t/dg4/education/minlang/Report/Recommendations/UkraineCMRec1_en.pdf (Accessed: 16 Dec 2014).

Diak, I. (2006) *Piata kolona v Ukraine: zagroza derjavnosti*. Kiyv

EMaidan (2014) 'In Kiev, an exhibition under the slogan "Do not Pass By: Kill" Colorado!' Available at: http://emaidan.com.ua/15448-v-kieve-otkrylas-vystavka-pod-lozungom-ne-proxodi-mimo-ubej-kolorada/ (Accessed: 28 January 2015).

Fakty.ua (2006) 'Prezident Ukrainy Viktor Yucshenko "Federalizm I separatism eto nosh v nashi korni"'. Available at: http://fakty.ua/46445-prezident-ukrainy-viktor-yucshenko-quot-federalizm-i-separatizm---eto-nozh-v-nashi-korni-quot (Accessed: 29 January 2015).

von Hagen, M. (1995) 'Does Ukraine Have a History?' *Slavic Review*, 54(3), pp. 658-673.

Himka, J. (1999) *Religion and Nationality in Western Ukraine: The Greek Catholic Church and the Ruthenian National Movement in Galicia.* McGill-Queen's University Press.

LB.ua (2014) 'Poroshenko Iklyuchaet Federalizatsiyu'. Available at: http://lb.ua/news/2014/11/27/287446_poroshenko_isklyuchaet_federalizatsiyu.html (Accessed: 29 January 2015).

Korrespondent.net (2014) 'At the charity fair in Nikolayev treated "The Blood of Russian babies"'. Available at: http://korrespondent.net/ukraine/comunity/3453219-na-shkolnoi-yarmarke-v-nykolaeve-uhoschaly-krovui-rossyiskykh-mladentsev (Accessed: 28 January 2015).

Khmelko, V. (2004) 'Linguistic and ethnic structure of Ukraine: regional differences and trends of change since independence. Scientific Notes of Kyiv-Mohyla Academy,' *Social science*, 32.

Miller, A. (2003) T*he Ukrainian Question: Russian Nationalism in the 19th Century*. Central European University Press.

Minakov, M. (2014) 'Moses und Prometheus. Die Ukraine zwischen Befreiung und Freiheit,' *Transit: Europäische Revue*, 45, pp. 55-70.

Mirror Weekly (2014). Available at: http://zn.ua/UKRAINE/okolo-30-ukraincev-schitayut-maydan-gosperevorotom-159252_.html (Accessed: 16 Dec 2014)

Pogrebinskiy, M. (ed.) (2013) *The Crises of Multiculturalism and Problems of National Politics*. Moskva Ves`mir.

Pogrebinskiy, M. (ed.) (2010) *Russian Language in Ukraine*. Khar'kov: HPMMS.

Pogrebinskiy, M. (ed.) (2005) *The "Orange Revolution":* Ukrainian version. Moskva: Evropa.

Part Two

POLITICS

8

Ukrainian Politics since Independence

ANDREW WILSON
UNIVERSITY COLLEGE LONDON

Ukraine became independent in 1991, but there was no real revolution – which is why the country tried to have two catch-up revolutions in 2004 and 2014. Independence came about when the collapse of central Soviet power in Moscow suddenly gave a hitherto minority nationalist movement the chance to make an alliance with the Communist elite – the deal being they would back independence, but keep their jobs. The costs of that bargain became clearer over the subsequent decades, as the economy stagnated and Ukraine became one of the most corrupt states in Eastern Europe.

Formal Institutions

Ukraine's neophyte status meant that it was the last post-Soviet state to adopt a new constitution, which took place in 1996. On paper, the document defines 'a democratic, social, law-based state', based on 'the principles of its division into legislative, executive, and judicial power', but in states like Ukraine, the constitution is only a guide to where power lies, not much more than a 'signal' of who the key patrons are and the 'focal points' that shape informal networks (Hale, 2014). The rule of law is weak and so is constitutionalism, defined as respect for the written document as defining the rules of the game, rather than it being the end-product of the game itself. The constitutional order has been radically reshaped three times; in 2004, 2010, and 2014, plus a failed attempt at similar wholesale change in 2000.

Nevertheless, the original document avoids many of the pitfalls of presidentialism. Technically, the system is semi-presidential, though with longer periods of greater presidential power in 1996-2005 and 2010-14, alternating with a premier-presidential system in 2006-10 and after 2014. The state is unitary, with one federal unit of Crimea, which ironically worked well enough as a compromise until 2014 – the local elite were allowed to enrich themselves as long as they did not play with the genie of separatism. An elaborate compromise on language rights ensured the reasonably peaceful coexistence of Ukrainian and Russian speakers before the crisis of 2014.

Informal Rules

The Constitution was only a guide to the real underlying informal system of power. By the time the commanding heights of the economy had been corruptly privatised under President Leonid Kuchma (1994-2005), Ukraine was really run by a cabal of oligarchs and regional bosses, in which the president was the chief arbiter. The chaotic early 1990s were followed by the recovery of state power under Kuchma, enforced by the use of so-called 'administrative resources' (including both the carrot of state patronage and the stick of a legal and tax system designed to reward friends and punish enemies), and disguised by 'political technology' (facade democracy and partly pluralism manipulated behind-the-scenes by Kuchma's presidential administration).

Kuchma's arbiter presidency was not followed by a true democratic breakthrough, but by a competitive diarchy or triarchy after the Orange Revolution; with new President Viktor Yushchenko, who had been Prime Minister under Kuchma from 1999 to 2001, constantly clashing with another insider-not-quite-turned-outsider Yuliya Tymoshenko when she was Prime Minister (2005 and 2007-10) and the Party of Regions headed by the leader of the most powerful regional clan from the Donbas, Viktor Yanukovych, which grew powerful in opposition and briefly controlled the government in 2006-7. Yushchenko was the former head of the Central Bank, while Tymoshenko had been a gas oligarch in the 1990s. In the 2004 election, Yushchenko was largely backed by voters in the West and Centre, while Yanukovych by voters in the East and South.

Constitutional reforms were agreed at the height of the Orange Revolution, to smooth Yushchenko's path to power, and introduced in 2006. They achieved a better balance between the president and parliament, but also helped entrench the bitter competition between the triarchy. Yushchenko and Tymoshenko fought each other into the ground, allowing Yanukovych to win the presidency by default in 2010. Yanukovych rapidly restored a traditional presidential monopoly of power, but then over-reached by attempting a hyper-centralisation of power. He broke the rules of the 2004 constitution, initially to win control of the legislature, where Tymoshenko was initially still Prime

Minister (in spring 2010), and then the judiciary with a highly centralising 'reform' entrenching executive control in the summer, leading to a string of 'political prosecutions' in 2011, including Tymoshenko. The strong-arming of the Constitutional Court to restore the 1996 Constitution in October only capped the process. But Yanukovych also broke two of the rules of post-Soviet non-democracy: he did not share within the elite and his predatory state made too many enemies outside of it.

The Worst Political Elite in Europe?

For almost a quarter of a century, Ukraine has been one of worst-governed states in Europe. The poor quality of the political class is because most are former Communists or co-opted opposition. Historical 'brain drain' and the effect of the purges and Holodomor (Stalin's famine in 1932-3) have also contributed to the situation. However, there are also post-independence factors, the most important of which is the difference between a resource state and a rentier state. Independent Ukraine did not have the abundant energy resources of Russia and Azerbaijan; instead, it had energy transit and raw materials, and a model of steel and chemical production based on rents from subsidised state inputs. So Ukraine had enough rent for the corrupt elite, but not enough to pay for a social contract, like in Russia, or even, using Russian money, in Belarus.

Except that was not enough to satisfy the elite. According to Yuliya Mostova, the editor of Ukraine's main opposition paper, *Dzerkalo tyzhnya*, understanding Yanukovych was always easy: 'He wanted to be the richest man in Eastern Europe' (Mostova, 2011). But that led in turn to a problem that was well identified by the leading economic and energy analyst Mykhailo Honchar: 'Yanukovych wanted to be both president and number one oligarch. Like all those other guys – Putin, Nazarbayev and Aliyev. Except they had energy and rents to distribute. Ukraine does not.' (Honchar, 2014).

But Yanukovych and his coterie carried on regardless. Under his rule, Ukraine became a pathologically predatory state, with an alleged 50% cut from all significant business and a tax-and-destroy policy against SMEs, driving the economy into the ground.

Ineffective Opposition

In the 1960s and 1970s, Ukraine had one of the biggest dissident movements in the USSR. Around 1,000 were in and out of trouble with the authorities, but the broader hinterland of passive supporters was much larger (Krawchenko, 1983). Normally, size would have been thought to be an advantage, but it was actually double-edged. A bigger movement meant more KGB control and more internal agents, and the KGB was always much tougher in Kiev than it was in Moscow. The same generation was still around to block more radical and more competent opposition forces when the Ukrainian Popular Front Rukh was formed in 1989. Rukh was always primed to cooperate with moderate Communists.

Rukh then split too early in 1992, when it still had some good arguments, and when its popular front function was still potentially intact. Significantly, it was the part of Rukh that cooperated with the new authorities that soon disappeared without trace; but Rukh, with its agenda essentially unfulfilled, was still around to come in second place in the 1998 elections. So the authorities encouraged it to split again in 1999.

The next reinvention of the opposition took place in 2002: Our Ukraine broke through to win almost a quarter of the vote by transcending traditional narrow cultural nationalism, but also by accepting leadership figures who had previously been part of Kuchma's elite, headed by Yushchenko, who saw Our Ukraine as a moderate balancing force. Kuchma was, however, weakened by scandal (the death of the journalist Hryhoriy Gongagdze in 2000), and was unable to stop the Donetsk group imposing Yanukovych as their candidate for the presidency in 2004. Yanukovych's candidacy upset the system of elite balance, and he had too few supporters when his crude attempts to fix the vote and deny Yushchenko the presidency led to the mass protests dubbed the 'Orange Revolution' in 2004.

However, although the protestors expressed a range of frustrations and inchoate demands, the Orange Revolution was really only about electing Yushchenko. He duly took office after a repeat vote and the protestors went home. Our Ukraine promptly re-absorbed itself into the political system. After the 2010 elections, its remnants and successors, including Tymoshenko's party, Fatherland, would only survive if they accepted Yanukovych's new rules of the game. The opposition parties, including Fatherland, took funding from oligarchs in order to survive. This also included the far-right Freedom Party, which provided the big surprise of the 2012 parliamentary elections by winning 10% of the vote, largely because it convinced a sufficient number of voters that it was the most radical opposition to Yanukovych – before a real opposition organised itself in 2014.

Underlying Pluralism

I have deliberately mentioned Ukraine's undoubted underlying pluralism late in the analysis. Ukraine is a new state with many underlying divisions of ethnicity, language, and religion, although the most powerful division of all is regional and regionally-based patronal networks. These well-known internal divisions would have been less of a factor if Ukrainian politicians had been brave enough, or competent enough, to transcend them. Instead, they have exploited and exacerbated them to stay in power. Moreover, it was politicians from East Ukraine who did most of the polarising. Ideology and the idea of European destiny were stronger forces in western Ukraine, so public opinion was harder to manipulate, although there were many nationalist politicians capable of alienating voters in the East. But a post-Soviet culture of paternalism, social atomisation, and Soviet Ukrainian mythology was still strong in the East and South, where politicians were able to win and retain power with a mixture of welfare and patronage and so-called 'political technology' that exploited anti-West Ukrainian stereotypes.

The Maidan as a Multiple Revolution

Yanukovych's presidency could not maintain that mixture. More exactly, its ability to distribute even limited economic benefits was increasingly circumscribed. The economy recovered briefly in 2010-11 from one of the worst recessions in Europe in 2009, when GDP fell by 15%, but Yanukovych's predatory state had destroyed growth by the second half of 2012. Yanukovych and the ruling Party of Regions began to lose support even in their East Ukrainian heartlands, and were increasingly dependent on fraud and political technology to divide and corrupt the opposition to stay in power.

One belated fruit of the Yushchenko Presidency was negotiations on a trade agreement with the European Union, which had only begun belatedly in 2007, and had produced a signable agreement by 2012. However, democratic deterioration, symbolised by the imprisonment of Tymoshenko, kept the agreement on ice. Russia, meanwhile, suddenly discovered an intense hostility to the agreement, driven by Putin's launching of the Eurasian Union project as one of the main themes for his re-election campaign in 2012.

The second 'Maidan' (the name of Kiev's central square where protestors gathered) was therefore about many things. It was triggered by Yanukovych succumbing to Russian pressure and refusing to sign the EU Association Agreement on the eve of a crucial EU summit in Vilnius in November 2013. But the real underlying fear was that Yanukovych would now have a free hand to consolidate his regime and undermine all vestiges of democracy. The protests were therefore also against the traditional opposition, which was a corrupted part of that system. The Maidan was an attempt to reinvent opposition politics in Ukraine after Rukh in the 1990s and Our Ukraine in the early 2000s, but this time with a stronger base in civil society.

The Maidan protests in 2013-14 therefore grew more radical, but were also beyond the control of traditional politicians. Yanukovych veered between a mixture of repression and concessions that only swelled protestors' ranks. The notorious 'repression laws', rammed through parliament on 16 January 2014, only created a sense of now-or-never.

Civil Society versus the System

Other chapters describe in detail the events before and after the February Uprising in Kiev. But several general points can be made. The protests revealed how much stronger Ukrainian civil society was in 2014 compared to 2004. And not just numerically; it was more proactive and much more modern than the political class. Civil society used technology, which the political class did not. New media sources like Hromadske TV tapped new audiences, and new media methods like stopfake.org counteracted Russian propaganda. Civil society groups used innovative crowd-sourcing methods and helped channel funds to the armed forces (the People's Project at narodniy.org.ua, and armyhelp.com.ua), setting a standard of transparency that shamed the Ukrainian state. Activists and journalists did excellent work analysing the incriminating documents left behind by Yanukovych at sites like yanukovychleaks.org and the Anti-Corruption Action Centre at antac.org.ua/en. One of the most effective technologies was the use of drones equipped with cameras to fly over the homes of mysteriously opulent politicians.

Civil society was also strongly motivated to do better this time than after 2004. We will never know, counterfactually, how good an attempt at transformation Ukraine might have made if Russia had not intervened. But once it did, the moment of what Leszek Balcerowicz called 'extraordinary politics' – front-loading radical measures to drive change while you are still popular – was in danger of being lost. The pseudo-patriotic argument that dramatic change was not possible while Ukraine was at war largely carried the day, even though preventing such change was one of the main objectives of Russia's action. The oligarch and political veteran Petro Poroshenko won the Presidency in May 2014, largely because he promised a safe pair of hands. But by the time pre-term parliamentary elections were held in October, a nominal cease-fire had been in place since 5 September and there was a popular mood to return to the reform agenda largely abandoned in February. Poroshenko's new eponymous Bloc failed to win its expected victory, though did well in former Party of Regions areas; voters in the West and Centre backed Prime Minister Yatseniuk's Popular Front and the new party Self-Help. The elections saw a much bigger turnover overall: 56% of all MPs, that is 236 out of 423, were new (27 seats in Crimea and the Donbas remained empty because of annexation or conflict) (Chesno.org, 2014).

Conclusions

Ukraine restored the 2004 Constitution on 21 February 2014, and the premier-presidential system with it. But unlike in 2006-10, after Yanukovych's flight and the collapse of the Party of Regions, parliament and presidency were in theory now controlled by the same political camp. Super-majorities were briefly possible in Spring 2014, then the old guard recovered its veto power in the summer, but they were much diminished in strength by the October elections. A new government with a healthy majority was then in place by December. Plans for yet another rewrite of the Constitution were much discussed in the summer, however, with so many pressing military and economic issues, they were less prominent in the new government's reform priorities.

But Ukrainian politics would clearly remain a general struggle between old-style politics and new. What is not clear is how much of the old informal politics had changed.

References

Chesno.org (2014) Parlamentskiy Brozhai, 30 October. Available at: http://chesno.org/media/gallery/2014/10/30/parl_results.jpg.

Hale, H. (2014) *Patronal Politics: Eurasian Regime Dynamics in Comparative Perspective*. Cambridge: Cambridge University Press, p. 10.

Honchar, M. (2014) Interview. 18 February.

Krawchenko, B. and Carter, A.J. (1983) 'Dissidents in Ukraine Before 1972: A Summary Statistical Profile,' *Journal of Ukrainian Studies*, 8(2), pp. 85-88, Winter.

Mostova, Y. (2011) Interview. 'Semostiinyi Yanukovych', Dzerkalo tyzhnia, 1 June 2012. Available at: http://gazeta.dt.ua/POLITICS/semostiyniy_yanukovich.html.

9

The Origins of Peace, Non-Violence, and Conflict in Ukraine

TARAS KUZIO
UNIVERSITY OF ALBERTA

Crimea was annexed by Russia in March 2014, a month after the Euromaidan revolution led to President Viktor Yanukovych fleeing from Ukraine. This was followed by the launch of a separatist rebellion that targeted the eight Russophone oblasts of Eastern and Southern Ukraine. In September 2014, a tenuous ceasefire was negotiated after five months of intense fighting that claimed 5,000 civilians and as many as 10,000 Ukrainian military, separatists, and Russian soldiers dead, wounded, and missing.[12] The very high number of combatant casualties reflects the viciousness and intensity of a relatively short war; in contrast, 600 soldiers and police officers were killed in Northern Ireland over a three-decade terrorist conflict. This is clearly not a terrorist conflict (despite Kiev's name given to its operations as ATO [Anti-Terrorist Operation]) but an insurgency; that is a conflict lying between a full-scale war and terrorism. As a result of the annexation of Crimea by the Russian Federation and the armed conflict in Ukrainian Donbas, over 921,000 people (as of 23 January 2015) have registered as internally displaced persons

---

[12] The official Ukrainian number of casualties is 1,300, far too low a figure as it does not include National Guard soldiers and nationalist volunteers. The separatists do not collect casualty figures of their own fighters, while Russia denies it has troops inside Ukraine; nevertheless, Russian NGOs have collected casualty lists ranging from 1,500 to over 5,000 Russian dead, which would suggest an even higher number of separatist casualties (Kuzio, 2014b). The Ukrainian and Russian armed forces do not wear dog tag identifications, as do European and North American armies, making it also difficult to compile true casualty lists.

(IDPs) within Ukraine, and over 524,000 have sought asylum or other legal status in the Russian Federation (PACE, 2015). Nevertheless, eighty percent of Ukrainians believe Ukraine is at war with Russia, according to a December poll. International organisations and human rights bodies have systematically reported widespread human rights abuses by separatist and Russian nationalist groups, while Ukrainian forces have been criticized for indiscriminate shelling of civilian areas (Amnesty International, 2014; Council of Europe, 2014; Human Rights Watch, 2014; Organisation for Security and Cooperation in Europe, 2014; United Nations, 2014).

This article seeks to understand why a bitter conflict took place in Ukraine after nearly two decades of peaceful inter-ethnic and inter-regional relations with a deepened partition following Russia's recognition of the 2 November 2014 'elections' in the Luhansk People's Republic (LNR) and Donetsk People's Republics (DNR). In the 1990s and 2000s, Ukraine resolved the Crimean separatist challenge at the same time as frozen conflicts emerged in Moldova, Georgia, and Azerbaijan, and Russia fought two wars in Chechnya.

Ukraine's transition from a state at peace to being in conflict with the Donbas and Russia is an outgrowth of four factors: first, rise of authoritarian and neo-Soviet political forces (Party of Regions, United Russia); second, reaction to Western-supported popular protests (Bulldozer, Rose and Orange Revolutions, Euromaidan); third, strong opposition to NATO and EU enlargement; and fourth, rise of nationalism and revisionism in Russian foreign policy.

Rise of Authoritarian and Neo-Soviet Political Forces

The Party of Regions and United Russia are united in their authoritarian, neo-Soviet, and populist-paternalistic operating culture. Both are difficult to classify using Western political science definitions because they unite oligarchs, attract former Communist Party voters, and uphold Soviet ideological tenets, such as state paternalism, anti-fascist discourse, and distrust of the West, particularly the US and NATO. The Party of Regions was allied to centrist parties during Leonid Kuchma's presidency (1994-2004) and therefore was routinely defined as 'centrist.' This, though, was misleading, as Eastern Ukrainian centrist parties had emerged from the Komsomol's (Communist Youth League) Democratic Platform within the Soviet Communist Party in the late 1980s and were seeking to build liberal parties targeting middle-class voters. The Party of Regions was very different, an ally of big business and indifferent or hostile to the middle class which twice led and financed rebellions against Yanukovych in the form of the Orange Revolution and Euromaidan.

At the same time, there are as many differences as there are similarities. United Russia is a typical Eurasian party of power that draws on senior former Soviet nomenklatura and security officials with their base in the country's central cities. The Party of Regions hails from the working-class and coalmining city of Donetsk (twinned with Britain's Sheffield) that never had influence in the central ruling organs of Soviet Ukraine, which was dominated by local elites from Kiev, Dnipropetrovsk, and Kharkiv. The Party of Regions is unique in the former Soviet space in being launched by a nexus of new oligarchs, old Soviet Red Directors, Pan-Slavic and regional activists, and organised crime figures (Kuzio, 2014a; Wilson, 2014, pp.126-128) that established a successful political machine that won four parliamentary and presidential elections in 2006-2012 (Kudelia and Kuzio, 2015). Mark Galeotti (2014) has pointed out that 'Crime, especially organised crime, has been at the heart of the events in Ukraine from the start,' and Russian and Ukrainian political leaders have a long record of collaboration with organised crime figures in the post-Soviet era (Dawisha, 2014, pp.15, 39, 62, 79, 83, 144, 158; Kupchinsky, 2009).

Another difference is nationalist ideology, which has always been present in United Russia, but not in the Party of Regions – a typical Eastern Ukrainian ideologically amorphous political force. Yanukovych and Putin are both kleptocrats, but the latter is also committed to building Russia as a great power, while the former starved the Ukrainian military of resources, mishandled its military reform launched in 2007, and then permitted a foreign power (Russia) to exert influence over the leadership of the presidential guard, military, and Security Service (SBU).

Although both were successful political machines, only United Russia and Putin could sustain genuine popularity through widespread public backing for Russian great power nationalism and high energy prices for much of the 2000s that increased living standards. Yanukovych's popularity had slumped to the low 20s in polls conducted just ahead of the Euromaidan, and without massive election fraud, he could not have won re-election in 2015. Ukraine's regional diversity made it impossible for the Party of Regions to dominate the country to the same extent as United Russia does in the Russian Federation. Yanukovych's failure to understand that Ukraine is not Russia, as the 2004 book by Leonid Kuchma is titled, ultimately led to his loss of power.

The Party of Regions did have some ideological members who included supporters of pan-Slavic and Soviet nationalism and integrated ideologues, such as Oleksandr Bazyliuk (Congress of Russian Organisations of Ukraine, Civic Congress renamed as the Slavic Unity Party), Vadym Kolesnychenko (Human Rights Public Movement "Russian-speaking Ukraine"), and Dmytro

Tabachnyk who was Education Minister in two Nikolai Azarov governments in 2010-2014 (Kryuchkov and Tabachnyk, 2008). They were members of Yanukovych's team that differentiated itself from Ukraine's earlier presidents in adopting Russia's position on the 1933 famine as a Soviet-wide tragedy (not genocide against Ukraine); emphasising the Great Patriotic War (not World War II); returning to Soviet denunciations of Ukrainian nationalism and Crimean Tatars as Nazi collaborators and 'fascists'; and distrust of the NATO, US, and the West in general. The Party of Regions, Communist Party of Ukraine (KPU), and Crimean Russian nationalists upheld Soviet dictator Joseph Stalin's justification for the 1944 deportation of Crimean Tatars when half their number died, a historic event viewed as genocide by them. In May 2014, only three months after Russia's annexation of the Crimea, the local authorities banned the annual commemoration of the deportation and closed down the unofficial Mejlis Tatar parliament (Coynash, 2014b, c, d; Council of Europe, 2014).

The Party of Regions was willing to countenance an alliance with Crimean Russian nationalists and the KPU, a step that would have been unpalatable to Kuchma, who defeated both political forces in 1995 and 1999, respectively. Kuchma marginalised Crimean Russian nationalists whilst the Party of Regions revived them after it cemented an alliance with United Russia in 2005, and a year later, Russian political technologist Konstantin Zatulin brokered an election alliance of the Party of Regions and Russian nationalists that won a majority in the Crimean parliament. In the 2014 Crimean parliamentary and local elections, many former Party of Regions deputies were elected by United Russia that won a majority of seats. In 2008, the Party of Regions, KPU, and Crimean Russian nationalists were the only political forces in the Commonwealth of Independent States (outside Russia and frozen conflict enclaves) who supported the independence of South Ossetia and Abkhazia breaking a long-standing consensus among Ukrainian elites in support of the territorial integrity of states. Yanukovych echoed Putin when he justified their support by referring to the independence of Kosovo and 'double standards.'

The Party of Regions was characterised by its willingness to use violence to achieve their goals. The party drew on sportsmen vigilantes for corporate raiding, election fraud, and violent attacks on civil society activists, journalists, and members of the political opposition (Kuzio, 2010a; Wilson, 2014; pp.49, 78-79; Zimmer, 2005). Yanukovych, with a twice-criminal record, is from Donetsk which, together with the Crimea and Odessa, experienced the most violent transitions in Ukraine during the 1990s. Yanukovych, the Donetsk clan, and the Party of Regions were therefore no strangers to violence, and brought their style of politics and business to the national level in the 2004 elections and from 2006, when they were first elected as an independent political force.

Violence was also more likely under Yanukovych for four reasons. First, unlike Kuchma, who left office in 2004 after two terms, Yanukovych in 2013-2014 was preparing for his re-election in 2015, and there was never any doubt but that he sought to remain in power. The second was his penchant for extravagant palaces, such as Mezhyhirya near Kiev, and the imprisonment of political opponents, both of which pointed to his desire to remain in power at all costs and indefinitely. The third was a willingness to use vigilantes and security forces for paramilitary operations against his opponents. During the 2004 elections, Kuchma forbade the entrance of Donetsk vigilantes, who waited in the city's outskirts, into central Kiev, where they would have clashed with Orange Revolution supporters. The fourth was his closer ties to Putin, who held kompromat (compromising materials) on him going back decades when he had worked as a KGB informer reporting on organised crime groups in Donetsk (Leshchenko, 2014, pp. 57, 210-215, 218; Judah, 2014; Wilson, 2014, p.122). Putin held two key meetings with Yanukovych in Sochi (October 2013) and Valdai (January 2014), where he pressured him to drop the EU Association Agreement in the first instance and introduce tough, repressive legislation in the second (which was adopted on 16 January). Yanukovych failed to keep his resolve in the face of a popular protest radicalised by the killing of the 'heavenly hundred' and pursue the security operations to their conclusion. Putin admitted that he assisted Yanukovych in fleeing from Kiev. Russia had supplied anti-riot equipment to Ukraine in December 2013 and January 2014, and FSB officers were based in Kiev assisting in drawing up 'Operation Boomerang' to destroy the protests using overwhelming force (Wilson, 2014, pp. 89-93). The Ukrainian military, which has cooperated with NATO's Partnership for Peace programme since 1994, refused to become involved, as it had during the Orange Revolution (Kuzio, 2010a), and Ukraine's police forces were insufficient in number for the task of suppressing a mass protest movement.

The plan was for Yanukovych to address a founding congress of the Ukrainian Front (founded on 1 February in Kharkiv by the local vigilante organisation Oplot, pro-Russian politicians, former police Berkut special forces, and Night Wolves hell's angels) that would have brought together delegates from Russian-speaking eastern and southern Ukraine (Wilson, 2014, pp. 78-79). They planned to declare Kharkiv the capital of a new autonomous entity (whether 'Novorossiya' – 'New Russia' – is unclear) and invite Russian forces to intervene to 'protect' Russian speakers. Kharkiv is symbolically important, as it was the first capital of Soviet Ukraine from 1922-1934.

The Kharkiv congress was to emulate the November 2004 separatist congress in Severdonetsk, Luhansk oblast, which had pressured opposition candidate Viktor Yushchenko to compromise during EU-brokered roundtable negotiations, except that the situation in 2014 was more critical, as the democratic revolution was unusual in not taking place during an election cycle. The Kharkiv congress did not attract sufficient delegates, and Yanukovych failed to attend after being advised by Donetsk oligarch Rinat Akhmetov and Kharkiv Governor Mykhaylo Dobkin that they would not support him. The Party of Regions (2014) had denounced Yanukoych in a strongly worded statement after he fled from Kiev, blaming him for the murder of protesters, and parliament had voted to remove him from power. He fled to Donetsk and Crimea, and eventually to Russia, from where he called for a Russian intervention in early March. These plans failed not only because Yanukovych left Ukraine, but also because pro-Russian uprisings failed to materialise in four out of Ukraine's eight Russian-speaking oblasts (Dnipropetrovsk, Zaporizhzhya, Kherson, Mykolayiv), and in another two swing regions (Kharkiv, Odessa). Pro-Maidan forces prevailed in the two crucial months of April and May 2014. Pro-Russian separatism only took hold in the Donbas (Donetsk, Luhansk), but even there it required the covert injection of Russian forces, some of whom had been involved in Russia's annexation of the Crimea, and by August, with separatists on the verge of being defeated, Russia's significant intervention, which turned the tide of battle. By the September ceasefire, Ukrainian forces controlled two thirds of the Donbas, and the DNR and LNR one third.

Western-supported Popular Protests (Bulldozer, Rose and Orange Revolutions, Euromaidan)

Putin came to power soon after NATO's bombardment of Yugoslavia, the detachment of Kosovo into a future independent state, and the bulldozer revolution in Serbia that was the first of what became called coloured or democratic revolutions. Kosovo had never been a Yugoslav republic and therefore, unlike the fifteen Soviet and six Yugoslav republics, it had no right under international law to become an independent state, a fact that Russian leaders have continually raised through to their justification of the annexation of the Crimea.

Russian and other post-Soviet leaders, including Yanukovych, were socialised within a conspiracy mindset and they therefore viewed these developments as one chain of events. This worldview deepened with the Rose and Orange Revolutions in 2003 and 2004, respectively, leading to calls in their legislatures (successful in Russia, unsuccessful in Ukraine) to clamp down on alleged Western intelligence support for NGOs and mass popular protests. Russian and Eastern Ukrainian leaders saw little difference between NATO's intervention in Serbia and the US invasion of Iraq, as both did not have UN authorisation.

The return to Soviet *conspiratology* was accompanied by a return to anti-Americanism first witnessed as early as during Ukraine's 2004 presidential elections. Yanukovych's election campaign, led by Russian political technologists (such as Gleb Pavlovsky) on loan from Putin, organised a 'directed chaos' strategy that portrayed Viktor Yushchenko, who has a Ukrainian-American spouse, as a US satrap and extreme nationalist. It was relatively easy to blame the Orange Revolution as a Western-backed putsch following such a negative campaign. Yanukovych's anti-Americanism took place while Ukrainians constituted the third largest military contingent in the US-led coalition in Iraq (and largest non-NATO force).

Needless to say, the Euromaidan that rocked Ukraine in November 2013 to February 2014 was also seen as a Western-backed putsch that overthrew a democratically elected President and brought 'fascists' to power. Yanukovych and Putin always believed the protests were led by extreme right nationalists ('fascists') in another example of the revival of Soviet ideological culture (Kryuchkov and Tabachnyk, 2008). Soviet ideological tirades were most prominent and vociferous against Baltic and especially Ukrainian 'bourgeois nationalists' through KGB-controlled institutions such as Tovarystvo Ukrayiny (shorthand for the Society for Cultural Relations with Ukrainians Abroad). Its two newspapers, *News from Ukraine* and *Visti z Ukrayiny*, specialised in uncovering alleged 'Nazi collaborators' in the Ukrainian diaspora.

Yanukovych could not comprehend the notion of individuals protesting as volunteers and unpaid civil society activists, as their experience is of a world where people attend rallies when they are induced by the threat of losing their state employment or receive payment in cash or kind. Yanukovych drew on 'political tourists' (i.e. paid rally participants) in the 2004 elections and when he was Prime Minister and President (2006-2007, 2010-2014). Differences between Eastern and Western Ukraine can be explained by the existence of a managed democracy and weak civil society in Sovietised Donetsk, and a far more active civil society, with its roots in the nineteenth century Austro-Hungarian Empire and inter-war Poland, in Western Ukraine (Beissinger, 2002; Kuzio, 2010b).

In the Soviet and Russian mindset towards Ukraine, seventeen million discriminated 'Russians' include ethnic Russians and Russian speakers who belong to the Russkii Mir (Russian World). Therefore, democratic revolutions propelled by large numbers of Western Ukrainian participants are inevitably anti-Russian, funded by the West, and dominated by 'nationalists' (equated as 'fascists'). Terms such as 'bourgeois nationalists' and 'fascists' in Soviet and post-Soviet usage have nothing in common with Western political science definitions of the term (Kryuchkov and Tabachnyk, 2008). In the USSR, such terms were applied against all shades of opinion that supported dissidents and Ukrainian cultural and political rights, and in the post-Soviet era against those who welcomed the Orange Revolution and Euromaidan and supported Ukraine's European integration. In the USSR, national communist Ivan Dzyuba, the author of *Internationalism or Russification?*, was therefore as much a 'bourgeois nationalist' as a Greek Catholic religious believer and member of the underground Ukrainian National Front in Soviet Galicia.

In a rather bizarre twist to the conflict in Eastern Ukraine, Donbas separatists have two extremist allies. The first are bona fide Russian fascists and neo-Nazis from the Russian Party of National Unity, who use a modified swastika as their party symbol and whose paramilitaries are fighting alongside separatists (see photographs at Shekhovtsov, 2014). Russian National Unity Party leader Aleksandr Barkashov's intercepted telephone conversation with Donetsk People's Republic leader Dmitriy Boitsov heard the former advising the latter to write that 89 per cent voted in favour in the May 2014 separatist referendum – a figure that became the official result (Barkashov and Boitsov, 2014; Wilson, 2014, p. 133). Crimean leader Sergei Aksyonov (with an organised criminal nickname of Goblin) is a long-time member of the Russian National Unity Party (Kuzio, 2014c). Moreover, Eurasianist ideologue Aleksandr Dugin was fired from Moscow State University after students protested against him saying Ukrainians 'must be killed, killed, killed' (Coynash, 2014a; Dugin, 2014).

The second are Europe's extreme left and right who have sent 'observers' to the March Crimean referendum and November 2014 'election,' and voted against ratification in the European Parliament of the EU Association Agreement (Coynash, 2014e; Orenstein, 2014). France's neo-Nazi Front National contributed the largest bloc of votes against the Association Agreement and has admitted receiving a large loan from a Russian bank.

NATO and EU Enlargement

Russia had always opposed NATO enlargement and this came to a head in the case of Georgia and Ukraine in 2005-2008, when enlargement received the enthusiastic support of the US Bush administration. In April 2008, Putin told the NATO-Russia Council at the Bucharest NATO Summit that Ukraine was a 'fragile' and 'artificial' state, warning it would disintegrate if it joined NATO. Yushchenko strongly backed President Mikhail Saakashvili when he visited Tbilisi after Russia's invasion in August of that year. In Summer 2009, President Dmitri Medvedev laid out a host of demands for the next Ukrainian President that Yanukovych fulfilled, such as extending the lease on the Black Sea Fleet base in Sevastopol until the middle of the century and ending support for NATO membership. Both of these Russian strategic objectives were threatened by Yanukovych's removal from power and replacement by what Moscow viewed as radical nationalists.

Russia's concerns about the Eastern Partnership (EaP), an EU initiative for post-Soviet states, was evident from its launch in 2009, even though it never laid out the prospect of future membership and was therefore derided by some Western scholars as 'enlargement-lite.' Russian worries were especially vociferous in the case of Ukraine, the largest of the EaP members. The effective separation of Ukraine's most pro-Russian regions (Crimea, Donbas) prevented their participation in the May 2014 presidential and October 2014 parliamentary preterm elections, which, coupled with the disintegration of the Party of Regions and unpopularity of its satellite Communist Party after Yanukovych fled from office, produced Ukraine's first pro-European parliamentary constitutional majority. Putin gained Crimea and part of the Donbas enclave, but lost Ukraine.

Russian Nationalism and Foreign Policy

The evolution of Putin and his militocratic regime beholden to nationalistic ideology took place during the fifteen years that Ukraine transitioned through four Presidents – Kuchma (2000-2004), Yushchenko (2005-2010), Yanukovych (2010-2014), and Petro Poroshenko (2014 to present). Putin's best relations were with Kuchma, an Eastern Ukrainian and therefore not ideologically suspect, who was a member of the senior Soviet nomenklatura (which Yanukovych never was). Yushchenko was anathema to Russian leaders who may have been behind his September 2004 poisoning. Yanukovych was more palatable because of his Donetsk background and willingness to implement Russian demands, work with Crimean Russian nationalists, and give free rein to Russia's intelligence services in Crimea (something that would become useful in Spring 2014). Medvedev's 2009 open letter to Yushchenko followed the expulsion of two Russian diplomats from Crimea and Odessa for espionage and covert support for separatists and the pro-Russian extremist Rodina party. Valentyn Nalyvaychenko, the then Chairman of the SBU, resumed this position in February 2014 with a more expanded campaign against Russian GRU and FSB agents backing 'directed chaos' and separatism (Kuzio, 2015).

Relations with Poroshenko should have been similar to those with Kuchma, as both are centrists and not anti-Russian; Poroshenko was born in Odessa and had business interests in Russia. Poroshenko was a founding member of the Party of Regions in 2000-2001 and had been a cabinet minister in the second Azarov government. Nevertheless, Poroshenko supported the Euromaidan early on, before it was known if it would succeed, and he came to power three months after the annexation of Crimea and two months after Donbas broke down into separatist violence. As his constitutional duty is to protect Ukraine's territorial integrity, he therefore had little choice but to act as Commander-in-Chief.

Russian nationalism is closely bound with Soviet myths and national identity, and these inevitably influence attitudes towards Ukraine. In this worldview, 'New Russia' – the Tsarist term for Southern Ukraine, but now expanded to include Donbas – includes Ukraine's Russian speakers. Chauvinistic derision towards the Ukrainian language was inherited from the USSR and has always been strongest in Crimea and Donbas and in Russia more broadly (Fournier, 2002). Putin has described Ukraine as an 'artificial state' whose territory was often changed in the course of the twentieth century. More importantly, Putin has repeatedly stated that 'the Russian and Ukrainian people is practically one people' with 'common historical roots and common destiny, we have a common religion, a common faith, we have a similar culture, language, tradition, and mentality' (Wilson, 2014, pp. 148-149). A 'common destiny' implies that Ukraine can only have a future alongside Russia – not outside Russia's sphere of influence in Europe – while Putin's conservative values project is promoted with Europe and the West vilified as decadent and of a lower civilisation to Russia's (BBC Monitoring, 2014). Controlling Ukraine is not only a strategic objective for Russia to regain its great power status, but an important component of its national identity that has always stressed unity of the three Eastern Slavic peoples, beginning in Kievan Rus' and continuing to Tsarist Russia and the USSR, with the CIS Customs Union-Eurasian Union the natural home (not NATO or EU). Spiritual unity is provided by the Russian Orthodox Church, which has a greater number of parishes in Ukraine than in the Russian Federation.

Conclusion

Ukraine descended into violence during and after the Euromaidan for the four reasons outlined above. Yanukoych and the Party of Regions had different social origins to Eastern Ukrainian centrists and were more willing to use violence and to back Russian objectives. The Euromaidan took place fourteen years after Putin first came to power, during which Russian nationalism and Soviet political culture began to be more influential, producing strongly negative attitudes to Ukrainian national identity defined outside the Russkii

Mir, democratic revolutions, and NATO and EU enlargement.

References

Amnesty International (2014) 'Ukraine: Mounting evidence of abduction and torture,' 10 July. Available at: http://www.amnesty.ca/news/news-releases/ukraine-mounting-evidence-of-abduction-and-torture.

Barkashov, A. and Boitsov, D. (2014) Telephone conversation on the upcoming May 2014 Donbas separatist referendum. Available at: https://www.youtube.com/watch?v=1xeCWGxGVUk.

BBC Monitoring (2014) 'Feature: Russian TV passes off porn parody as West's depravity,' BBC, 1 December.

Beissinger, M.R. (2002) *Nationalist Mobilization and the Collapse of the Soviet State*. Cambridge: Cambridge University Press.

Coynash, H. (2014a) 'Russian fascist ideologue Dugin: Why stop with Donetsk and Luhansk?' *Kharkiv Human Rights Protection Group*, 1 September. Available at: http://khpg.org/en/index.php?id=1409512010.

Coynash, H (2014b) 'Targeting the Crimean Tatar Mejlis as pro-Russian euphoria fades in Crimea,' *Kharkiv Human Rights Protection Group*, 19 September. Available at: http://khpg.org/en/index.php?id=1411135890.

Coynash, H. (2014c) 'Crimean Tatar TV channel ATR accused of 'extremism,' *Kharkiv Human Rights Protection Group*, 25 September. Available at: http://khpg.org/en/index.php?id=1411646632.

Coynash, H. (2014d) 'Moscow endorses offensive against Crimean Tatar Mejlis,' *Kharkiv Human Rights Protection Group*, 26 September. Available at: http://khpg.org/index.php?do=print&id=1411739009.

Coynash, H. (2014e) 'The Crimean referendum's neo-Nazi observers,' *Kharkiv Human Rights Protection Group*, 16 March. Available at: http://khpg.org/en/index.php?id=1394946269.

Dawisha, K. (2014) Putin's Kleptocracy. *Who Own's Russia?* New York: Simon and Schuster.

Dugin, A. (2014) video, 'Putin's Advisor Dugin says Ukrainians must be killed, killed, killed.' Available at: https://www.youtube.com/watch?v=MQ-uqmnwKF8.

Fournier, A. (2002) 'Mapping Identities: Russian Resistance to Linguistic Ukrainianisation in Central and Eastern Ukraine,' *Europe-Asia Studies*, 54(3), pp. 415-433.

Galeotti, M. (2014) 'How the Invasion of Ukraine Is Shaking Up the Global Crime Scene,' *Vice*, 6 November. Available at: http://www.vice.com/read/how-the-invasion-of-ukraine-is-shaking-up-the-global-crime-scene-1106.

Human Rights Watch (2014), 'Ukraine: Rebel Forces Detain, Torture Civilians,' 28 August. Available at: http://www.hrw.org/news/2014/08/28/ukraine-rebel-forces-detain-torture-civilians.

Judah, B. (2014) 'Putin's Coup,' *Politico*, 19 October. Available at: http://www.politico.com/magazine/story/2014/10/vladimir-putins-coup-112025_Page3.html#.VIAbJDGUcrU.

Kryuchkov, H. and Tabachnyk, D. (2008) *Fashizm v Ukraine: ugroza ili realnost?* Kharkiv: Folio.

Kudelia, S. and Kuzio, T. (2015) 'Nothing personal: explaining the rise and decline of political machines in Ukraine,' *Post-Soviet Affairs*, 31(1).

Kupchinsky, R. (2009) 'The Strange Ties between Semion Mogilevich and Vladimir Putin,' *Eurasia Daily Monitor*, 6(57), 25 March. Available at: http://www.jamestown.org/single/?no_cache=1&tx_ttnews%5Bswords%5D=8fd5893941d69d0be3f378576261ae3e&tx_ttnews%5Bany_of_the_words%5D=PKK&tx_ttnews%5Bpointer%5D=3&tx_ttnews%5Btt_news%5D=34753&tx_ttnews%5BbackPid%5D=381&cHash=2cf5525019#.VIAoYDGUcrU

Kuzio, T. (2010a) 'State-Led Violence in Ukraine's 2004 Elections and Orange Revolution,' *Communist and Post-Communist Studies*, 43(4), pp. 383-395.

Kuzio, T. (2010b) 'Nationalism, Identity and Civil Society in Ukraine: Understanding the Orange Revolution,' *Communist and Post-Communist Studies*, 43(3), pp. 285-296.

Kuzio, T. (2014a) 'Crime, Politics and Business in 1990s Ukraine,' *Communist and Post-Communist Politics*, 47(2), pp. 195-210.

Kuzio, T. (2014b) 'In Ukraine, it is time to call a war a war,' *Financial Times*, 27 November. Available at: http://blogs.ft.com/beyond-brics/2014/11/27/guest-post-in-ukraine-it-is-time-to-call-a-war-a-war/.

Kuzio, T. (2014c) 'Crime and Politics in Crimea,' *Open Democracy*, 14 March. Available at: https://www.opendemocracy.net/od-russia/taras-kuzio/crime-and-politics-in-crimea-Aksyonov-Goblin-Wikileaks-Cables.

Kuzio, T (2015) 'Is Russia a State Sponsor of Terrorism,' *New Eastern Europe*, 22 January. Available at: http://neweasterneurope.eu/articles-and-commentary/1461-is-russia-a-state-sponsor-of-terrorism.

Leshchenko, L. (2014) *Mezhyhirskyy Syndrom. Diahnoz vladi Viktora Yanukovycha*. Kiev: Bright Star Publishing.

Muižnieks, N. (2014) 'Report by Commissioner for Human Rights, following his mission in Kiev, Moscow and Crimea, from 7 to 12 September 2014,' *Council of Europe*, 27 October. Available at: https://wcd.coe.int/ViewDoc.jsp?Ref=CommDH(2014)19&Language=lanEnglish.

Orenstein, M. A. (2014) 'Putin's Western Allies. Why Europe's Far Right Is on the Kremlin's Side,' *Foreign Affairs*, 25 March. Available at: http://www.foreignaffairs.com/articles/141067/mitchell-a-orenstein/putins-western-allies.

Organisation for Security and Cooperation in Europe (2014) 'Ukraine, Human Rights Assessment Mission: Report on the Human Rights and Minority Rights Situation,' The Hague/Warsaw, 12 May. Available at: http://www.osce.org/odihr/118476.

Parliamentary Assembly of the Council of Europe (PACE) (2015) 'The humanitarian situation of Ukrainian refugees and displaced persons,' Committee on Migration, Refugees and Displaced Persons report, *Council of Europe*, 23 January. Available from: http://assembly.coe.int/nw/xml/XRef/Xref-XML2HTML-en.asp?fileid=21335&lang=en.

Party of Regions (2014) 'Statement by the Party of Regions Faction,' 23 February. Available at: http://partyofregions.ua/en/news/5309dfd9f620d2f70b000031.

Shekhovtsov, A. (2014) 'Neo-Nazi Russian National Unity in Eastern Ukraine.' Available at: http://anton-shekhovtsov.blogspot.co.uk/2014/08/neo-nazi-russian-national-unity-in.html.

Office of the United Nations High Commissioner for Human Rights (2014) 'Report on the Human Rights Situation in Ukraine,' 15 May. Available at: http://www.ohchr.org/Documents/Countries/UA/HRMMUReport15May2014.pdf.

Wilson, A. (2014) *Ukraine Crisis. What it Means for the West.* New Haven: Yale University Press.

Zimmer, K. (2005) 'The Comparative Failure of Machine Politics, Administrative Resources and Fraud,' *Canadian Slavonic Papers*, 47 (3-4), pp. 361-384.

10

The Ukrainian Crisis and its Impact on Transforming Russian Nationalism Landscape

MARLENE LARUELLE
GEORGE WASHINGTON UNIVERSITY

The Ukrainian crisis shattered the ideological status quo in Russia, the place of so-called 'Russian nationalists' in the public space, and the competition between different groups claiming to represent the authentic interests of the Russian state. In this article, I discuss the three main impacts of the Ukrainian crisis on the landscape of Russian nationalism: its division in interpreting the several crises, its successes in framing the Novorossiya narrative, and its ambivalences at debating the relationship between an imperial appeal and xenophobic feelings.

Three Ukrainian Crises – Three Responses by Russian Nationalists

The first phase of the crisis in Ukraine – the Euromaidan – has created deep divisions within nationalist movements. The so-called 'national-democrats' expressed solidarity with Maidan, seeing it as an example of successful grassroots democratic revolution against a corrupt and authoritarian regime. This minority supported the Ukrainian nationalist Svoboda movement in its struggle for 'national liberation'. Some of them, often with neo-Nazi sympathies, still today fight on the side of the pro-Ukrainian Azov volunteers' battalions. On the other side of the spectrum, majority movements that can be defined as statist and/or imperialist shared the Kremlin's vision of Euromaidan as a neo-fascist coup organised with the support of the United States.

The second stage of the crisis – the annexation of Crimea – abruptly changed the stakes, creating a moment of near-unanimity around Vladimir Putin. Very few nationalist figures have had the courage to challenge the annexation. Many of pro-Maidan nationalists, for instance Konstantin Krylov, shifted toward the defence of ethnic Russians and the 'right to self-determination', while remaining critical toward Putinism. There have been a few exceptions among the national-democrats, for instance Aleksei Navalny, who saw it as a violation of international law and did not want to see a new area subjected to the Russian non-democratic and corrupt regime. For all other groups, the time had come for reconciliation with a regime some had for years denounced as leading an a-national, or even anti-Russian, policy, and to celebrate the statesmanlike stature of Vladimir Putin.

With the third stage of the conflict – the pro-Russian secessionism in the Donbas region – the nationalist circles had to elaborate a more complex positioning. They support Putin in his interpretation of the conflict – Russia has the 'right to protect' Russian minorities abroad when they are threatened by an unfriendly regime – but accuse him of having insufficient courage to defend militarily the secessionist regions. For the more radical, the correct solution was not to create a new frozen conflict against the Kyiv authorities, but to turn the Donbas into a second Crimea, a successful example of an almost blood-free annexation. The current situation of a humanitarian crisis, with several thousand dead, hundreds of thousands of displaced, a destroyed industrial fabric, and no political solution in sight, is apprehended more a failure for Russian great-powerness than a success. For those calling for a general 'awakening' of the Russian population – suddenly ready to fight not only for Donbas, but to export a 'national liberation' war in Russia itself – against Western presence and oligarch domination, the disillusion is even greater. Russia's population supports the Kremlin's reading of the crisis and the need to protect Donetsk and Lugansk. However, it shows a growing fatigue linked to the ongoing crisis and is mostly concerned about the impact of sanctions on standards of living; two elements that have disappointed Russian nationalist circles.

The Novorossiya Narrative and its Main Propagandists

Although disappointed, Russian nationalists try to take advantage of the current patriotic atmosphere for consolidating their media reach. The fight for Donbas offers them a unique narrative. For the first time since the battle between Yeltsin's troops and the defenders of the Supreme Soviet in October 1993, Russian nationalists finally have a story that celebrates their achievements in both words and images (and in music), offering the whole array of heroic battles and martyrs. Igor Strelkov, who was transformed into a living icon before being 'recalled' by the Kremlin and slowly marginalised, embodied this narrative. One of the main successes of nationalists has been the widespread use of the term of 'Novorossiya' to define not only the Donbas, but also other potentially secessionist regions of Ukraine. With origins dating from the second half of the 18th century, the term was revived during the Ukraine crisis and gained indirect official validation when Russian President Vladimir Putin used it during a call-in show in April 2014 to evoke the situation of the Russian-speaking population of Ukraine.

As I explored in other papers, the 'Novorossiya' term can be understood through a triple lens: 'red', 'white', and 'brown'. The first 'red' ideological motif nurturing Novorossiya emphasises Soviet memory. The 'red' reading of Novorossiya justifies the Donbas insurgency in the name of geopolitical arguments, Russia's destiny as a large territory, and Soviet perceptions of the Donbas as a region proud of its industrial legacy and one that shows the way to a new oligarchic-free Russia. The 'white' approach to Novorossiya sees the Donbas insurgency as a vehicle that can open the way to a renewal of political Orthodoxy. This, in turn, will confirm Russia's status as a herald of conservative values and Christianity and, for some adherents of this view, popularise the notion of a new monarchy. It sees in Orthodoxy both a civilisational principle that makes Russia a distinct country, and a political value that resonates with the regime. Novorossiya also became the engine of the so-called Russian Spring, which claims that the ongoing 'national revolution' should not only fight Kyiv, but export itself to Russia. This motif can be defined as neo-fascist and therefore 'brown'; it calls for a totalitarian national revolution that would overthrow the current regime and transform society. It combines an allegedly leftist discourse denouncing corporations and oligarchs, and a focus on the dangers threatening the survival of the nation, two features typical of fascist movements.

The most vocal and organised group that has been able to make the most of the Ukrainian crisis is the Izborsky Club. Created in late 2012 as a response to the Bolotnaya protests organised by the liberal opposition, the Izborsky Club brings together almost 30 nationalist or conservative ideologists and politicians – who often have contradictory views and conflictual personal relations – under the leadership of an old but always vigorous Alexander Prokhanov. Prokhanov, who presented himself as a Soviet imperialist, cultivated his own network of friends in the military and the security services, and uses the Club as a platform to develop a nationalist storyline that can then be transmitted to the upper echelons of power. The Club's main members – Prokhanov first, followed by the co-founder Vitali Averyanov, and then by the Eurasianist geopolitician Alexander Dugin – have been able to consolidate media visibility through their personal contacts at Channel One – Mikhail Leontyev, among many others – to get high visibility on television and online journals. Three other Club members have also used their visibility in the Russian public space to support 'Novorossiya': Natalia Narochnitskaya, director of the Paris-based Institute of Democracy and Cooperation, and famous promoter of political Orthodoxy; Father Tikhon (Shevkunov) a prominent cleric and best-selling writer, the editor of the conservative web-portal Pravoslavie.ru, and rumoured to be Vladimir Putin's personal confessor; and Sergey Glazyev, adviser to the president for regional integration issues, in charge of supervising the Eurasian Union project.

Eurasia or Russian World? Empire or Xenophobia?

Despite this visibility, the concept of 'Novorossiya' and the rapid production of new ideological narratives to explain the Ukrainian crisis failed in resolving the apparent contradiction between the Eurasian Union project and the notion of the 'Russian world' (Russkii mir) advanced by the Russian state to protect Russian minorities abroad. The Eurasian strategy does not aspire to recreate the Soviet Union, as US officials unfortunately stated. Rather, it is based on the need for a more modern approach to reassert Russia's role in its periphery in a more competitive way, based on economic integration. It calls for Russia to look south to Central Asia and east to Asia to balance Western influence, and to accept multi-ethnicity in the name of this regional hegemon status. The 'Russian World' narrative originally was based on an ethnocentric vision of Russians as a divided nation, with 25 million 'compatriots' abroad. In the 2000s, it was able to bypass this ethnic/linguistic focus to broaden its scope, and now looks at boosting Russia's soft power abroad by shaping a 'Russian voice' in the world. However, the terminological inexactitude, which blurs the distinction between the Russian world, Russian compatriots, and Russian-speaking population, continues to endow this notion with an ethnocentric tone that contradicts the multiethnic appeal of Eurasianism.

The 'Eurasia' and 'Russian World' narratives seem to compete, offering a multinational versus an ethnocentric definition of Russia's role in Eurasia. However, several layers in fact need to be dissociated. First, if 'Russian World' is understood as Russia's 'civilisational project' and 'voice' in the world – claiming the respect of established regimes against street revolutions as in Syria, or family-oriented Christian values against gay marriage – then the Eurasian Union is only the economic side of the country's reassertion as a regional hegemon. If 'Russian world' is understood as the defence of ethnic Russians or Russian-speaking population in the near abroad, it is a purely instrumental tool used when the Eurasian appeal fails: only those countries which refuse to integrate into Russia's regional hegemon strategy – Georgia, Moldova, post-Yakukovich Ukraine – see their Russian minorities 'activated'; those who play according to the rules, such as Nazarbaev's Kazakhstan, do not have to face Moscow's support for their Russian minorities. In both cases, the 'Eurasia' and 'Russian World' narratives imbricate in each other more than they conflict.

The real contradictory point in the Russian nationalists' narrative is thus not linked to the near abroad or foreign policy issues, but to domestic stances: how can Russia become an (imperial) regional hegemon when society is massively xenophobic? Two thirds of the population asked for a visa-regime with the Central Asian and South Caucasian republics and would like to see immigration stopped. On that issue, only the 'national-democrats' came up with a logical solution, accepting the idea of a 'retracting' Russia, looking for integration with the West, and establishing a new iron curtain with Central Asia and Asia globally, to avoid being 'invaded' by migrants. This 'national-democratic' group lost its popularity during the Ukrainian crisis: its pro-Maidan stance destroyed its legitimacy to define Russia's identity. The nationalist groups that won from the Ukrainian crisis are on the opposite side of the spectrum, giving priority to the regional hegemon scheme without risking addressing openly the xenophobia issue. On that, they follow the presidential administration line of postponing the moment of choosing a national identity narrative and hoping to maintain the lowest common denominator without defining the level of inclusiveness and exclusiveness of Russia's nationhood.

Conclusion

The Ukrainian crisis has affected the landscape of Russian nationalism by fragmenting the 'national-democrat' scene and strengthening nostalgic aspirations for the recreation of Soviet great-powerness, of Russia's imperial mission, and of the Eurasian Union project. However, media saturation around the Ukrainian crisis will not be eternal, and the disappearance of the migration issue from the spotlight is probably only temporary. Both the regime and the nationalist milieu close to it as the Izborsky Club gained time, but the 'national-democrat' narrative, both xenophobic and pro-European, could return sooner rather than later.

11

An Unnecessary War: The Geopolitical Roots of the Ukraine Crisis

PETER RUTLAND
WESLEYAN UNIVERSITY

To a large degree, the tragic events that unfolded in Ukraine in 2013-14 were driven by developments beyond Ukraine's borders. Of course, domestic factors also played a crucial role, and Ukrainian political actors at all points across the political spectrum must share in the blame for what transpired. But it was Ukraine's ambiguous geopolitical position, and the clumsy interventions of competing outside powers pursuing their own self-centred agendas, that pushed Ukraine's log-jammed domestic politics over the brink into violent civil war.

The three main protagonists were Russia, the European Union, and the United States, in roughly descending order of importance.

The Evolution of Russia's Relations with Ukraine since 1991

Moscow has had difficult, testy relations with Ukraine ever since the two countries split off from the Soviet Union in 1991. The relationship with Kiev is a sub-set of Russia's problematic relationship with the outside world at large following the Soviet collapse. In 2014, Ukraine became the touchstone of two decades of Russian frustration and insecurity, with tragic consequences.

First Mikhail Gorbachev, and then Boris Yeltsin, wanted to be treated as an equal partner by the United States. However, the Soviet collapse meant that Russia was stripped of half its population, a third of its territory, and all its bloc of ideological allies and client states. In the 1990s, the loss of superpower status combined with economic collapse and an ideological vacuum created a profound identity crisis in Russia. Yeltsin was humiliated by his dependence on loans from the West, and by NATO's decision to expand the alliance to include former Warsaw Pact countries. The bombing of Yugoslavia by NATO forces in 1999, in a bid to stop human rights violations in Kosovo, was a turning point. It underlined the geopolitical marginalisation of Russia, unable to protect Serbia – its traditional ally. In the 2000s, on the foundation of a growing economy (thanks to rising world oil prices) Vladimir Putin forged a new Russian identity – that of a great power, able to stand up to the depredations of the US, the world's 'sole superpower.' The idea of Russia as a great power was something which resonated strongly with the Russian public, and which of course had deep roots in Soviet and Russian history (Mankoff, 2011; Trenin, 2014).

Ukraine was a litmus test of Russia's resurgence. With 46 million people, it was by far the largest of the states that had split away from Moscow's control in 1991, and it was strategically located between Russia and the West. Zbigniew Brzezinski famously argued that 'without Ukraine, Russia ceases to be a Eurasian empire' (Brzezinski, 1997, p. 46). Ukraine's new leaders were keen to build a sovereign, independent country – even those who were Russian-speakers and came from eastern Ukraine, such as Leonid Kuchma, president from 1994-2005. Ukraine joined the Commonwealth of Independent States, the loose association of 11 former Soviet states, but was wary of any closer military or political alliance with Russia. Ukrainians complained that Russia never fully accepted their existence as a sovereign nation. Putin himself reportedly told President George W. Bush in 2008 that Ukraine 'is not even a country' (Bohm, 2013). Ukrainians resented the policies of the Soviet era, which were aimed at suppressing Ukrainian culture – above all the 1932 famine (the Holodomor) that followed Stalin's collectivisation drive. Traditionally, Russians treated Ukrainians as a 'younger brother,' with a language and culture that were rooted in the countryside, and that were but a pale shadow of Russian civilisation. Russia also objected to Kiev's efforts to persuade the country's Russian-speakers, who amount to half the population, to adopt the Ukrainian language, and its refusal to legally protect the rights of Russian-speakers.

On the other hand, the two countries continued to maintain close economic ties. Russia remained Ukraine's largest trading partner, and much of Ukraine's export industry (focused on steel and chemicals) was based on the supply of cheap energy (principally gas) from Russia (Balmaceda, 2013). Russia, in turn, was dependent on Ukraine for the transit of half its natural gas exports to Europe, and Russia's defence industry relied on some crucial components from Ukrainian factories (such as the engines for ballistic missiles).

In the 1990s, Russia and Ukraine established a modus vivendi of sorts. Under the 1994 Budapest Memorandum, brokered by the US, Russia recognised Ukraine's sovereignty and territorial integrity – in return for which Kiev gave up any claim to the former Soviet nuclear weapons which were still located on Ukrainian territory. In 1997, Kiev gave Russia a 20-year lease on the Sevastopol naval base in Crimea, home of Russia's Black Sea Fleet. In the mid-1990s, Russian nationalists agitated for the return to Russia of Crimea, which had been given to Ukraine in 1954 to mark the 300th anniversary of Ukraine's unification with Russia. However, Yeltsin refused to give any support to this campaign and it fizzled out.

Russia found itself bogged down in testy horse-trading with Ukrainian leaders over the course of the next two decades. Whether the leaders of Ukraine were 'pro-Russian,' such as Presidents Kuchma or Viktor Yanukovych, or 'pro-Western,' such as President Viktor Yushchenko or Prime Minister Yulia Tymoshenko, the issues remained the same – above all, hard bargaining over the price Ukraine paid for Russian gas. The fragile equilibrium between Moscow and Kiev was threatened by the 2004 Orange Revolution, which saw the electoral defeat of Viktor Yanukovych – Kuchma's chosen successor and Russia's favourite candidate – at the hands of his West Ukrainian rival, Viktor Yushchenko. A wave of 'colour revolutions' in Georgia (2003), Ukraine (2004), and Kyrgyzstan (2005) saw authoritarian leaders toppled by popular protests demanding fair elections. Putin saw this as an orchestrated campaign by the West to spread democracy – and pro-Western governments – into the post-Soviet space, and he took decisive steps to prevent this phenomenon from reaching Moscow, tightening restrictions on the opposition while creating pro-Kremlin popular movements.

The colour revolutions came against the backdrop of the eastern enlargement of the two key Western regional organisations – the European Union and NATO. Putin became convinced that Russia was subject to a deliberate strategy of encirclement and containment by the US. Russia's relations with the US deteriorated after the invasion of Iraq in 2003, which Putin bitterly opposed. He was further angered by the Western recognition of the independence of Kosovo in February 2008. Things came to a head in August 2008, when Georgian President Mikhail Saakashvili sent his forces into the breakaway region of South Ossetia, killing several Russian peacekeepers in the process. Russia responded with a full-scale invasion, driving back the Georgian forces and going on to grant recognition to South Ossetia and Abkhazia. In retrospect, we can see Russia's actions in Georgia in 2008 as setting a precedent for what would happen in Crimea in 2014: Moscow used military force to change internationally-recognised borders.

In 2009, the newly elected President Barack Obama tried to revive the partnership with Russia's new president, Dmitry Medvedev, launching a 'reset' of relations with Moscow. This produced some positive results – a New Strategic Arms Reduction Treaty was signed in 2010 and the US started using the Northern Distribution Network across Russia to ferry troops and equipment into Afghanistan. However, relations deteriorated once more in the wake of the 2011 Arab Spring, which Russia saw as yet another example of America's aggressive democracy promotion. Moscow was angered by the toppling of Muammar Gaddafi in Libya following NATO air strikes and, in 2012, vetoed proposed UN action to halt the Syrian civil war. In September 2013, Russia scored a diplomatic coup by persuading President Bashar Assad to decommission Syria's chemical weapons, allowing Obama to step back from his threat to attack Syria if chemical attacks continued. This showed that Russia and the US could still cooperate where areas of common interest were found.

The US Position

In the 1990s, the Clinton administration treated Russia as an emerging democracy, a friend and partner of the United States. Yeltsin was offered economic assistance to help with the painful transition to a market economy and, in 1998, Russia joined the G7 group of advanced industrial nations (which became the G8). However, Washington saw a security vacuum opening up in Eastern Europe in the wake of the Soviet collapse. It seemed logical to plug the gap by offering membership in the North Atlantic Treaty Organisation – a defensive alliance – to the newly democratic Central and East European countries that were eager to join. The victory of Vladimir Zhirinovsky's nationalist party in the 1993 State Duma election was a wake-up call that Russia could 'go bad' and return to its imperialist ways. As early as 1994, President Clinton publicly supported the idea of expanding NATO membership. In order to join the alliance, applicants had to be democracies and willing to put their forces under NATO command (which meant learning English, buying compatible weapon systems, accepting NATO bases on their territory, and so on). In return, under Article V of the NATO charter, the alliance pledged to come to the defence of any member state that was attacked. Poland, Hungary, and the Czech Republic joined NATO in 1999, and seven other countries (Estonia, Latvia, Lithuania, Bulgaria, Romania, Slovakia, and Slovenia) entered in 2004. Croatia and Albania also joined in 2009.

Russia objected to NATO expansion, pointing out that the Soviet-led Warsaw

Pact alliance had dissolved in 1991. NATO expansion meant that Russia was still seen as a potential enemy – although Western leaders insisted that this was not the case. Some steps were taken to create a special relationship between NATO and Russia. In 1997, the NATO-Russia Founding Act created a Permanent Joint Council in Brussels and, in 2002, the Rome Summit created the NATO-Russia Council. President George W. Bush was keen to enlarge NATO further east as part of his post-9/11 'Freedom' agenda. However, at the April 2008 Bucharest Summit, NATO's European members blocked Bush's plan to offer Ukraine and Georgia a membership action plan (Stent, 2014, pp. 165-74). In consolation, they were told that the door was still open to NATO membership in the future – which redoubled Russia's determination to prevent such a development.

After the 1994 Budapest Memorandum that led to the denuclearisation of Ukraine, US policy towards Ukraine was mostly subordinate to US policy towards Russia. Ukraine's transition to democracy and a market economy suffered from the same ills as neighbouring Russia: the rise of a wealthy oligarch class who stifled competition, while colluding with a deeply corrupt political elite. There was a surge of optimism after the Orange Revolution in 2004, but that soon dissipated as the Yushchenko administration fell prey to the same kind of corruption and infighting that had dogged its predecessor. With the victory of the pro-Russian Yanukovych in more or less free elections in 2010, US strategy seemed to have reached a dead end. Washington effectively sub-contracted Western policy towards Ukraine to its partners in Brussels.

The European Union's Position

The collapse of communism in Eastern Europe caught the European Union – and everyone else – by surprise. The EU itself was in the process of introducing deepening social and economic integration under the 1992 Maastricht Treaty, which renamed the European Community the European Union. The 1995 Schengen agreement saw the abolition of border controls between participating countries, and a common currency, the Euro, was introduced in 1999. In 1998, Brussels began accession talks with Central and East European applicant countries. Applicants had to be functioning democracies ('Copenhagen criteria') and harmonise their domestic legislation with the body of EU law (the 108,000 documents of the *acquis communautaire*). These conditions were more stringent than those for NATO membership; as a result, Central-East Europeans started joining NATO five to ten years before they joined the EU.

The decision to enlarge the EU was controversial. The living standard in the former communist countries was less than half that of the EU, and massive investment would be needed to bring their infrastructure up to EU levels. Existing EU members feared an influx of cheap labour from the new states, and that all the regional development funds would be diverted to the East. Nevertheless, a political consensus for enlargement did emerge. Germany pushed for enlargement as a way to stabilise its relationship with neighbouring Poland – which accounted for 40 of the 76 million citizens in the new states. Britain and Denmark supported enlargement as an alternative to 'deepening' EU integration, figuring that it would be harder to agree on the creation of stronger federal institutions if there were 28 members instead of 15.

In 2004, 10 new members joined the EU: Estonia, Latvia, Lithuania, Poland, Czech Republic, Slovakia, Hungary, Slovenia, Malta, and Cyprus. Romania and Bulgaria followed in 2007, and Croatia in 2013. Enlargement did contribute to a delay in deepening. A new draft EU constitution, introducing qualified majority voting, was rejected by referenda in France and the Netherlands in 2005. It was not until 2009 that a watered-down version, the Lisbon Treaty, came into effect. The EU's eastern enlargement was a major advance for the cause of democracy in Europe. However, it came at a price. One problem was what to do with the countries lying outside the expanded EU. While there is still hope that the remaining countries in the Balkans (Bosnia, Macedonia, Montenegro, and Serbia) will eventually join the EU, it was hard to see Belarus, Moldova, or Ukraine joining anytime soon. They were even poorer than the new wave of member states, and they were far from democratic. Belarus was ruled by Alexander Lukashenko, 'the last dictator in Europe,' while Moldova was riven by the secession of the Russian-speaking republic of Transnistria. With 46 million inhabitants, Ukraine was too large and too politically unstable to be a serious candidate for EU entry in the foreseeable future, although some EU states, notably Poland, thought that an action plan for membership should be on the table.

In the meantime, in 2003, the EU launched a new European Neighbourhood Policy to provide a framework for cooperation with countries that were not going to be put on the membership track. The policy included 10 countries of North Africa and the eastern Mediterranean (the 'Southern Neighbourhood'), in addition to Armenia, Azerbaijan, Belarus, Georgia, Moldova, and Ukraine. The relationship with the post-Soviet states was formalised as the 'Eastern Partnership' at a summit in Prague in May 2009 (Korosteleva, 2012; Korosteleva, 2013). Russia was invited to join, but declined, preferring to keep its more privileged bilateral relationship with Brussels. The EU signed a Partnership and Cooperation Agreement with Russia in 1994, followed up with an agreement on four 'Common Spaces' in 2003. Since 1997, Russian and EU leaders have held biannual summits (suspended since January

2014).

The carrot offered to the Eastern partners was 'association status,' which carries some of the benefits of membership such as the lowering of trade barriers and possibly the lifting of visa requirements. The granting of such benefits was conditional on partner countries respecting democratic values and the rule of law, and bringing their policies into line with EU procedures. With the Schengen visa-free zone challenged by a flood of refugees from North Africa, Brussels urgently needed to maintain secure borders to the east. Visa waivers would be offered in return for cooperation in tighter border controls and agreement on the return of refugees to the country from which they entered the EU.

In 2011, Brussels re-launched the European Neighbourhood Policy, tying aid to benchmarks in economic and political reform – that is, more money for more reform and, presumably, less money for less reform (European Union, 2011). The EU spent 7 billion Euro ($10 billion) on the ENP for 2011-13, but two-thirds of the money went to the Mediterranean countries. Optimists argued that association status would stimulate states to improve their domestic governance. Cynics saw it as an empty gesture that had no real political or financial commitment from Brussels. One crucial factor that was largely ignored was Moscow's determination to disrupt and prevent the efforts of its neighbours to reach association agreement status with the EU. While the EU insisted that its Eastern partnership policy was just about establishing good relations with neighbouring states, Russia viewed it through a geopolitical lens (Gretsky, 2014). Russian Foreign Minister Sergei Lavrov complained, 'What is the Eastern Partnership, if not an attempt to extend the EU's sphere of influence?' (Pop, 2009).

The 2013 Crisis

The EU began negotiations for a free trade and association agreement with Ukraine in 2008. However, after Yanukovych won election to the presidency in February 2010, he moved quickly to centralise political power and bring Ukraine back into Moscow's orbit. In April 2010, Medvedev and Yanukovych signed a deal to extend Russia's 1997 lease of the Sevastopol naval base for 25 years beyond 2017, in return for a 30% cut in the natural gas price. In June 2010, the Ukrainian parliament voted to abandon NATO membership aspirations. In October 2010, the Constitutional Court overturned the limits on presidential power introduced in 2004. In November 2011, former prime minister Yulia Tymoshenko was sentenced to seven years on spurious abuse of office charges (connected to the signing of the 2009 gas deal with Russia). In April 2013, the European Court of Human Rights declared Tymoshenko's sentence illegal. Yanukovych's actions left Brussels in a quandary. Some Europeans pushed for the introduction of sanctions on Ukrainian leaders and the suspension of talks on the creation of a free trade zone until Tymoshenko was released. Others argued that isolating Yanukovych would drive him further into the arms of the Kremlin. A similar tension between democratic principles and the logic of realpolitik dogged EU policy towards Belarus.

The EU's plan to open up the Ukrainian economy brought it into conflict with Putin's efforts to create a deeper economic union in the post-Soviet space. This was a priority for Putin, who was determined to forestall the expansion of EU influence and the presumed democratisation that would accompany it. In January 2010, Russia launched a Customs Union with Belarus and Kazakhstan, introducing tariff-free trade between the three countries. This was the precursor to the Eurasian Economic Union, launched on 1 January 2015. In September and December 2013, Armenia and Kyrgyzstan agreed to join the Union. Putin hoped to persuade Ukraine to join as well, but this would not be possible if Ukraine signed the free trade agreement with the EU.

The EU pressed ahead with its plans for Ukraine, despite misgivings over the state of democracy and the rule of law there. The association and free trade agreements were initialled in Brussels in July 2012, and were due to be signed at a summit in Vilnius on 29 November 2013. However, European parliamentarians were insisting on Tymoshenko's release as a condition for final approval. In the course of the summer, Putin increased the pressure on Ukraine – for example, in July, Russia banned the imports of Ukrainian chocolates from the Roshen company (owned by the man who would later become Ukraine's president, Petro Poroshenko). On 21 November, Yanukovych abruptly announced that he would not, after all, sign the association agreement in Vilnius, and the parliament rejected the EU's demand to release Tymoshenko. Yanukovych's refusal to sign the agreement triggered the Euromaidan protests, which spiralled out of control over the winter.

It is unclear whether Yanukovych refused to sign the agreement because of the Tymoshenko issue, or because he was conducting a bidding war between Russia and the EU. EU Enlargement Commissioner Štefan Füle said Yanukovych had been asking for $27 billion in aid to sign the agreement. On **17 December,** Putin agreed to lend Ukraine $15 billion, and to cut the price of gas by a third (from $400 to $268 per 1000 cubic meters). However, by then it was too late to prevent Yanukovych's loss of control of the situation on the streets.

International players (Russia, the EU, and the US) were heavily involved in the unfolding political conflict. Ironically, each accused the other of interference in Ukrainian affairs. The EU's Catherine Ashton and the US Assistant Secretary of State, Victoria Nuland, encouraged Yanukovych and the protestors to reach a compromise - while Russia was pushing Yanukovych to hold firm. Russian propaganda portrayed Nuland as the architect of the protests, playing video of her giving out food on the Maidan square, boasting that the US had spent $5 billion on democracy promotion in Ukraine, and playing tapes of an intercepted 6 February phone conversation in which she discussed the composition of the future Ukrainian government. Putin's advisor, Sergei Glazyev, opined that 'the entire crisis in Ukraine was orchestrated, provoked, and financed by American institutions in cooperation with their European partners' (Simes, 2014). The collapse of the 21 February agreement in the face of insurgent demonstrators and the flight of Yanukovych was seen by Moscow as the point of no return. They assumed the new government would sign the association agreement with the EU, apply to join NATO, and revoke the agreement granting Russia the use of the Sevastopol base. Putin responded with force and vigour – annexing Crimea and using surrogates to launch an insurrection in east and south Ukraine.

Putin's decision to annex Crimea on 16 March caught the international community by surprise. Recognition of national sovereignty and the inviolability of borders are central to the international state system and, since 1991, the Russian Federation (like the Soviet Union before) had been an ardent defender of these principles. The EU and the US responded swiftly with 'smart' sanctions, imposing asset freezes and travel bans on a few dozen politicians directly involved in the Crimean annexation. German industrialists doing business with Russia urged Chancellor Angela Merkel not to bow to US pressure to introduce broader sanctions. As the surrogate war raged in east Ukraine, on 16 July, the US introduced 'sectoral' sanctions on strategic corporations, barring them from long-term borrowing. The next day, separatists apparently shot down Malaysian Airlines Flight 17. This atrocity, and Russia's seeming unwillingness to help bring those responsible to justice, caused a groundswell of support for tougher action, particularly in the Netherlands and Germany. On 25 July, the EU expanded its sanctions to an additional 15 top Russian government officials (though it was not until 12 September that they imposed sectoral sanctions). Putin responded on 6 August by introducing a one-year ban on imports of fruits and vegetables, dairy products, and meat from countries that had imposed sanctions on Russia.

The political association agreement with the EU was signed on 21 March 2014, and the economic chapters on 21 June. Implementation of the economic dimension was postponed for a year as an incentive to Russia to help bring peace to East Ukraine. Negotiations in Minsk, under the auspices of the OSCE, resulted in a shaky ceasefire on 26 August, but agreement on a permanent solution remained out of reach. Kiev refused to yield to Russian demands that Ukraine would abjure from NATO membership and would grant full autonomy to the secessionists in Donetsk and Luhansk. Russia had suspended gas deliveries through Ukraine in June, which was not an immediate problem since demand is low in summer and Ukraine had ample reserves. Negotiations continued over supplies for the next winter. On 31 October, Ukraine agreed to pay Russia $3 billion in arrears and $1.5 billion as prepayment for 2015 gas at a price of $378 per 1000 cubic metres.

Conclusion

Ukraine is a struggling, fragile, and poorly governed state that found itself torn apart by the forces of shifting tectonic plates. On one side was the shrinking 'plate' of the Russian state, and on the other side the expanding 'plate' of the Euro-Atlantic community. Cooperation between the rival parties was complicated by the fact that Russia was looking at the world through a military-strategic lens, focusing on issues such as NATO enlargement, missile defence, and protection of its hard power assets such as the Sevastopol base. In contrast, the EU is a post-modern entity that builds long-term relationships based on human rights and the free movement of goods and services.

The chances for miscommunication were high. The Western players underestimated the importance of Ukraine to Putin and his willingness to break the rules of the post-1991 international system in order to prevent what he saw as threats to Russia's national interests. There was a mismatch between the incremental carrots being offered by Brussels and the big sticks being wielded by Moscow. As Andrew Wilson put it, the EU 'took a baguette to a knife fight' (Wilson, 2014).

Nevertheless, the US and EU stood their ground, and deployed economic sanctions to counter Putin's use of not-so-covert military force. At the G20 meeting in Brisbane in November 2014, Merkel said that 'old thinking in spheres of influence together with the trampling of international law must not be allowed to succeed' (Lough, 2014). The collapse in the oil price in the second half of 2014 (it fell from $115 a barrel in June to $60 at year's end) multiplied the impact of the financial sanctions, and plunged Russia into a currency crisis and recession. The baguette may yet prevail over the knife.

References

Balmaceda, M. (2013) *Politics of Energy Dependency: Ukraine, Belarus, and Lithuania between Domestic Oligarchs and Russian Pressure.* Toronto: University of Toronto Press.

Bohm, M. (2013) 'Ukraine is Putin's favorite vassal,' *Moscow Times*, 25 December.

Brzezinski, Z. (1997) *The Grand Chessboard.* New York: Basic Books.

Dutkiewicz, P. and Sakwa, R. (eds) (2014) *Eurasian Integration – The View from Within.* London: Routledge.

European Union (2011) *A New Response to a Changing Neighborhood.* Brussels: European Union. Available at: http://eeas.europa.eu/enp/pdf/pdf/com_11_303_en.pdf.

Gower, J. and Timmins G. (eds) (2011) *The European Union, Russia and the Shared Neighbourhood.* London: Routledge. Also a special issue of *Europe-Asia Studies* (2009) 61(10).

Gretsky, I. et al. (2014) 'Russia's perceptions and misperceptions of the EU Eastern Partnership,' *Journal of Communist and Post-Communist Studies*, 47 (3-4), pp. 375-383.

Korosteleva, E.(ed.) (2012) *Eastern Partnership: A New Opportunity for the Neighbours?* London: Routledge. Also a special issue of *The Journal of Communist Studies and Transition Politics*, (2011) 27(1).

Korosteleva, E. et al. (eds) (2014) *EU Policies in the Eastern Neighbourhood: The Practices Perspective.* London: Routledge. Also a special issue of *East European Politics*, (2013) 29(3).

Lough, J. (2014) 'Ukraine crisis prompts a sea change in Germany's Russia policy,' *Chatham House*, 24 November. Available at: http://www.chathamhouse.org/expert/comment/16320?dm_i=1TYG,30AET,BLOMTE,ATMQX,1#sthash.IWFC1y0J.dpuf.

Mankoff, J.(2011) *Russia: The Return of Great Power Politics.* Lanham, MD: Rowman and Littlefield.

Pop, V. (2009) 'EU expanding its 'sphere of influence,' Russia says,' *EU Observer,* March 21. Available at: http://euobserver.com/foreign/27827.

Simes, D. (2014) 'An interview with Sergei Glazyev,' *The National Interest*, 24 March. Available at: http://nationalinterest.org/commentary/interview-sergey-glazyev-10106.

Stent, A. E. (2014) *The Limits of Partnership. US-Russian Relations in the 21st Century.* Princeton University Press.

Trenin, D. (2014) 'Russia's breakout from the post-cold war system,' *Carnegie Endowment*, 22 December. Available at: http://carnegie.ru/2014/12/22/russia-s-breakout-from-post-cold-war-system-drivers-of-putin-s-course/hxsm.

Wilson, A. (2014) 'Ukraine's 2014: a belated 1989 or another failed 2004?' *Open Democracy*, 18 February. Available at: https://www.opendemocracy.net/od-russia/andrew-wilson/ukraine%E2%80%99s-2014-belated-1989-or-another-failed-2004.

12

Between East and West: NATO Enlargement and the Geopolitics of the Ukraine Crisis

EDWARD W. WALKER
UNIVERSITY OF CALIFORNIA, BERKELEY

With the breakup of the Soviet Union on 31 December 1991, the United States and its Western allies faced a critical challenge: building a post-Cold War security architecture for Europe that would prevent conflict and institutionalise cooperation in what former Soviet leader Mikhail S. Gorbachev had called 'our common Europe home.' In particular, a decision had to be made about what to do with the North Atlantic Treaty Organization (NATO), the purpose of which had been to defend Western Europe from invasion from a Soviet Union and Warsaw Pact that no longer existed.

The question of NATO's post-Cold War role had already come up in 1990 during negotiations between Western and Soviet officials over German reunification. Initially, Moscow insisted that a unified Germany within NATO was unacceptable. When it became clear that Western governments would not accept, and Moscow could not block a unified Germany within the Alliance, Moscow pushed for guarantees that NATO forces would not move eastward into the territory of the former German Democratic Republic.

As it turned out, negotiations over reunification were effectively mooted by the rapid collapse of communism in Eastern Europe and growing political and economic turmoil in the USSR. Unification took place with Germany as a NATO member and without formal restrictions on NATO's conventional or nuclear force dispositions on German territory (Sarotte, 2014a; Sarotte, 2014b; Shifrinson, 2014). The Alliance also made clear at its July 1990 London Summit that it had no intention of dissolving itself even if Soviet troops pulled out of Central Europe (NATO London Summit Declaration, 1990). The consensus in Western capitals was that NATO, and America's military presence in Europe, should remain the cornerstone of Western security.

Nonetheless, Washington and its allies tried to accommodate Moscow's security concerns by advocating new arms control measures that would entail deep cuts in conventional and nuclear forces in Europe. They also called for the strengthening of the conflict prevention and cooperation functions of the Conference for Security and Cooperation in Europe (CSCE, since renamed the Organization for Security and Cooperation in Europe, or OSCE), which included all NATO and former Warsaw Pact countries as members. Finally, they indicated that NATO would gradually become a political rather than military organisation, and that it would commit to regular consultations with Soviet officials on security and political matters. To that end, a North Atlantic Cooperation Council (NACC) was established on 20 December 1991, with participation by all NATO and former Warsaw Pact member-states, including (eventually) all 15 of the Soviet successor states.

That was more or less where matters stood when the Soviet Union dissolved at the end of 1991. As the USSR's legal successor, Russia faced a host of internal problems, including a collapsing economy that diverted attention from national security concerns and increased Moscow's already considerable need for Western financial assistance. Nevertheless, Russian foreign policy officials, the bulk of whom had served as Soviet officials, continued to suggest that NATO be disbanded, but if not, that it should at least refrain from moving forces further east or engaging in 'out of area' operations in Europe without Russian permission, notably in the Balkans, which by then was descending into violence.

The extent to which NATO was a sore point for the new Russian leadership was highlighted at the end of December, when Russia's pro-Western foreign minister, Andrey Kozyrev, made a startling speech at a CSCE meeting in Stockholm that *The New York Times*' William Safire would characterise as a 'peek at Cold War 2' (Safire, 1994). Pretending to be an anti-Western successor to himself, Kozyrev complained, *inter alia*, about,

> the strategies of NATO and the WEU [the West European Union, a now defunct military arm of the European Community – EWW], which are drawing up plans to strengthen their

military presence in the Baltic and other regions of the territory of the former Soviet Union and to interfere in Bosnia and the internal affairs of Yugoslavia (Rotfield, 2009).

As Kozyrev later explained, his mock speech was intended as a warning about what might happen should the West fail to help Russia economically, isolate it politically, or contain it militarily.

In fact, Russian suggestions for a new European security's architecture based on the Europe-wide CSCE/OSCE received little consideration in the West at the time, positive or negative. In part, the reason was that Western officials were preoccupied with other problems, notably the violent unravelling of Yugoslavia. But Western officials also assumed that Russia was, and would remain, too weak to become a serious security problem for the foreseeable future, and that as a result its security concerns could be safely ignored.

Another critical decision was made by Western governments in this period that would have important, and unforeseen, consequences. On 7 February 1992, just a few weeks after the Soviet dissolution, the European Community (EC) signed the so-called Maastricht Treaty, which entailed a commitment to 'deepening' the organisation and transforming it into what would become the European Union (EU). Among other measures, the treaty would lead to the establishment of a common currency, the Euro, in January 1999.

This commitment to deepening came, to no small degree, at the expense of 'widening.' In part, this was because deepening raised the bar for accession, but it was also because deepening used up political capital that might otherwise have been spent on widening. As the historian John Lewis Gaddis would put it in a 1998 article, the EU's 'single-minded push to achieve a single currency among its existing members' meant that it was 'left to NATO to reintegrate and stabilise Europe as a whole, which is roughly the equivalent of using a monkey wrench to repair a computer' (Gaddis, 1998, p. 147). A decade later, design flaws with the Euro would also make Europe's Great Recession all the worse and threaten to undo the entire European project.

It was not until mid-1993, however, that the question of NATO enlargement began to be seriously discussed in the West. The issue was raised by Presidents Vaclav Havel of the Czech Republic and Arpad Goncz of Hungary, who, on a visit to Washington in April 1993, informed US President Bill Clinton that their countries wished to join NATO as soon as possible. Other Central European governments, notably Warsaw, followed suit. Their reasoning was clear. As Lennart Meri, the Estonian president, told one of Clinton's senior foreign policy advisors, 'the only way to keep Russian troops from reoccupying his country when Yeltsin gave way to a more traditional Russian leader was for Estonia to be in NATO and protected by the American nuclear umbrella' (Talbott, 2002, p. 94).

Russian President Boris Yeltsin was preoccupied at the time by an intensifying struggle with oppositionists in the Russian parliament, and initially he seemed to take the possibility of NATO enlargement in stride. On a trip to Poland in August, he indicated that he 'understood' Warsaw's desire to join NATO, and he would make similar statements on trips to Prague and Bratislava. As it turned out, this would be the only moment when the Kremlin expressed anything but firm opposition to enlargement.

Yeltsin's position changed after the violent showdown with the opposition on 21 September 1993. Reportedly under pressure from the Russian military, whose support had been critical to Yeltsin in his victory over his opponents, Yeltsin wrote to several Western leaders, including Clinton, that his earlier 'understanding' of NATO expansion was conditional on Russia having a central role in the new European security system. While he had indicated previously that Russia might be willing to join the Alliance at some point, his government would not accept membership for Poland or other East European countries without simultaneous admission for Russia.

Yeltsin's letter caused considerable debate within the Clinton administration, and it ultimately convinced the White House to postpone offering membership to particular countries (Talbott, 2002). Instead, Washington proposed that NATO adopt a 'Partnership for Peace' (PfP) programme for the former communist countries of Eastern Europe and the Soviet successor states. PfP members would carry out joint military exercises with NATO, work on 'interoperability' with NATO equipment and procedures, participate in joint peacekeeping and humanitarian operations, and consult with NATO in the event of security threats. The White House hoped that the PfP would mollify Russia, which would be encouraged to join, but it also described the program as a kind of 'halfway house' for eventual membership and enlargement down the road (Chollet and Goldgeier, 2008). And it was clear, given that the demand for enlargement was driven by fears of a resurgent Russia that NATO membership was off the table for Moscow.

Not surprisingly, PfP was received coldly by most Central European governments, which continued to push for full and rapid accession. This was particularly true after a far-right nationalist party, Vladimir Zhirinovsky's LDPR, won an unexpected 17% of the party list vote in Russian parliamentary elections on 12 December 1993. The strong performance by Russian nationalists raised new alarms in Poland, the Baltic states, and elsewhere about Russian efforts to carve out a sphere of influence not just on the territory of the former Soviet Union – what Russians were calling 'the Near Abroad' – but in Central Europe as well.

Nonetheless, the PfP was approved at NATO's Brussels Summit in January 1994. The Alliance also made clear that it expected to take in new members on its eastern borders in the reasonably near future, as stated in its Final Declaration:

> We expect and would welcome NATO expansion that would reach to democratic states to our East, as part of an evolutionary process, taking into account political and security developments in the whole of Europe (NATO Brussels Summit Declaration, 1994).

By then, NATO enlargement had become an important partisan issue in Washington, with Republicans pushing the White House to offer membership to Central European countries in short order. Leading Republicans also argued that enlargement was needed to protect democratic governments in Central Europe from Russia intimidation and military pressure. The White House, they asserted, was adopting a 'Russia first' policy that mistakenly assumed that 'as went Russia, so went the rest of Eurasia.' Accommodating Moscow on security matters, they argued, would do nothing to keep Russia from 'backsliding' on democracy and engaging in neo-imperialist policies in former Soviet space and East-Central Europe.

Pressure on the administration to come up with a firm plan for enlargement intensified in the lead up to the November 1994 Congressional elections. Newt Gingrich, soon to be Speaker of a Republican-controlled House, included a demand in his 'Contract for America' that a first round of enlargement take place no later than 1999. Of particular concern to the administration was the possibility that Republican criticism of its 'Russia first' policy would undermine support for Democrats among Central European heritage voters, particularly Polish-Americans, in important swing states in the mid-West.

As a result, Clinton stated repeatedly over the course of 1994 that he expected PfP to lead eventually to full membership for countries that met NATO's criteria as democratic, law-governed states with institutionalised civilian control of the military. He also argued that the PfP was open to all former Warsaw Pact countries, including Russia, and that as a result, enlargement would neither isolate Moscow nor lead to a new division of

Europe. Why Russian participation in the PfP programme but enlargement for post-communist countries other than Russia would be acceptable to Moscow was never made clear.

At any rate, by the end of 1994, the Clinton administration had effectively committed to NATO enlargement, even if it left open the timing and extent of the process (Goldgeier, 1999). Pressured by post-communist countries in Central Europe that were worried about Russian aggression down the road, concerned about a loss of political support from Central European heritage voters, but hoping at the same time not to provoke Russia unduly, it settled on PfP and delayed enlargement as the least-worst option. The fact that domestic political considerations were an important factor in driving the most important strategic policy for the United States after the collapse of the Soviet Union was widely recognised at the time.

As it turned out, the Democrats lost control of both houses of Congress in the November elections regardless, and the PfP failed to placate Moscow. The intensity of Russian opposition to enlargement was made clear by Yeltsin in September 1995, when he asserted that it 'will mean a conflagration of war throughout Europe for sure' (Erlanger, 1995). These objections only intensified after the pro-Western Kozyrev was replaced by the 'realist' and former FSB director Evgeny Primakov as Russian Foreign Minister in January 1996.

NATO moved ahead with its enlargement plans nonetheless. In September 1995, it issued an Enlargement Study laying out criteria for accession. Applicant countries were invited to start a dialogue on accession early the next year, and the Alliance confirmed that it would announce its decision on the first round of accession countries at its July 1997 summit. As it turned out, the first round was limited to Poland, the Czech Republic, and Hungary, which joined in early 1999. Bulgaria, Estonia, Latvia, Lithuania, Romania, Slovakia, and Slovenia joined in March 2004, and Albania and Croatia did so in April 2009, bringing the total to 28 member states today.

It is important to emphasise that enlargement was opposed, in many instances passionately, by many influential American foreign policy experts, Democrats and Republicans alike (Kupchan, 1994; Ikle, 1996; Rosner, 1996; Mandelbaum, 1996; Kline, 1997; Lieven, 1997; Kennan, 1998; Gaddis, 1998; Waltz, 1998). Most notably, more than 40 influential foreign policy experts, including former US Senators from both sides of the aisle, former ambassadors, former cabinet officials, and academics who were not known as particularly pro-Russian or dovish, wrote an open letter to President Clinton dated 26 June 1997, which began as follows:

> We, the undersigned, believe that the current US-led effort to expand NATO, the focus of the recent Helsinki and Paris Summits, is a policy error of historic proportions. We believe that NATO expansion will decrease allied security and unsettle European stability' (Burton et al., 1997). It went on to list a host of reasons, all of which were by then familiar to anyone following the controversy, why NATO expansion was a mistake of 'historic proportions.'

Moscow's continuing objections to enlargement, along with widespread domestic criticism of the policy establishment, led the Clinton administration to make another effort to arrive at an institutional arrangement that would square the enlargement circle. On 27 May 1997, NATO and Russia signed the Founding Act of the Russia-NATO Permanent Joint Council. Among other provisions, the Act called on the signatories to support the conflict prevention efforts of the CSCE and respect the UN Security Council's sole right to authorise the use of force against a sovereign member state. In a key passage on NATO force dispositions, it also stated that NATO agreed that,

> in the current and foreseeable security environment, the Alliance will carry out its collective defence and other missions by ensuring the necessary interoperability, integration, and capability for reinforcement rather than by additional permanent stationing of substantial combat forces (Russia-NATO Permanent Council Founding Act, 1997).

NATO would interpret this to mean that it could send 'rotational' forces to the territory of new member states but not establish permanent bases there 'in the current and foreseeable security environment.' Again, the hope was that the Council would allow enlargement to proceed with Moscow's acquiescence.

Initially, there were indications from Moscow that it might go along with a first round of enlargement if the Council gave Russia real discretion over NATO's force dispositions and out-of-area operations (Simes, 1998). That this was not going to be the case was soon made clear by NATO's bombing campaign against Serbia in 1999. Washington and its allies pressed the UN Security Council to authorise NATO to use force to prevent what Western governments considered the forced displacement of hundreds of thousands of Albanians by Serbian forces. When China and Russia vetoed the resolution, NATO proceeded regardless, on the grounds that it was exercising its right of collective self-defence, despite the fact that it was clearly engaging in an out-of-area operation. For Russia, NATO's bombing campaign without UNSC authorisation made clear that the Alliance had no intention of allowing Russia a meaningful veto over NATO operations. For Western governments, the episode suggested that Russia had no interest in a peaceful, democratic, and stable Europe.

NATO was again a critical factor in the next major crisis in Russia's relations with the West, the August 2008 Russo-Georgia war. In late 2007, it became clear that the George W. Bush administration was pressing its allies to offer Membership Action Plans (MAPs) to Georgia and Ukraine at NATO's April 2008 Bucharest Summit. The plan was rejected by key NATO members, including France and Germany, among other reasons because they were aware that doing so might well cross a red line for the Kremlin (Lieven, 2008). But the Bush administration did manage to convince its allies to accept a compromise whereby MAPs would be offered to Ukraine and Georgia in the future. As the summit's concluding declaration made clear, that day might well come soon:

> NATO welcomes Ukraine's and Georgia's Euro Atlantic aspirations for membership in NATO. We agreed today that these countries will become members of NATO… Therefore we will now begin a period of intensive engagement with both at a high political level to address the questions still outstanding pertaining to their MAP applications (NATO Bucharest Summit Final Declaration, 2004).

Not surprisingly, Moscow concluded that NATO membership for Georgia or Ukraine might well happen in the not-so-distant future.

The Bucharest Summit came on the heels of another event that the Kremlin considered a serious and gratuitous provocation. With encouragement from the United States and many of its European allies, Kosovo declared independence from Serbia on 17 February 2008. Washington, London, and Paris announced they were affording Kosovo diplomatic recognition the next day, and most European countries, including Germany, followed suit over the course of the next month.

This was the first and only time that United States and its allies offered recognition to a government that was seceding unilaterally from a UN member state. The Western argument about recognising the successor states of the Soviet Union, Czechoslovakia, and Yugoslavia had been that these three federations dissolved into their constituent units, not that any one of the latter was seceding from a surviving rump state (Walker, 2004). That, however, was clearly not the case with what the State Department by then was referring to as 'the Former Republic of Yugoslavia,' because rump Serbia was not a formal federation and Kosovo had never had equal status with Serbia proper.

As Serbia's traditional patron, Russia reacted sharply to Western recognition of Kosovo's independence. It made clear that it would use its Security Council veto to block UN membership for the region, and it argued that recognising Kosovo would serve as a destabilising precedent. To emphasise the latter point, it indicated that it might well follow the Western lead and recognise the independence of some or all of the breakaway regions in its neighbourhood – Abkhazia, South Ossetia, Transnistria, and Nagorno-Karabakh.

After more than eight years of robust economic growth and the consolidation of Russian President Vladimir Putin's 'power vertical,' the Kremlin was signalling that its security concerns and political interests, particularly but not only in post-Soviet space, could no longer be ignored. Accordingly, 2008 witnessed a ratcheting up of Russian pressure on Georgia. Among other measures, Moscow increased military presence in Abkhazia and South Ossetia, intensified its already harsh criticism of the Georgian government, and carried out large-scale military exercises along its border with Georgia. As the summer progressed, artillery exchanges and small-scale skirmishes escalated along the line of control separating South Ossetian and Abkhazian forces from Georgian troops. Despite multiple warnings against using military force against South Ossetia or Abkhazia from Western officials, the Georgian president, Mikheil Saakashvili, finally took the bait and ordered his military into South Ossetia in August. The result was a Russian invasion and a decisive military defeat for Georgia, which ended any hope that Tbilisi had of reasserting its sovereignty in Abkhazia or South Ossetia for the foreseeable future.

The August 2009 Russo-Georgia War marked the low point in Russian relations with the West in the post-Cold War era. A number of factors, including the election of Barack Obama as US president and his administration's commitment to a 'reset' with Moscow, contributed to a reduction of tensions over the next several years, but little was done to address the underlying cause of those tensions, which was a security system for Europe that Russia rejected. The result was an even worse crisis at the end of 2013.

The immediate trigger for the Ukraine crisis was not, however, NATO enlargement. Rather, it was an EU plan to offer association agreements, coupled with so-called Deep and Comprehensive Free Trade Agreements, to Moldova, Armenia, Georgia, and Ukraine at its Vilnius Summit in late

November 2013. Ukraine was politically unstable, highly corrupt even by the standards of the region, and in dire economic straits at the time, and as a result, European government and EU officials assumed that Moscow realised that EU membership for Ukraine was a very distant prospect at best. This was particularly true because the EU was itself in serious trouble, thanks to the 2008 global financial crisis, design flaws with the Euro, and the rise of Eurosceptic parties. The last thing the EU needed at the time was a larger, poorer, and more economically distressed Greece on its hands.

The Kremlin, however, viewed EU accession very differently. From its perspective, association agreements for Armenia, Georgia, Moldova, and Ukraine were direct challenges to Putin's principal geopolitical objective in his third term as president, which was the establishment of a 'Eurasian Union' of former Soviet republics, one that would institutionalise Russia's sphere of influence in post-Soviet space. This would be accomplished by creating, and then deepening and widening, a Eurasian Economic Union that, like the European Community before, would lead eventually to a full-blown economic-political union. The Eurasian Union, along with the Collective Security Treaty Organization (CSTO), would become a Russian-dominated equivalent of the EU and NATO. It would also become one pole in what Russian officials described, correctly, as an increasingly multipolar world.

Central to this project – not only for security, but also for economic and cultural reasons – was Ukraine. Particularly galling to the Kremlin was the EU's insistence that signing the association agreement would preclude Kiev from joining the Eurasian Economic Union. It also viewed EU accession as an irrevocable step toward full-blown incorporation into the Western institutional order and a backdoor path to eventual NATO accession.

As a result, Moscow responded by using all means at its disposal short of war to put pressure on Armenia, Moldova, Georgia, and Ukraine to reject EU membership. Russia's leverage was varied but powerful, including offers of financial assistance, threats of economic reprisals, below market prices for natural gas, and political pressure, some open and some covert. Its task was made easier when financial tightening by the US Federal Reserve Bank – so-called tapering – caused a spike in interest rates on emerging market debt, including Ukraine's. The rate spike turned what was an already serious economic slowdown in Ukraine into a debt-servicing crisis over the summer of 2014 (Steil, 2014).

The first country to change course on EU accession was Armenia, which announced in early September 2013 that it was no longer interested and would join the Eurasian Economic Union. For whatever reason, the Ukrainian president, Viktor Yanukovich, held out, perhaps because he hoped to get the best economic deal possible from Russia or the EU. Nevertheless, in the end Kiev followed Armenia and announced that it was accepting a generous aid package from Russia and would not sign the EU association agreement.

The result was the Euromaidan uprising in Kiev, violence on the streets of Kiev, the mobilisation of anti-Maidan forces in eastern and southern Ukraine, the fall of the government, and the flight of Yanukovich, who was by then hated across Ukraine, to Moscow. With a government taking power in Kiev that would be hostile to Moscow, that would seek to join the EU and reject membership in the Eurasian Economic Union, and that might press to join NATO at some point, the Kremlin reacted by putting into place what were doubtless long-standing contingency plans for the occupation of Crimea and the destabilisation of Ukraine's already volatile eastern and southern regions.

Conclusion

There can be no doubt that NATO enlargement has brought many benefits to its new members. It has helped integrate former Warsaw Pact members into Europe, reduced the risk of interstate conflict among the former communist countries of Central Europe, and allowed new member-states to spend less on security while modernising their defence forces. Above all, it has meant that the small and militarily vulnerable Baltic states can be reasonably confident that NATO membership will deter Russia from intimidating, or invading, their countries in the current standoff between Russia and NATO.

That said, it is also true that NATO expansion has contributed to – indeed, one can reasonably argue that it has been the principal cause of – a dangerous geopolitical struggle for influence in the countries to Russia's West and South, above all Ukraine. The Russian political elite is virtually unanimous in viewing NATO as Russia's most serious security threat and a direct challenge to its interests as a Great Power. It likewise views enlargement as an unjust and unnecessary incursion into Russia's rightful sphere of influence, and EU expansion and democracy promotion as stalking horses for NATO and Western hegemony in post-Soviet space.

One cannot know with confidence what would have happened had the Clinton administration rejected NATO expansion in favour of a concerted effort to build a European security architecture that included, rather than excluded, Russia. The obvious mechanism for doing so was the CSCE/OCSE. As many Western foreign policy experts advocated at the time, NATO could have remained in place, with a reunited Germany as a member, and it could have assisted with the transformation of post-Communist countries through a PfP-type program. At the same time, Western governments could have worked with Russia to transform the OSCE/CSCE into an authoritative organisation overseeing dispositions, arms control measures, monitoring missions, and armed peacekeeping operations. Above all, the West could have postponed enlargement unless and until a genuine security threat to Central Europe emerged from Russia.

As is turned out, NATO enlargement eventually ran up against the countervailing power of a resurgent Russia with a preponderance of hard power along its borders. It did so first in Georgia in 2008, and it did so again in Ukraine in 2014.

References

Burns G. et al. (1997) *Open Letter to President Clinton.* Available at: http://www.bu.edu/globalbeat/nato/postpone062697.html.

Chollet, D. and Godgeier J. (2008) 'American Between the Wars: From 11/9 to 9/11,' *Public Affairs*.

Editorial Board of The New York Times. (1994) 'Don't Russia to Expand NATO,' *The New York Times*, 30 November.

Erlanger, S. (1995) 'In a New Attack Against NATO, Yeltsin Talks of a 'Conflagration of War,' *The New York Times*, 9 September.

Gaddis, J. L. (1998) 'History, Grand Strategy, and NATO Enlargement,' *Survival*, 40(1).

Goldgeier, J. M. (1998) 'NATO Expansion: The Anatomy of a Decision,' *Washington Quarterly I,* 21(1).

Goldgeier, J. M. (1998) *Not Whether But When: The U.S. Decision to Enlarge NATO*. Brookings Institution Press.

Ikle, F. (1995) 'How to Ruin NATO,' *International Herald Tribune*, 18 January.

Kennan, G. F. (1997) 'A Fateful Error,' *The New York Times*, 5 February.

Kupchan, C. A. (1994) 'Expand NATO—And Split Europe,' *The New York Times*, 27 November.

Kupchan, C. A. (1995) 'It's a Long Way to Bratislava: The Dangerous Folly of NATO Expansion,' *The Washington Post*, 14 May.

Lieven, A. (1997), 'Restraining NATO: Ukraine, Russia, and the West,' *The Washington Quarterly*, 20(4), pp. 55-77.

Lieven, A. (2008) 'Three Faces of Infantalism: NATO's Bucharest Summit,' *The National Interest*, 4 April.

NATO (1990) *London Declaration On A Transformed North Atlantic Alliance*, 5-6 July. Available at: http://www.nato.int/docu/comm/49-95/c900706a.htm.

NATO (1994) *The Brussels Summit Declaration*, 11 January. Available at: http://www.nato.int/cps/en/natolive/official_texts_24470.htm?selectedLocale=en.

NATO (2008) Bucharest Summit Declaration, 3 April. Available at: http://www.nato.int/cps/en/natolive/official_texts_8443.htm.

Mandlebaum, M. (1996) 'Don't Expand NATO,' *Newsweek*, 23 December.

Mearsheimer, J. J. (2014) 'Why the Ukraine Crisis is the West's Fault: The Liberal Delusions that Provoked Putin,' *Foreign Affairs*, September/October.

Rosner, R. (1996) 'NATO Enlargement's American Hurdle,' *Foreign Affairs*, July/August.

Rotfield, A. D. (2009) *Does Europe Need a New Security Architecture?* Finnish Institute of International Affairs and Ministry of Foreign Affairs.

Safire, W. (1992) 'Kozyrev's Wake-up Slap,' *The New York Times*, 17 October.

Sarotte, M. E. (2014) *The Collapse: The Accidental Opening of the Berlin Wall*. New York: Basic Books.

Sarotte, M. E. (2014) 'A Broken Promise? What the West Really Told Moscow About NATO Expansion,' *Foreign Affairs*, September/October.

Sciolino, E. (1994) 'Yeltsin Says NATO Is Trying to Split Continent Again,' *The New York Times*, 6 December.

Shifrinson, J. and Itzkowitz R. (2014) 'Put It In Writing: How the West Broke Its Promise to Moscow,' *Foreign Affairs*, 19 October.

Simes, D. K. (1999) *After the Collapse: Russia Seeks Its Place as a Great Power*. New York: Simon and Shuster.

Steil, B. (2014) 'Taper Trouble: The International Consequences of Fed Policy,' *Foreign Affairs*, July/August.

Talbott, S. (2002) *The Russia Hand: A Memoir of Presidential Diplomacy*. New York: Random House.

Walker, E. W. (2002) *Dissolution: Sovereignty and Dissolution of the Soviet Union*. Rowman & Littlefield.

Waltz, K. N. (1998) 'The Balance of Power and NATO Expansion', *Center for German and European Studies Working Paper,* 5.66, University of California, Berkeley.

Part Three

PROPAGANDA

13

'Hybrid War' and 'Little Green Men': How It Works, and How It Doesn't

MARK GALEOTTI
NEW YORK UNIVERSITY

When Russian special forces seized Crimea at the end of February 2014, without their insignia, but with the latest military kit, it seemed as the start of a new era of warfare. Certainly, the conflict in Ukraine has demonstrated that Moscow, in a bid to square its regional ambitions with its sharply limited resources, has assiduously and effectively developed a new style of 'guerrilla geopolitics' which leverages its capacity for misdirection, bluff, intelligence operations, and targeted violence to maximise its opportunities. However, it is too soon to declare that this represents some transformative novelty, because Moscow's Ukrainian adventures have not only demonstrated the power of such 'hybrid' or 'non-linear' ways of warfare, but also their distinct limitations.

The Genesis of the Idea

The essence of Russia's tactics was precisely to try and avoid the need for shooting as much as possible, and then to try and ensure that whatever shooting took place was on the terms that suited them best. To this end, they blended the use of a range of assets, from gangster allies to media spin, in a manner that draws heavily on past political operations, not least the *aktivnye meropriyatiya* ('active measures') of Soviet times (Madeira, 2014).

While not entirely new, their tactics were given a particular novelty simply by the characteristics of the contemporary world, something recognised by the Chief of the General Staff Valerii Gerasimov, in a crucial article from 2013, in which he noted that 'The role of non-military means of achieving political and strategic goals has grown, and, in many cases, they have exceeded the power of weapons in their effectiveness' (Gerasimov, 2013). In what is ostensibly a piece on the lessons of the 'Arab Spring' – which Kremlin orthodoxy presents as the result of covert Western campaigns of regime change – he outlines a new age in which:

> Wars are no longer declared and, having begun, proceed according to an unfamiliar template... [A] perfectly thriving state can, in a matter of months and even days, be transformed into an arena of fierce armed conflict, become a victim of foreign intervention, and sink into a morass of chaos, humanitarian catastrophe, and civil war.

There are a variety of reasons why today's Russia may find itself favouring operations in which, still to quote Gerasimov, 'The open use of forces – often under the guise of peacekeeping and crisis regulation – is resorted to only at a certain stage, primarily for the achievement of final success in the conflict.' For a start, despite the still-formidable size of its military, in practice, many of its forces remain antiquated, poorly trained, and scarcely operational. Moscow clearly has the preponderance of military and economic muscle in post-Soviet Eurasia, the region in which it feels it has hegemonic rights. However, not only is this apparent advantage to a considerable extent neutralised by the risk of involving the USA, China, or even the European Union in case of obvious aggression, it is also often not so overwhelming as to guarantee a quick and above all risk-free adventure. Even the five-day war against Georgia in 2008, while a victory, was a sufficiently painful one – with friendly fire incidents, communications mix-ups, and vehicle break-downs – that it galvanised meaningful military reform for the first time in more than two decades (Cohen and Hamilton, 2011).

Non-Linear Instruments

Instead, Russia finds itself in a situation where many of its strengths are either less decisive than it might like, or else are constrained because of economic or geopolitical realities. Put bluntly, a country with an economy somewhere between the size of Italy's and Brazil's is seeking to assert a great power international role and agenda. To this end, Russia has turned to this new 'guerrilla geopolitics' as a means of playing to its strengths and its opponents' weaknesses. It has also invested disproportionate resources into the assets most useful for such conflicts.

These are, broadly speaking, three, and they reflect how this is a way of war which even more explicitly than most targets not the opponent's military or even economic capacity, but their will and ability to fight at all. Of course there is a 'kinetic' element – the need to deploy armed forces and sometimes for them to fight – but the forces required for this will tend to have to operate with more autonomy than has in the past been usual for Russian troops, and likewise with greater precision. Thus, Russia has been developing its special and intervention forces, especially its 12,000 or so *Spetsnaz*. These are generally described as special forces, but they are highly mobile and effective light infantry akin to US Rangers or the French Foreign Legion, rather than true commandos (Galeotti, 2015). Instead, the newly established Special Operations Command (KSO) has perhaps 500 true operators in what in the West would be called 'Tier One' akin to the British SAS or US Delta force. Nonetheless, the *Spetsnaz*, like the VDV Airborne Troops or the Naval Infantry marines, represent an 'army within an army' able to operate professionally, decisively, covertly if need be, and outside Russia's borders.

There is an 'intelligence-war' dimension beyond the 'military war'. The Kremlin has devoted particular resources in its intelligence community. The Foreign Intelligence Service (SVR), the Main Intelligence Directorate (GRU, military intelligence), and even the Federal Security Service (FSB), which is increasingly involved in overseas operations, are not only agencies tasked with gathering information about foreign capabilities and intentions. Rather, they are also instruments of non-linear warfare, spreading despair and disinformation, encouraging defections, and breaking or corrupting lines of command and communications.

The third particular focus for Kremlin efforts has been its capacity to fight the 'information war,' to broadcast its own message and undermine and contest those of others in the name of winning the war in their hearts and minds (Pomerantsev and Weiss, 2014). The RT international television station, for example, has become a crucial player not only in espousing the Kremlin line, but, perhaps more importantly, in challenging Western media orthodoxy with a glitzy mix of genuine investigation, bizarre conspiracy theory, and cynical disingenuousness (Ioffe, 2010; O'Sullivan, 2014). Its 2015 budget is due to increase by almost 30%, suggesting the Kremlin appreciates its role.

Crimea: When It Works

The application of these new, deniable, and politically driven tactics in Ukraine has proven their potential value, but also the risks. In so many ways, Crimea was the perfect context in which the Russians could test out their new approach. The Peninsula already had Russian Black Sea Fleet facilities including the 810th Independent Naval Infantry Brigade, amongst whom KSO operators could quietly be secreted under cover of regular troop rotations. The local Ukrainian military forces, which in any event would never get clear orders from Kiev, were essentially technicians and mechanics, not front-line combat troops. The local population, alienated by twenty years of neglect and maladministration by Kiev, were largely willing to join richer Russia, and there were political and also criminal powerbrokers especially eager to become the agents of a new Muscovite order.

On 27 February, KSO and Naval Infantry seized the Crimean parliament building and began blockading Ukrainian bases on Crimea. Despite their modern Russian uniforms and weapons, the lack of insignia on these 'little green men' and Moscow's flat denial that they were Russian troops was enough to inject a moment's uncertainty into the calculations in both Kiev and NATO. Were they mercenaries, could it be Crimean vigilantes, or was this some unsanctioned adventure by a local commander? This deliberate *maskirovka*, or deception operations, was enough to give the Russians and their local allies the time to take up commanding positions across Crimea, including blockading Ukrainian garrisons, such that even if they had then been ordered to fight, they would have been in a very weak position. Ultimately, they surrendered after at most the demonstrative use of a few tear gas grenades, and Russia was able to seize Crimea without a single fatal casualty (Howard and Pukhov, 2014).

The reasons for the success were several. The new government in Kiev was already in disarray and mistrustful of its military commanders, something Moscow could encourage. The Russians had not only good troops already in-theatre and the opportunity covertly to introduce more, they also had a broadly supportive local population. Ukrainian forces, by contrast, were largely not combat ready, scattered in smaller garrisons, demoralised and in some cases sympathetic to or suborned by the Russians. Likewise, the local police and even Ukrainian Security Service (SBU) were penetrated by the Russians, while there were ample allies within the Crimean political and criminal elite to provide both compliant front men and a supply of thuggish 'local self-defence militias.'

For Moscow, these were the ideal possible conditions. They precluded the need to destabilise the target before intervention, allowed Russia to wage a pre-emptive information war to establish grounds for its mission, and allowed it to use its troops to assert and maintain a near-bloodless fait accompli with, if not deniability, at least a degree of ambiguity.

The Donbas: When it Doesn't

However, the subsequent adventure into south-eastern Ukraine – *Novorossiya* in the new Russian lexicon – while undoubtedly also following the non-linear war playbook, has shown how this is by no means the guaranteed war-winner some had initially assumed. Again, the Russians armed and supported irregular allied detachments, backed by a deniable force of their own special forces, while presenting this as an entirely spontaneous and local response to an illegal transfer of power in Kiev. The full panoply of Russian propaganda was deployed to muddy the waters in the West, especially by presenting the new Ukrainian regime as comprising or depending on 'fascists.'

The expectation appears to have been again that this would be a quick operation that would capitalise on Western hesitancy and its need for consensus politics. Chaos would be stirred up in Novorossiya to demonstrate to Kiev just what could happen if it failed to appreciate its place within Moscow's sphere of influence. Rather than face a Russian-backed insurgency just at the time it was trying to build a new Ukraine, the government would make suitable obeisance and concessions, above all ruling out further movement towards the European Union and NATO and also constitutional guarantees for Moscow's allies and clients in the east. Russian active operations would be ended, and all before the West had had a chance to decide what to do.

So much for neat plans, and the Kremlin's glib assumptions that all would run smoothly epitomises a cocky attitude that prevailed in government circles after Crimea. As one senior military advisor told me at that time, 'Russia is back. And we now know of what we are capable.' The very disarray in Kiev, which had worked to Moscow's advantage over Crimea, now proved a serious problem, as there was no one there able or willing to make the kind of politically ruinous concessions the Russians were demanding. Instead, a 'short, victorious little war' (as Interior Minister Plehve invoked before the disastrous 1904-5 Russo-Japanese War) turned into a 'bleeding wound' (as Mikhail Gorbachev characterised the 1979-88 invasion of Afghanistan).

Militarily, Russia could maintain the war, not least by the drip-fed addition of military matériel for the fighters of the self-proclaimed Donetsk and Lugansk People's Republics. Russian troops maintain a role on the battlefield in the guise of 'volunteers' alongside locals, mercenaries, and adventurers, including many Russians and Cossacks marshalled and armed by the GRU in Rostov and moved across the border into Ukraine (RFE/RL, 2014). Others provide training or technical support for the heavy weapons Russia has provided. In situations where it looks as if government troops might even make serious headway on the battlefield, such as in August, a large body of Russian troops were deployed across the border directly to ensure that the insurgent forces were not defeated, only then to be withdrawn – all without any formal acknowledgement of their role.

Russia has been able to maintain an insurgency which, by all accounts, has some genuine local support, but which in military terms is really best considered a loose coalition of local warlords, gangsters, opportunists, and Kremlin proxies. However, it has done so at catastrophic cost, considering the economic impact of the consequent Western sanctions regime, and with no evidence of any successful outcome. Both Kiev and Moscow now want the conflict to end, but unless one side or the other is willing to make greater concessions than have yet been placed on the table, Novorossiya risks becoming an unviable frozen conflict, a pseudo-state dependent on Moscow for its security and economic survival, while in return dooming Russia to continuing international opprobrium and economic crisis.

Conclusions: Politics Is All

Why such a different outcome? The first crucial difference was in the intended outcome: seizing Crimea was a relatively simple objective and although the issue would have been more complicated had the Ukrainians fought, either on Kiev's orders or local initiative, ultimately it was up to the Russians to win or lose. Their subsequent adventure, though, was a political gambit to influence Ukrainian politics and, as such, dependent on a multitude of factors beyond Moscow's control, or even imagination.

Most of the same operational advantages were present. A contiguous border allowed for the quick deployment of forces and reliable resupply of men and matériel. The Russians had and have near-absolute command of the air and a preponderance of artillery. Ukraine's forces have proven largely of indifferent quality; their capacity is undermined by Russian intelligence activity, including the presence of foreign agents within the ranks of their command structure (Galeotti 2014). Moscow had the initiative, and could also rely on local allies and agents.

But while in military terms, the operation was a success, the military is purely a part of the political campaign, and that has been a disastrous failure. What this highlights is that this new style of war, which seeks to rely on multiple military and non-military shocks to paralyse the enemy and break their will to resist, depends above all on a clear and accurate understanding of the political context in which it will operate. Putin gambled that over Crimea, Kiev would be unable to respond meaningfully and on time, and that Western anger and dismay would likely soon ebb, not least as new crises and challenges arise to direct its attention elsewhere. He was probably right. But perhaps over-emboldened by the effortless victory in Crimea, he overreached dangerously in his subsequent intervention into mainland Ukraine.

The Russian state won the 'military war' to create Novorossiya. It won the 'intelligence war' to support combat operations. It even had successes in the 'information war' to undermine Western enthusiasm for direct involvement, at least until the tragic blunder which was the shooting down of MH17. However, the essence of 'non-linear war' is that all these diverse components must effectively combine to win the underlying 'political war' to achieve the desired aim, and here Moscow is losing, and losing badly.

Does this mean that 'non-linear war' is just a temporary fad? No. In an age of interconnected economies, expensive militaries, and the 24/7 news cycle, if anything the fusion of a range of different types of conflict will become the norm. Indeed, arguably the combination of Western military aid on the battlefield, economic sanctions, and political pressure represent a similarly non-linear and asymmetric response. Where Russia leads, the West – but also perhaps China, India, and other powers looking to asserting their power in restrictive and non-permissive political environments – may well follow, albeit carefully learning the lessons of Crimea and Novorossiya alike.

References

Cohen, A. and Hamilton, R. (2011) *The Russian Military and the Georgia War: lessons and implications*. Carlisle: US Army Strategic Studies Institute.

Galeotti, M. (2015) 'Behind enemy lines: the rising influence of Russia's special forces,' *Jane's Intelligence Review*, January.

Galeotti, M. (2014) 'Moscow's Spy Game: Why Russia Is Winning the Intelligence War in Ukraine,' *Foreign Affairs*, 30 October. Available at: http://www.foreignaffairs.com/articles/142321/mark-galeotti/moscows-spy-game.

Gerasimov, V. (2013) 'Novye vyzovy trebuyut pereosmyslenniya form i sposobov vedeniya boevykh deistvii,' *Voenno-promyshlennye kur'er,* No. 8.

'The "Gerasimov Doctrine" and Russian Non-Linear War' (2014) *In Moscow's Shadows*, 6 July. Available at: https://inmoscowsshadows.wordpress.com/2014/07/06/the-gerasimov-doctrine-and-russian-non-linear-war/#more-2291

Howard C. and Pukhov, R. (eds) (2014) *Brothers Armed: military aspects of the crisis in Ukraine*. Minneapolis: East View Press.

Ioffe, J. (2010) 'What is Russia Today?' *Columbia Journalism Review*, 28 September. Available at: http://www.cjr.org/feature/what_is_russia_today.php.

Madeira, V. (2014) 'Russian subversion – haven't we been here before?' *Institute of Statecraft*, 30 July. Available at: http://www.statecraft.org.uk/research/russian-subversion-havent-we-been-here.

O'Sullivan, J. (2014) 'The difference between real journalism and Russia Today,' *The Spectator*, 6 December. Available at: http://www.spectator.co.uk/features/9390782/the-truth-about-russia-today-is-that-it-is-putins-mouthpiece/.

Pomerantsev P. and Weiss, M. (2014) 'The Menace of Unreality: How the Kremlin Weaponizes Information, Culture and Money,' *The Interpreter*. Available at: http://www.interpretermag.com/wp-content/uploads/2014/11/The_Menace_of_Unreality_Final.pdf.

RFE/RL (2014) video, 'Interview: I was a separatist fighter in Ukraine,' 13 July. Available at: http://www.rferl.org/content/ukraine-i-was-a-separatist-fighter/25455466.html.

14

Putin's Nationalism Problem

PAUL CHAISTY & STEPHEN WHITEFIELD
UNIVERSITY OF OXFORD

The crisis in Ukraine has produced a new narrative about Vladimir Putin's leadership. In contrast to the stated modernising goals of his first two presidencies – the achievement of greater state efficacy and the improvement of living standards and prosperity for ordinary Russian citizens – Putin has been recast as the saviour of the Russian nation. This new narrative includes a mission to protect the citizens of the 'Russian World' that live beyond the borders of the Russian Federation. In some analysis, this has led to parallels with Slobodan Milosevic's political journey in the former Yugoslavia (Whitmore, 2014).

Yet, while Vladimir Putin has shown strong patriotic instincts throughout his political career, he is not a natural nationalist. In an article titled 'Russia: The Ethnicity Issue,' which Putin published in January 2012 ahead of the presidential election, his ambiguous support for ethnically-based nationalism was apparent. He warned about the dangers that ethnic chauvinism posed to the territorial integrity of the Russian state: 'I am convinced that the attempts to preach the idea of a "national" or monoethnic Russian state contradict our thousand-year history,' he averred, 'this is a shortcut to destroying the Russian people and Russian statehood, and for that matter any viable, sovereign statehood on the planet' (Nezavisimaya Gazeta, 2014). Moreover, his regime's relationship with the nationalist leadership in eastern Ukraine, and their ideological backers in Russia, has not always been cordial during the Ukrainian conflict. Putin's commitment to the creation of a new territory, 'Novorossiya,' which would lead to the breakup of Ukraine, has been questioned by nationalist ideologues and militia leaders throughout the crisis (Sonne, 2014).

Nor has Putin's public support base been drawn over the years mainly from the nationalist political camp. Rather, public opinion evidence from the early and mid-2000s (Whitefield, 2005, 2009) indicates that Putin and his government was significantly less likely to be supported by nationalist and anti-Western citizens and that there were only very limited differences socially and ideologically between his supporters and those for so-called liberal politicians. Indeed, Putin's political success may have been founded on his relative centrist and modernising stances: an organised and strong state, and one which deliberately made political use of the Soviet past, but not ethno-nationalist or anti-Western.

To explain the new narrative of Putin and Putinism, we argue, it is necessary to examine the political strategy that defined Putin's return to power in 2012. This strategy emerged in response to the threat that Russian nationalism posed the Putinite system in the aftermath of the 2008-09 financial crisis. This crisis discredited the modernising agenda that framed Putin's first two presidencies, and undermined the regime's previous support base. The potential for a nationalist backlash was evident in the nationalist support for the electoral protests against the Putin regime in 2011-12, and in the strategies for counter-mobilisation that drove Putin's fight back in 2012. Thus, we argue that the Ukrainian crisis has reinforced a trend that was already present prior to Russia's annexation of Crimea. But we also contend that the crisis has raised the stakes for the Putin regime. If Putin fails to deliver in Ukraine, the possibility of a challenge to his authority from a more radical nationalist agenda is likely to be greater than it was before the start of the crisis.

Putin's Contentious Return

Putin's third presidential term was always going to be different from his previous stints in the Kremlin. In contrast to the relatively trouble-free election victories in 2000 and 2004, Putin's election in 2012 occurred within the midst of the first serious popular political revolt against his rule. His controversial decision to return to presidential office in September 2011 – in place of incumbent Dmitry Medvedev – took place at a time of declining support for the ruling party, United Russia. Opposition forces were in the ascendant, and the proposed switching of roles with Medvedev – with the sitting president lined up as the next prime minister – divided his political allies. In the event, the parliamentary elections that were held in December 2011 provided the focus for significant protest against the regime. Mass protest took place on the streets of Russia's main cities, with thousands of Russian citizens claiming that the elections were fraudulent.

The break that Vladimir Putin took from the presidency between 2008 and 2012 also coincided with the global financial crisis, which hit Russia in 2008.

This crisis undermined the appeal of the programme of economic modernisation, which had kept Putin in power for the previous eight years. The crisis slowed down earnings growth, challenged the government's capacity to manage the economy, and made those who were directly affected by the financial crisis less willing to put up with the negative features of Putin's rule, such as corruption and the overconcentration of political power. It also undercut whatever vestiges of support remained for the neo-liberal, globalisation, and pro-Western model of economic development. The West was now seen to have feet of clay, while at the same time it could even more credibly be blamed for Russia's national humiliations over the previous two decades.

Crucially, the global financial crisis eroded support and confidence in the regime. In the summer of 2009, we conducted a nationally representative survey of 1,500 Russian citizens, and found that respondents who were directly affected by the financial crisis were more likely to respond negatively to questions concerning popular support for the political leadership of the country, the efficacy of the political authorities, and the actual practice of democracy in Russia (Chaisty and Whitefield, 2012). Importantly, our analysis found that individuals who were adversely affected by the financial crisis were less willing to pledge their support either to Putin or Medvedev in a future presidential election (Chaisty and Whitefield, 2012, p. 201), and were more likely to believe that the social and political situation in the country had become less stable as a result of the global financial crisis (Chaisty and Whitefield, 2012, p. 202).

Therefore, declining support for the regime was already apparent before United Russia announced Putin as their presidential candidate in September 2012. Throughout 2011, support for the governing party fell, and claims of corruption were skilfully used by opposition leaders against the authorities. Putin's decision to return to the Kremlin acted as the trigger for underlying discontent, which focused on the 2011-12 electoral cycle. The parliamentary elections of 2011 provided an opportunity for protest from opponents of the regime who held a variety of grievances. Significantly, support for the protests came not only from the usual suspects – supporters of Western-style political democracy – but also from nationalists who rejected the Western path of political and economic transition.

The Nationalist Threat

Radical nationalist opposition to Putin's decision to return to the presidency was evident in the political makeup of the protests that took to the streets of Russia's cities, in particular Moscow. The sight of nationalist yellow-and-black

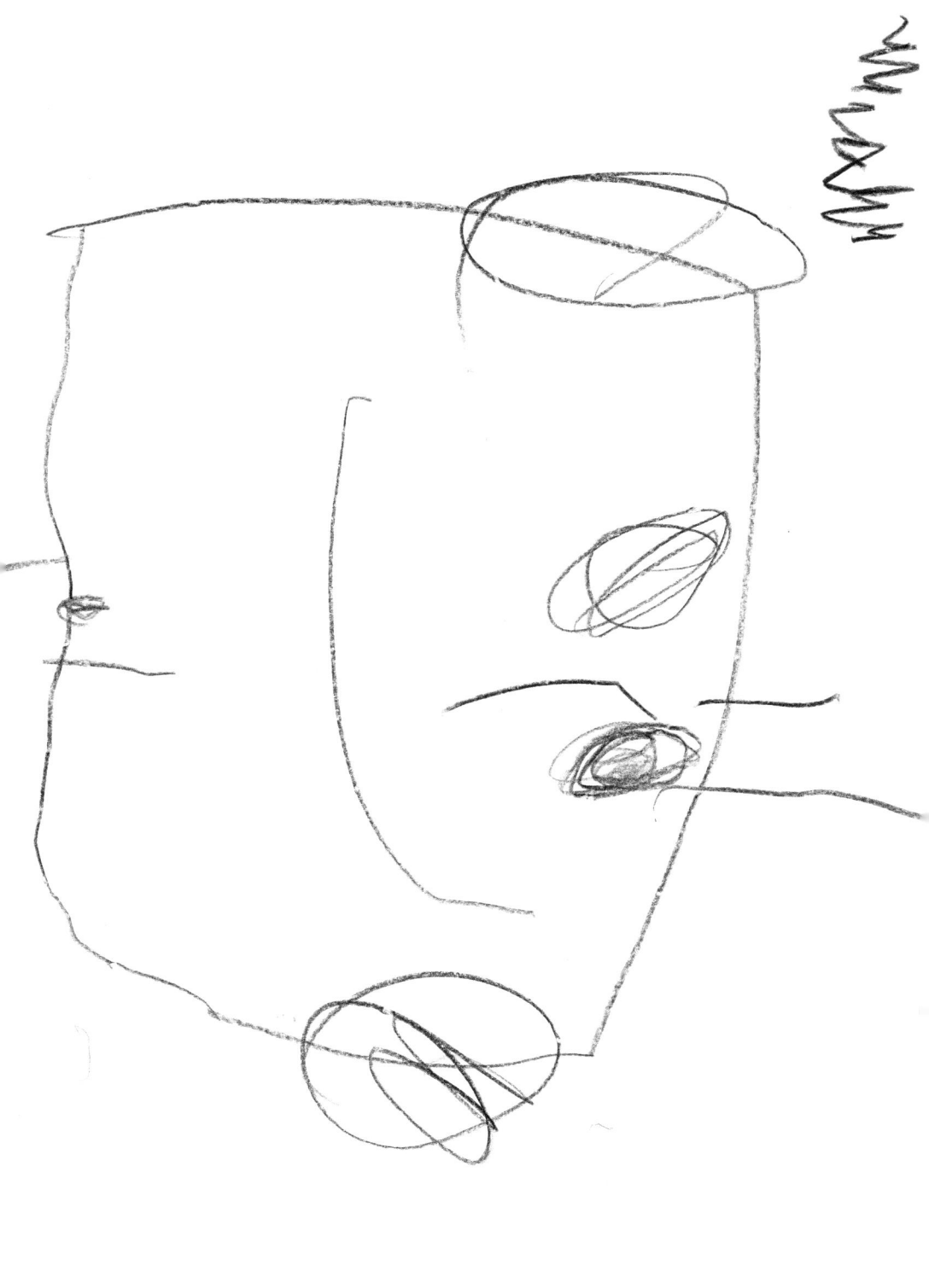

banners, mixed in among the distinctive colours of Russia's leftist and democratic opposition, was a vivid signal to the Kremlin that protest against the regime covered the entire political spectrum. Yet, this opposition was not only confined to the relatively small numbers of committed nationalist activists who took to the streets in December 2011. A far greater problem for the Kremlin was the mass basis for such views among citizens who supported the protests.

In our work, we have researched the attitudes of those who supported the electoral protests of 2011 (Chaisty and Whitefield, 2013). We conducted a nationally representative survey of 1,200 Russian citizens in the week after the presidential elections of 2012. Of those that we surveyed, almost half (47 per cent) agreed with the statement that the protests were justified. This figure was comparable to the results of Russian polling agencies, notably the Levada Centre, at this time. Our analysis of the demographic and attitudinal characteristics of the supporters of the electoral protests was revealing. We found that supporters of protest tended to be concentrated in the main metropolitan centres of Moscow and St. Petersburg; their support for the protests was motivated by opposition to Putin's decision to return to the presidency; and their political attitudes were not, as was a common narrative in the Western press at the time, supportive of a Western path of political transition as in the Orange Revolution – instead, supporters of protest were more likely to support authoritarian solutions to Russia's problems, and were likely to hold strong ethno-nationalist views.

This normative orientation of those who backed the electoral protest against the regime posed Putin a number of serious problems on his return to power. The potency of authoritarian and ethno-nationalist attitudes among his critics were in addition to the effects of metropolitan residence and opposition to his decision to return for a third term. For example, controlling for other predictors, we found that those who strongly agreed with ethno-nationalist statements (e.g. Jews have too much power and influence in Russia) were 18 per cent more likely to support protest than those who disagreed, and those who agreed that the overthrow of democracy would be justified if it solved the country's problems were 25 per cent more likely to support protest (Chaisty and Whitefield, 2013, p. 9).

Given the underlying problems facing Russia's leadership – predictions of future economic crises and growing discontent with systemic corruption – the regime was particularly sensitive to this opposition. In response, the Kremlin set about building a new majority that would drive Putin's third presidential campaign. This campaign involved more direct engagement with nationalist themes.

Putin's Fight Back

The Kremlin's concern about the nationalist threat can be seen in the nature of the counter-mobilisation campaign that was organised in the immediate aftermath of the December protests. Pro-Kremlin rallies centred on patriotic themes that would provide the basis for Putin's presidential election campaign. In place of the earlier emphasis on modernisation, which had been the buzzword of the Medvedev presidency, the focus moved in a conservative direction, with greater prominence given to themes of order and the need to protect the state.

Particularly revealing were the individuals involved in the counter-mobilisation activities of early 2012. Conservative and nationalist intellectuals like Sergei Kurginyan and Alexander Dugin participated in events aimed at rallying support for the authorities, as well as other individuals associated with late Soviet-era patriotic and nationalist politics. This constituency had been largely peripheral in front-line Russian politics since the early 1990s. They have advocated a worldview that has been sharply critical of the direction of change that has taken place in Russia since the collapse of the Soviet Union. Thus, the authorities were compelled to draw strength from individuals who were not natural bedfellows. During the constitutional crisis of October 1993, for example, many of these individuals had backed an uprising against the regime that Putin helped to consolidate. The fact that, twenty years later, this voice was called on to help the same regime to revive its support, and later provide intellectual and military leadership for an armed insurgency in eastern Ukraine, underlines the leadership's predicament.

Nonetheless, this strategy was successful politically. Putin succeeded in mobilising enough support to win the presidential elections on the first round with 64 per cent of the vote. Since then, the regime has promoted a conservative agenda that has consolidated this support and marginalised those opposition politicians who threatened to make a breakthrough in late 2011. The conservative campaign – energised by such high-profile incidents as the arrest and imprisonment of the Pussy Riot punk rock feminists for their performance of an anti-Putin stunt in Moscow's Cathedral of Christ the Saviour – succeeded in keeping Putin's core support mobilised and, crucially, it reconnected Putin with conservatively-inclined citizens who had threatened to join with the opposition.

The Impact of Crimea

The direction of travel had therefore been established before the start of the Ukrainian crisis. The conservative agenda that emerged was politically more authoritarian, as illustrated by the backsliding over initiatives aimed to raise political competition; socially more conservative, as highlighted by the measures against sexual minorities; and more critical of Western action in the area of foreign policy. Although the effects of this strategy require more systematic analysis, which is the focus of our current research, in general the conservative agenda appears to have been successful in consolidating and mobilising Putin's core support: state employees who have seen their living standards rise significantly under his leadership. This group shares the government's conservative and patriotic agenda.

However, the Ukrainian crisis and Russia's annexation of Crimea was significant in nullifying the criticisms of those who were sympathetic to anti-regime protest. It extended Putin's support to encapsulate a broad constituency of Russian citizens, which includes both moderate patriots, who are ideologically supportive of political and economic modernisation, and more radical nationalists who reject the Western path of development (Bunin, 2014). For the moment, at least, Putin appears to have assuaged the radical constituency. The decline in anti-Kremlin nationalist mobilisation, which was evident in the comparatively low turnout by anti-regime activists in the National Unity Day marches in November 2014, provides some evidence for this.

What, then, do we conclude about Putin and Putinism? We do not see the man and the regime as defined by principled ideological nationalism. Rather, this turn to nationalism reflects a political strategy – likely to preserve the existing 'kleptocratic' political economy – that classically mobilises nationalism to divert attention from the regime's failings and to put the blame for the humiliation widely said to be felt by Russians on the West and on internal political and social enemies. It is also a means of incorporating actors who were the strongest and most dangerous opponents of the regime. These, of course, were not the almost completely marginalised liberals, but rather the mobilised nationalists who took to the streets in 2011-12.

This broad coalition of core supporters, moderate patriots and more radical nationalists, accounts for the sharp spike in support for Putin during the Ukrainian crisis. Yet, the ability of the regime to maintain this coalition presents a new set of challenges. Unless the Ukrainian crisis has radically transformed the attitudes of Russian citizens, which we doubt, the Kremlin will have to satisfy a diverse range of conflicting demands. This task will be rendered more difficult by economic crisis and the international limitations to territorial expansion in eastern Ukraine. The regime's willingness to engage with more radical nationalist ambitions, such as the creation of "Novorossiya", may have raised expectations beyond realistic limits. This may become a new focus of opposition to the regime as the conflict in Ukraine grinds on. Thus, Putin's nationalism problem has not been resolved by the Ukrainian crisis, and it could define the remainder of his presidency.

References

Bunin, I. (2014) 'Novoye putinskoye bol'shinstvo: faktory konsolidatsii,' *Politikom*. Available at: http://www.politcom.ru/17679.html (Accessed 4 June 2014).

Chaisty, P. and Whitefield S. (2012) 'The Effects of the Global Financial Crisis on Russian Political Attitudes,' *Post-Soviet Affairs,* 28(2), pp. 187-208.

Chaisty, P. and Whitefield, S. (2013) 'Forward to democracy or back to authoritarianism? The attitudinal bases of mass support for the Russian election protests of 2011-2012,' *Post-Soviet Affairs,* 29(5), pp. 387-403.

Sonne, P. (2014) 'Russian Nationalists Feel Let Down by Kremlin, Again,' *The Wall Street Journal*. Available at: http://www.wsj.com/articles/russian-nationalists-feel-let-down-by-kremlin-again-1404510139 (Accessed 4 July 2014).

Whitefield, S. (2005) 'Putin's Popularity and Its Implications for Democracy in Russia' in Pravda, A. (ed.) *Leading Russia: Putin in Perspective*. Oxford: Oxford University Press, pp. 139-160.

Whitefield, S. (2009) 'Russian Citizens and Russian Democracy: Perceptions of State Governance and Democratic Practice, 1993-2007,' *Post-Soviet Affairs*, 25(2), pp. 1-25.

Whitmore, B. (2014) 'Slobodan's Ghost', *RFE/RL,* 14 July.

15

Vladimir Putin: Making of the National Hero

ELENA CHEBANKOVA
UNIVERSITY OF LINCOLN

Isaiah Berlin (2006, p. 17), in his essay titled 'Politics as a Descriptive Science,' argues that the central issue of political philosophy is the question of 'why should any man obey any other man or a body of men?' Bearing this in mind, any attempts to account for the public support of a particular political leader could be approached from this broad philosophical standpoint. Why are some politicians admired and why do people submit to them freely? Why some are not? How do popular politicians become so popular? Why are some occasionally treated as national heroes and thereby enjoy the compliance and support of their compatriots? How can we account for these developments in the Russian case, in which Vladimir Putin almost achieved the status of 'national hero' and a public approval rating unthinkable for many of his counterparts in the West? To what extent has the Ukrainian crisis contributed to these developments?

Some analysts may indeed feel tempted to reduce their explanations of Putin's 'national hero' status to the pressure of events in Crimea and Ukraine. Some may relate his success to Russia's impressive economic performance that, within a decade, pulled the country out of poverty and created a stable and resilient economic structure with a healthy trading balance, impressive gold reserves, and the virtual absence of state debt. Some others may look even deeper and hope to find answers in the emergent political stability that, although looking to many liberals like political stagnation, gave Russians a welcome breathing space much required in the wake of the turbulent era of the 1990s. While we should not dismiss such empirical factors entirely, mere economic and political stability, as well as Russia's geopolitical successes in Crimea, cannot provide satisfactory answers to the question that we are trying to deal with. Crimea indeed contributed to the surge of national consolidation, while economic and political stability initially led to the shifting away from issues of mere survival to a host of existential questions, such as 'who are we?', 'how should we live?', and 'who is responsible?' (see similar theoretical critiques in the Western context by Habermas, 1981, p. 36; Edwards, 2004, p. 115; Ingelhart, 1989; Giddens, 1990). At the same time, we must continue our search on deeper existential levels rather than empirical ones for the answer to the question of a leader's political popularity is unavoidably philosophical. Such explanations belong to the discursive, and not the economic, military, or political, realm. This article will argue that the secret of Putin's 'national hero' status can be found in the way that he has presided over a fundamental paradigmatic shift from a liberal to a traditionalist episteme that took place in the discursive sphere of Russian society.

From a theoretical point of view, it is important that the birth of the post-modern world has seriously elevated the significance of the discursive realm. It is discursive practice that shapes much of today's politics and it is dominant interpretations of historic events and socio-cultural structures of society that define the redistribution of power, form the 'regime of truth', and compel one group of people to obey another. Discursive mapping of human history now challenges the universalist, rationalist, and positivist accounts that aspired empirically to explain the development of societal relationships. The central question becomes: how can a dominant discourse be identified and what factors and actions are responsible for its criticism, change, and transition? Truth, therefore, becomes particular and contingent on idiosyncratic interpretations that are firmly embedded in the spatial and chronological context. Quentin Skinner (2002, p. 53), following Barry Barnes and David Bloor, observes that 'the only possible judge of the truth of our beliefs must be whatever consensus over norms and standards may happen to prevail in our local culture'. Hence, we can narrow our search by asking whether one or another 'regime of truth' accurately reflects the 'needs of society under which it had originated' (Taylor, 1998, p. 223; Skinner, 2002, p. 28; Mouffe, 1988, p. 37; Gray, 2000, p. 14; Kymlicka, 2004, pp. 117-9). Within these conditions, the role of political ideas, words, and statements becomes consequential. In many ways, we could depend on them for explaining social change, shifts in the redistribution of power, and the rise of influential political figures.

Foucault, Skinner, and Wittgenstein share this explanatory approach of social change emphasising, each at their theoretical level, the importance of discursive, linguistic events and treat the language of politics as a 'tool' responsible for political action, which is subject to manipulation, criticism, modification, and change (Tully, 1988, pp. 5-8). Foucault (1989) in *The Archaeology of Knowledge* introduces the idea of a 'discursive event' that represents a 'basic unit of communication... unique as event and repeatable as thing' (Flynn, 2005, p. 53). A radically new statement, a book, a work of an author, a political idea – all feature in such discursive historic events. These events are 'epistemic' for they have the power to alter the entire paradigm of social self-perceptions, the web of socio-political relationships, and the redistribution of political power (Foucault, 1989, p. 172). Hence, these events work as 'epistemological acts and thresholds' for they 'suspend the continuous accumulation of knowledge, interrupt its slow development, and force it to enter a new time, cut it of its imaginary complicities' (Foucault, 1989, p. 4). The emergence of an epistemic event results in the relevant commentary and in the gradual accumulation of a pool of similar discursive statements. These statements, as Skinner (1978) notes, incrementally manipulate the established political, moral, and ideological conventions of the age until such manipulations enter into insurmountable contradictions with the dominant use of hegemonic ideology. This dynamic steadily changes society's self-perceptions, appreciation of the outside world, and its attitudes to historic events. It prompts this society to redefine moral conventions and create a new regime of power and truth. Hence, we witness a certain 'paradigmatic shift' that changes 'speech-act potentials of normative terms' and significantly redefines society morally (Tully, 1988, p. 13; Skinner, p. xi). Those politicians who manage to ride the wave of discursive change often become 'national heroes' for they manage accurately to reflect the subtle and innermost changes of their societies and preside over the ineluctable paradigmatic change.

Another question of importance is: how can we historically demarcate the emergence of a discursive event that achieves a change of a paradigm? What induces the change of conventional discourse in the first place? It could be argued that discursive events do not spring up out of the blue. Their surfacing always reflects the needs of the society under which they had originated. As Skinner (1978, p. xi) notes, 'political life itself sets the main problems for the political theorist, causing a certain range of issues to appear problematic, and a corresponding range of questions to become the leading subject of debates'. Thus, political problems of the age get their initial reflection in the discursive realm before proceeding to become a formed political action. On the one hand, socio-political changes within a society must be sufficient enough to produce new demands and expectations. On the other hand, an appropriate discursive event must surface and start to provide gradual but steady shifts within the socio-political and socio-cultural structure. This situation does not necessarily or immediately lead to a radical transformation of the dominant political paradigm, but it may well change the way in which such a paradigm is narrated.

This explanation invokes Berlin's (2002, pp. 28-9) argument that knowledge plays a leading role in the legitimation of certain regimes of compliance in which knowledge satisfies 'ignorance, curiosity, doubt' and responds to the question of 'why should I obey?' Such knowledge must tend to the compelling desire of humans to resolve existential issues such as the nature of 'truth, happiness, reality... for this is what they [humans] mean by "good"' (Berlin, 2002, pp. 32-3). Due to the particular nature of truth, such knowledge often comes in the shape of new historic and political myths, as well as new interpretations of old conventions. These myths, which constitute the projection of the culture's unconscious values, form the basis of paradigmatic and structural narratives (Giddens, 1979, p. 21; Harkin, 2009, pp. 45-6; Hroch, 1985; Breuilly, 1985; Sorel, 1999; Casirer, 1946). From this follows that historic and political myths, as well as epistemic 'discursive events', are created to match our expectations (Skinner, 2002, p. 28). Therefore, we may treat discursive events as a new form of knowledge that strives to address the most pressing political problems of the age and reflects slow but unavoidable paradigmatic shift. Here again, the ability of a political leader to satisfy 'curiosity and ignorance' by appealing to an appropriate *type* of knowledge and the ability to operate a particular *type* of discursive statement – which reflect the longing for unconventional interpretations of existing ideology and the production of new myths – contribute decisively to his/her standings.

To reflect these theoretical stipulations in the Russian case, we must divide the analysis between two distinct but interconnected spheres: political structural and discursive. In the first case, we must select some problematic areas of the political age that generated expectations and societal requests for the creation of new myths and narratives. In the discursive realm, we must distinguish those epistemic, historical events that led to a change in the paradigmatic narrative and contributed significantly to the formation of new myths. In this light, to account for Putin's public success is to map out the point in history at which ideological transition had begun and to ascertain the way in which he led such a change.

One stable feature of Russian political life is seen in a permanent struggle between two competing paradigms: liberal and traditional. These two paradigmatic views, explaining the politics of an age and trajectories of a country's development, compete and replace each other over the course of Russia's history (Kara-Murza, 2008; Filatov, 2006). Both paradigms have different tasks, priorities, and objectives, and tend to differing needs generated by Russian society. The traditionalist (statist) paradigm is concerned with the preservation of the country's territorial integrity, security, refuting the external threat and consolidating domestic political and economic stability. The liberal paradigm challenges the traditionalist perspectives at the existential level. It is geared towards the issues of social justice, fairness, transparency of government, and keeping the state's authoritarian tendencies in check (Yanov, 2003; Shevtsova, 2008). The duality and struggle between these two radically different paradigms constitutes the essence of Russian political life. These two competing paradigms are narrated differently at different historic periods, each time depending on a particular historic context. It is important that each paradigm creates different historic myths that tend to different needs and requirements of Russian society, and hence uses different modes of societal and political interpretation. The rupture of the previous paradigm and its subsequent change takes place through the accumulation of discursive events that somehow reflect the growing cultural and economic needs of Russian society.

These two cardinal paradigms of Russian political life have been redefined in a variety of different ways during the past hundred years. The first serious redefinition of Russia's existential narrative took place in the aftermath of the October 1917 Revolution. Then the previously liberal tendencies of the age seen in the quest for social justice spawned by the Russian Revolution were replaced by statist traditionalist interpretations disguised in the form of Soviet Communism. It created a watershed in Russian history and necessitated the formation of qualitatively new Russian myths. Those myths, though existentially and, above all, unconsciously, repeated the general socio-psychological pattern of the Russian Empire, still rested on a qualitatively different discourse. Soviet ideological and mythical constructs have been met by practical historical necessities of Russia's industrialisation and the building of military potential capable of fighting the Nazi invasion and subsequently responding to the challenges of a bipolar world, of which Russia was a central part. This was an invariably traditionalist discourse that was skilfully embedded within Soviet rhetoric.

The collapse of the Soviet Union provoked a serious existential crisis through the radical destruction of previously established epistemic myths. It was important that the dissolution of the Soviet narrative did not coincide chronologically with the actual collapse of the Soviet state. The liberal counter-myth emerged as early as in the late 1960s and early 1970s (Byzov, 2006; English, 2000. Some historians date it back to the 1940s; see Lukin, 2009, p. 71; Kharkhordin, 2005, pp. 83-7; Timashev, 1946) and had become gradually entrenched in the Soviet societal landscape. The need to recast the Soviet system to account for unsatisfied consumer demand contributed to the emergence of a new public political ideal based on hedonistic tendencies and demands for higher living standards. Towards the end of the 1980s and early 1990s, the transition to the liberal paradigm was complete. However, this was an epistemic shift of formidable magnitude. Hence, the final and irretrievable loss of the traditionalist Soviet epistemic foundation resulted in the profound loss of a sense of direction and paradigmatic uncertainty. It destroyed the coherent narrative that linked Russian Imperial and Soviet history into a single comprehensive unit. This atmosphere of epistemological uncertainty fuelled the quest for a new knowledge and narrative. True to form, those narratives had to have a traditionalist flavour.

A difficult web of Russia's societal relationships was formed towards the end of the 1990s and pointed in the direction of an emerging consensus over the need to reinvent the structural narrative in a way which would be embedded in a sense of national self-awareness, tradition, statism, and dignity. Some subtle messages on Russia's new particular self-consciousness began to appear within the commercial advertising sphere – an area that is exceptionally sensitive to the innermost needs of society. They have also emerged in the cinematic art. A prime example is the nationalist film *Brother*, which struck a chord with the absolute majority of Russians. In the realm of international relations, this subtle shift has been visible through the replacement of liberal and pro-Western Russian foreign minister Andrei Kozyrev with the more pragmatic and traditionalist Yevgeniy Primakov. Russia's questioning and distinct stance on the NATO bombing of Yugoslavia has reflected that change well.

In the domestic political sphere, discursive events have been seen during the second Chechen campaign, when Putin declared his determination to tackle the problem in the most decisive and radical manner. His statements on the need to pacify the region and his practical support of the army elicited a response among many Russian military personnel, thus creating an avalanche of patriotic commentary and discussion (Troshev, 2001; Medvedev, 2001). All these events signified the rupture of Russia's previous liberal narrative that had dominated the discourse, formally and informally, most probably from the *détente* period, when the need for structural reform of the Russian political system became apparent.

The subsequent growth of similar discursive events – seen in the calls to revise Russian history (Putin's 2013 Valdai speech), to find an appropriate place for the country within the international arena (Putin's 2007 Munich speech), to reinvent Russia's anthropology on some traditionalist perceptions of stable identities – gave birth to profound epistemic shifts and transformations that became clearly visible within a decade. The general change of Russia's discourse, an epistemic shift from the liberal to traditionalist myth created a new atmosphere, a new regime of truth, a new ideological environment, which, though not fully formed, had an air of great expectations and a sense of a return to the Russian traditionalist mission.

It could be argued that the explanations of Putin's popularity may be found in the fact that he was rightly attuned to the gradual change of the paradigmatic narrative that was taking place, moving from liberalism to traditionalism at the time of his arrival to the presidency. Putin, through an attempt to create a new coherent socio-historic narrative, came close to a situation in which his ideas became 'true to the needs' of Russia's society. He was well-attuned to the requirements of the new traditionalist paradigm that could provide new answers to existential questions, that could meet the challenge of contextualising concrete Russian peoples within the historical, political, and international scene. From this point of view, an extremely positive response from Russians to Putin's actions during the Ukrainian crisis has been entirely logical. Ukraine and Crimea represented, using Foucault's terminology, a 'population of events in the space of discourse in general' (Flynn 2005, p. 51). It was an instance, or perhaps the apex, of the decade-long process of Russia's epistemic shift – a shift that involved the creation of a new leader and the formation of radically new historic and contemporary social narratives. The secret of Putin's success, in the view of the author, is his attempt to recreate a narrative of the Russian structure in a new form. His attempted myths resonated well with the majority of the Russian public. The Ukrainian crisis unmasked those hidden passions of Russian society and became the focal point for this long search for self-rediscovery within the broader context of Russia's history.

References

Berlin, I. (2006) *Political Ideas in the Romantic Age*. Princeton: Princeton University Press.

Breuilly, J. (1985) *Nationalism and the State*. Manchester: Manchester University Press.

Byzov, L. (2006) 'Konservativnaia Volna v Rossii', *VTsIOM*, 2 October. Available at http://wciom.ru/arkhiv/tematicheskii-arkhiv/item/single/3298.html?no_cache=1&cHash=a4c273c90e.

Cassirer, E. (1946) *The Myth of the State*. New Haven: Yale University Press.

Davidson, D. (1984) 'On the Very Idea of Conceptual Scheme' in *Inquiries into Truth and Interpretation*. Oxford: OUP, pp. 183-98.

Edwards, G. (2004) 'Habermas and Social Movements: What's "New"?' in Crossley N. and Roberts J.M. (eds) *After Habermas: New Perspectives on the Public Sphere*. Oxford: Blackwell Publishing.

English, R. (2000) *Russia and the Idea of the West.* New York: Columbia University Press.

Filatov, V. (2006) 'Osobennosti liberalizatsii i modernizatsii Rossii vo vtoroy polovine XIX–nachale XX vekov v kontekste Yevropeyskogo razvitiya' in *Rossiya: Varianty institutsional'nogo razvitiya*, Proceedings of the Internet Conference at the Higher School of Economics, Moscow, 25 October to 15 December. Available at: http://ecsocman.hse.ru/text/16207777/.

Flynn, T. (2005) *Sartre, Foucault and Historical Reason. A Post-Structuralist Mapping of History.* Chicago: University of Chicago Press.

Foucault, M. (1989) *Archaeology of Knowledge.* London: Routledge Press.

Giddens, A. (1979) *Central Problems in Social Theory: Action, Structure and Contradiction in Social Analysis.* Berkley: University of California Press.

Giddens, A. (1990) *The Consequences of Modernity.* Cambridge: Polity Press.

Gray, J. (2000) *Two Faces of Liberalism.* New York: The New Press.

Habermas, J. (1981) 'New Social Movements', *Telos*, Vol. 49, pp. 3-31.

Harkin, M. (2009) 'Levi-Strauss and History' in Wiseman B. (ed.) *The Cambridge Companion to Levi-Strauss.* Cambridge: Cambridge University Press, pp. 39-59.

Hroch, M. (1985) *Social Preconditions of National Revival in Europe: A Comparative Analysis of the Social Composition of Patriotic Groups among the Smaller European Nations.* Cambridge: Cambridge University Press.

Kara-Murza, A. (1998) 'Dualizm Rossiyskoy identichnosti: Tsivilizovannoye Zapadnichestvo versus geopoliticheskoye Yevraziystvo,' *Russkiy Zhurnal,* 27 October.

Kharkhordin, O. (2005) *Main Concepts of Russian Politics.* Maryland: University Press of America.

Kymlicka, W. (2004) 'Dworkin on Freedom and Culture' in Burley, J. (ed.) *Dworkin and His Critics*. Oxford: Blackwell, pp. 113-133.

Lukin, A. (2009) 'Russia's New Authoritarianism and the Post-Soviet Political Ideal,' *Post-Soviet Affairs*, 25(1), pp. 66-92.

Medvedev, R. (2001) *Vremya Putina?* Moscow: Prava Cheloveka.

Mouffe, C. (1988) 'Radical Democracy: Modern or Post-modern?' in Ross A. (ed.) *Universal Abandon: The Politics of Post-Modernism*. Minneapolis: University of Minnesota Press, pp. 31-45.

Shevtsova, L. (2008) *Russia: Lost in Transition*. Washington, DC: Carnegie Endowment for International Peace.

Skinner, Q. (1978) *The Foundations of Modern Political Thought. Volume 1*. Cambridge: CUP.

Skinner, Q. (2002) *Visions of Politics. Volume I. Regarding Method*. Cambridge: CUP.

Sorel, G. (1999) *Reflections on Violence*. Cambridge: Cambridge University Press.

Taylor, C. (1988) 'The Hermeneutics of Conflict' in Tully, J. (ed.) *Meaning and Context: Quentin Skinner and his Critics*. Cambridge: CUP, pp. 218-28.

Timasheff, N. (1946) *The Great Retreat*. New York: Dutton.

Troshev, G. (2001) *Moia Voina. Chechenskii Dnevnik Okopnogo Generala*. Moscow: Vagrius.

Tully, J. (1988) 'Pen is a Mighty Sword' in Tully, J. *Meaning and Context. Quentin Skinner and his Critics*. Princeton: Princeton University Press.

Yanov, A. (2003) 'Ideynaya voina. Epigony, Liberaly, Rossiya i Yevropa,' *Polis*, February 3, 2014. Available at: http://www.politstudies.ru/universum/dossier/03/yanov-2.htm.

16

Dominant Narratives in Russian Political and Media Discourse during the Ukraine Crisis

STEPHEN HUTCHINGS, UNIVERSITY OF MANCHESTER
&
JOANNA SZOSTEK, UNIVERSITY COLLEGE LONDON

The Russian leadership views mass communication as a crucial arena of global politics, in which rival powers work to undermine each other and further their own interests at others' expense. The ability to project narratives to foreign audiences is therefore considered a matter of national security, as is the ability to control the circulation of narratives at home. In its Foreign Policy Concept of 2013, Russia declared that it must 'create instruments for influencing how it is perceived in the world', 'develop its own effective means of information influence on public opinion abroad', and 'counteract information threats to its sovereignty and security' (Russian Foreign Ministry, 2013). In line with these goals, the Russian government has invested heavily in media resources that can convey its point of view to other countries, such as the TV news channel RT.

Meanwhile, independent and critical voices have been increasingly stifled within Russia's domestic media environment. State control over news on the main television channels (Pervyy Kanal, Rossiya 1, NTV) has been tight for years – all of them reflect and support the government's stance. There is still pluralism in the press, on the radio, and on the Internet. However, the Ukraine crisis has coincided with a clampdown even in these 'freer' parts of Russia's media landscape: the popular news website lenta.ru has had its editorial team replaced and the Internet and satellite channel Dozhd has been evicted from its premises.

The narratives described in this chapter can be observed throughout the Russian media which are aligned with the state – from state-owned federal channels to commercial tabloids like *Komsomolskaya Pravda* and the widely-used state news agency/website RIA Novosti. Some of the narratives have caused considerable consternation in Kiev. The post-Yanukovych Ukrainian government quickly banned Russian channels from Ukrainian cable networks, fearing that tendentious Russian reporting was stoking unrest in the eastern regions. It has certainly caused widespread offence in other parts of the country. Ukraine has set up a Ministry of Information in an attempt to 'repel Russia's media attacks' (Interfax-Ukraine, 2014). The conflict in Ukraine has thus become an 'information war' as much as a conventional one. Studying Russia's main narratives can tell us much about the ideas, fears, and goals that drive its foreign and domestic policy.

Narratives of 'the West', the USA and the EU

Anti-western narratives were already a salient feature of Russian political and media discourse before the crisis in Ukraine began (Smyth and Soboleva, 2014, pp. 257-275; Yablokov, 2014, pp. 622-636), but the crisis has imbued them with particular vitriol. These narratives attribute various negative characteristics to the USA and EU states via an interrelated set of plotlines that explain current developments with reference to 'historical' patterns. Negative narratives about the West serve the goals of the Russian leadership in a number of ways: they diminish the credibility of western criticism of Russia, they legitimise Russian behaviour in the eyes of the public, and they defend Russia's self-identity as a European great power. At the same time, the narratives frame how Russians at all levels of society, including the elite, interpret world politics. Therefore, the fact that they are used instrumentally to bolster support for the Russian authorities should not obscure the fact that the narratives have also been internalised among those in authority and thus influence the direction of policy.

Characteristics attributed to western governments by the Russian media include hypocrisy, risibility, arrogant foolishness, and a lack of moral integrity to the point of criminality. Russian television finds evidence of these characteristics in events both past and present. At one point in summer 2014, for example, it referred back to US President Woodrow Wilson promoting democracy and self-determination 'just for export' while denying rights to African and Native Americans. The presenter claimed that the USA had demanded 'the right to judge everyone by its own very flexible standards for a hundred years' (Rossiya 1, 2014). Such claims undermine the validity of international condemnations of Russian actions in Ukraine by conveying that those doing the condemning have only their own selfish interests at heart –

not any real moral values.

'Double standards' (*dvoynyye standarty*) is a charge that is levelled against the West time and time again by the Russian state media as they report and echo the words of the Russian president, foreign minister, and other officials. President Vladimir Putin, for instance, pointed out that American troops and military bases were all over the world, 'settling the fates of other nations while thousands of kilometres from their own borders'. This makes it 'very strange', he argued, that the Americans should denounce Russian foreign troop deployments so much smaller than their own (Putin, 2014). Not only does such a line of argument again attack the moral standing of Russia's critics, it also implies, through a comparison of Russian actions with 'similar' American actions, that Russia is just behaving as great powers do – for few doubt the USA's great power status.

The Russian media frequently mocks western leaders and officials for their lack of understanding and for making foolish errors. When Putin gave an interview to French journalists, a Russian presenter said the president had 'patiently and politely engaged in tackling illiteracy, as if warming up ahead of meetings with colleagues from America and Europe' (Rossiya 1, 2014a). Sometimes the mockery is personal. US State Department spokeswoman Jen Psaki became a target, with Russian television alleging that internet users had adopted the word 'psaking' to mean issuing categorical statements without first checking their accuracy (Rossiya 1, 2014b). The implication is clearly that condemnation of Russia originating from such sources should not be taken seriously.

The Russian media do differentiate, however, between the USA and Europe. The USA is more often accused of outright criminality. Over summer 2014, US 'war crimes' in Ukraine were highlighted regularly and the charges reinforced through parallels with history. In June, for instance, a Russian presenter claimed:

> Ten years ago the Americans used white phosphorous against people in the Iraqi town of Fallujah. Afterwards the White House lied that it hadn't done so… Now the USA is covering up its accomplices in the criminal deployment of incendiary ammunition in Ukraine. (Rossiya 1, 2014c)

A report about the tragic crash of flight MH17 similarly observed that there had been only a few cases of the military shooting down civilian aircraft, but the most serious had been Iranian Air flight 655, downed by the US Air Force in 1988, for which 'America didn't even apologise' (Rossiya 1, 2014d).

Vesti Nedeli presenter Dmitriy Kiselev interprets events against a photo of Obama and the Ukrainian Prime Minister, Arseny Yatsenyuk, captioned 'The West - Sponsor of Genocide'.

European states, on the other hand, were generally portrayed as being led astray against their own best interests by malign American influence. Russian Foreign Minister Sergey Lavrov claimed that international attempts to 'restrict Russia's possibilities' were led primarily by the USA, not the European powers; he argued that the Americans were 'trying to prevent Russia and the EU from uniting their potentials' due to their goal of 'retaining global leadership' (Lavrov, 2014). According to Russian television, the sanctions imposed on Moscow were forced through by the USA 'to weaken the Europeans along with the Russians and get them hooked on [American] shale gas' (Rossiya 1, 2014e). Germany and France are the countries which – in the Russian narrative – the USA is particularly desperate to prevent drawing closer to Russia. Around the anniversary of the outbreak of World War I, Russian television again drew on history to make its point, reporting:

> Then, as now, Germany and Russia were acquiring strength. With their peaceful cooperation, the old world had every chance for prosperity and influence. Then, as now, the English and Americans had a common goal – to sow discord between Russia and Germany and in doing so, exhaust them. Then, as now, willingness to destroy part of the Orthodox world was used to bring Russia into a big war. Then, it was Serbia, now it is eastern Ukraine. (Rossiya 1, 2014f)

This plotline is used to suggest that Russia and Europe would enjoy a close and untroubled relationship were it not for American interference. Tensions with the EU can thus be accounted for without having to acknowledge any fundamental differences that might threaten Russia's European sense of self.

When used strategically in an international context, narratives 'integrate interests and goals – they articulate end states and suggest how to get there' (Miskimmon, O'Loughlin, and Roselle, 2013, p. 5). Three dominant plotlines point particularly to the Russian leadership's goals vis-à-vis western countries. The first relates to western 'interference' causing instability around the world. This plotline situates unrest and violence in Iraq, Syria, Libya, Afghanistan, Georgia, Ukraine, and elsewhere all within the same explanatory paradigm: the West (led by the USA) gets involved, then countries fall apart. The resolution proposed – either implicitly or explicitly – is for the West (above all the USA) to adopt a less interventionist foreign policy. Russia's desire to see the USA less involved in the domestic affairs of other states relates particularly to Ukraine and the post-Soviet region, but extends similarly to parts of the world where Russia's comfortable and profitable dealings with entrenched autocratic leaders (Saddam Hussein, Muammar Gaddafi, Bashar al-Assad) have been disrupted by American support for such leaders' removal.

A second goal-oriented plotline relates to the West (above all the USA) seeking global dominance and acting without due consultation with others. The logical resolution to this plotline favoured by the Russian leadership is to grant non-western countries such as Russia (or perhaps, more accurately, Russia and those who agree with Russia) a greater say in international decision-making. This goal is expressed in Russian calls for 'multipolarity' and endorsement of formats such as BRICS and the G20.

A third major goal-oriented plotline relates to the 'inevitable' continuation of Russia's cooperation with Europe. The narrative projected by Russian leaders and state media insists that commercial and business ties between Russia and the EU are continuing to develop, despite political tensions, because both sides have so much to gain from 'pragmatic cooperation'. The end state which Russia's leaders envisage to resolve security problems in Europe is a 'single economic and humanitarian space from Lisbon to Vladivostok' (a space which obviously attaches Europe to Russia while detaching it from the USA) (Putin, 2014a).

All these Russian goals are associated with the Russian state's preferred identity as a European great power. By opposing western 'interference' abroad, the Russian leadership hopes to block political changes – particularly in the post-Soviet region – which might diminish the international influence which it 'must', as a great power, exert. By rejecting international formats in which Russia's preferences are overridden in favour of formats where Russia's voice is louder (e.g. BRICS), the Russian leadership is claiming the right to be heeded, which great powers 'must' enjoy. By pushing for greater economic cooperation with the EU and promoting the idea of a common space from Lisbon to Vladivostok, Russia is asserting its membership of Europe, while striving to minimise Europe's 'western-ness' – the aspect of Europe's identity that connects with the USA and excludes Russia.

Narratives of Russian Nationhood

The narratives by which Russia projects its position on Ukraine in the international arena are inextricably linked to the grand nation-building mission that has been underway on the domestic stage since the tail end of the El'tsyn era, and which has intensified significantly under Putin. It must be remembered that, unlike other post-Soviet nations (including Ukraine), when communism fell in 1991, Russia's centuries-long history as the core of a larger, imperial entity ended abruptly, and it was left with no clear sense of what it was, of its 'natural' boundaries and basis for 'belonging', or of its key national myths. The fact that remnants of its former imperial conquests (including the Muslim regions of the North Caucasus) remained within its borders, and that Russia is still a vast, multi-ethnic, multi-lingual country, have not made the task of answering those questions any easier.

It is unsurprising, therefore, that the anti-westernism that has recently defined Russia's post-Ukraine international stance, and that has recurred periodically throughout Russia's history, has also dominated its domestic nation-building programme. Crucially, it has been at the heart of efforts to establish the basis for national belonging. This was crystallised in the extensively reported address that Putin gave to the two houses of the Russian Duma following the annexation of Crimea. One of the most striking lines of the speech made reference to 'a fifth column… a disparate bunch of "national traitors" with which the West now appears to be threatening Russia' (Putin, 2014b). The reference to 'national traitors', a term associated with the Stalin-era repressions, had a chilling effect on Russia's now beleaguered opposition movement, but it was in keeping with the scapegoating of west-leaning liberals and other marginal groups that had been growing over the past two years. The label soon gained currency among prominent pro-Kremlin television commentators. During a special edition of the *Voskresnyi vecher* programme broadcast on the Rossiya channel on 21 March 2014, and in response to a question from the host, Vladimir Solovev, Dmitrii Kiselev attributed his inclusion in the list of individuals named in western sanctions against Russia to the actions of such national traitors (Kiselev, 2014).

It is commonly assumed that the anti-US and anti-European hysteria which gripped the Russian public sphere in 2014 is attributable solely to a Kremlin strategy implemented with an iron hand and from the top down. However, this is not entirely the case. First, Russia is not the Soviet Union, and certain prominent media figures linked to (but not necessarily coincident with) the Kremlin line are given the freedom to develop Kremlin thinking to extremes well beyond what might be permissible in official circles. When punitive sanctions were imposed on Russia, Kiselev was at the centre of a frenzy of cold-war rhetoric, using the platform of his *Vesti nedeli* programme to point out that Russia alone among nations has the capacity to turn the USA into 'radioactive dust' (Rossiya 1, 2014h). He was echoed by extreme right-wing writer Aleksandr Prokhanov, like Kiselev a frequent presence on Russian television, who announced that his 15-year-long dream of a return to the Cold War had been fulfilled (Barry, 2014). The two commentators, both close to Putin's inner circle, offer a sobering demonstration of the dependency of Russian national pride in its distortive, Putinesque manifestation on the 'treacherous, conspiratorial West' that in the aftermath of the Ukraine crisis is Russia's constant nemesis.

Secondly, Kremlin thinking itself is developed in part in response to, and under the influence of, ideological currents circulating at a level below that of official discourse, which employs the state-aligned media to 'mainstream' those currents and thus legitimate the accommodations it makes with them. In the months following the annexation of Crimea and the peak of hostilities in Eastern Ukraine, for example, the Eurasianist and extreme nationalist Aleksandr Dugin, who has been influential in shaping official discourse, once again stalked Russian talk shows. He had been somewhat sidelined prior to this and his re-emergence was an indicator of the new pathway the Russian political elite had now embarked upon. In an interview with the well-known presenter Vladimir Pozner, Dugin advocated the outright invasion of Ukraine by Russia (Dugin, 2014).

Dugin's account of Russia as the leader of a powerful union of Slavic and Central Asian states capable of reconciling Islam and Christianity is only one of a set of core ideological narratives with which news and current affairs programmes are framed. In addition, there is the isolationist Russian nationalism[13] which rails against migration, privileging the status of ethnic Russians and showing little interest in engagement beyond Russia's borders. This competes with an imperialist variant that is nostalgic for the Soviet Union and keen to preserve the Russian Federation as a multicultural state.

---

[13] http://www.thenation.com/article/176956/how-russian-nationalism-fuels-race-riots

Finally, a narrative[14] has emerged positing Russia as a global standard bearer for 'traditional values', with either an Orthodox Christian, or a dual Orthodox and Muslim, inflexion. Each carries its own brand of anti-western sentiment and each has its champions on Russian state-aligned television. The Kremlin has sometimes struggled to navigate these narratives, but in justifying Russia's actions in Crimea and Eastern Ukraine, Putin succeeded in blending several of them, bringing one or more of them to the fore for particular purposes.

The pretext for Russia's actions in Crimea, and later for both its tacit and its explicit support for the separatist rebels in Eastern Ukraine, focused on the protection of its 'compatriots' (*sootechestvenniki*). The conflation of this term with 'ethnic Russians' (*etnicheskie russkie*) and 'Russian speakers' (*russkoiazychnye*) reflects the ethnicisation of national identity characteristic of isolationists such as Arkadii Mamontov, host of *Rossiia's Spetsialnyi* correspondent show. But the 'compatriots' theme also had resonance for pseudo-imperialists like Prokhanov and the Eurasianist Dugin. News broadcasts, including Channel 1's *Novosti*, gave sympathetic treatment to demonstrations throughout Russia and called to endorse the resistance of Russian speakers in Crimea and the Donetsk and Luhansk regions of Ukraine to the new Kiev authorities. The demonstrators' slogans and demands were quoted at length:

> Russia doesn't abandon its own'; 'Sevastopol – we are with you'... with slogans like this the inhabitants of Petropavlovsk came to a meeting in support of their compatriots. They spoke both Russian and Ukrainian... 'We Ukrainians are with the Russians; we are one country, one nation; we have both Ukrainian and Russian blood in us; there is no separate Ukraine and no separate Russia'... 'The fraternal people of Ukraine are connected to us historically, culturally and by their spiritual values. Our grandfathers and great grandfathers fought together on the front and liberated our great Soviet Union. (Channel 1, 2014)

The different forms of nationalism did not always work in harmony, however, as illustrated by shifts and contradictions in coverage of the resistance of the Muslim Tatar popular to the annexation of Crimea. Some pre-annexation news broadcasts acknowledged the Tatar community's unease about the possibility of a Russian takeover, even including open admissions that many

---

[14] http://www.thedailybeast.com/articles/2014/06/29/iraq-s-christians-see-putin-as-savior.html

Crimean Tatars were not pro-Russian. Later broadcasts echoed Putin's triumphal annexation speech which insisted (against all the evidence) that most Crimean Tatars supported reunification with Russia. In this representation, the Crimean Tatars were used as a symbol of Crimea's and Russia's unity in diversity. This ambivalent recognition and simultaneous denial of the 'Crimean Tatar problem' exposed the tension between Putin's neo-imperialist/Eurasianist variant on Russian patriotism (one which, like its nineteenth and twentieth century predecessors, aspires to square the need for inclusivity and inter-ethnic harmony with the imperative to maintain the dominant ethnic group's power), and the isolationist nationalists, for whom 'Muslim minorities' constitute a problem.

The slogans quoted above were indicative of a further powerful narrative of nationhood driving Russian media responses to the consequences of regime change in Ukraine: the myth of the Great Patriotic War and the shared struggle of the Russian and Ukrainian peoples against fascism. This in turn was linked to the purported role of Nazi extremists in the Euromaidan movement and the new Ukrainian regime. Accusations that the new Kiev regime is packed with, tolerant of, or manipulated by Nazi extremists have continued to remain at the centre of Russian media accounts of the Euromaidan uprising and their efforts to discredit and de-legitimise the post-Yanukovich government and its actions. Emotive references to *Banderovtsy* (followers of the Ukrainian war-time Nazi collaborator Stepan Bandera) abounded in the discourse not only of media commentators, but Russian political leaders including Putin himself. Pro-Kremlin outlets have consistently emphasised the role of volunteer soldiers from the right-wing *Pravy sektor* in prosecuting Kiev's 'punitive operation' in Eastern Ukraine.

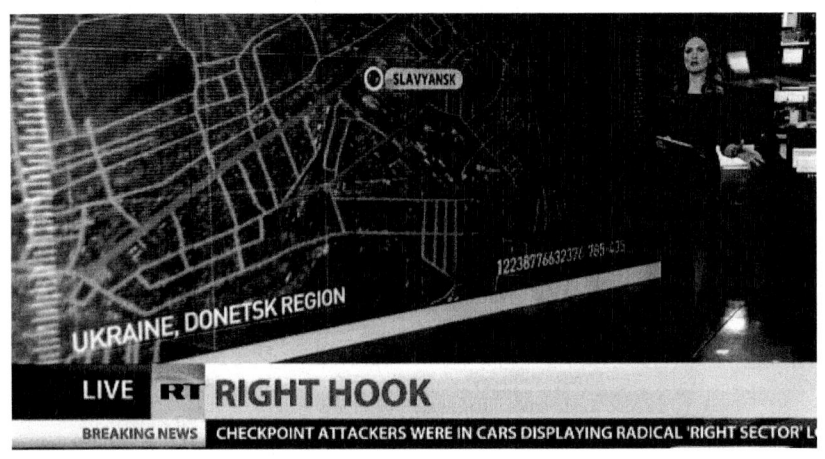

Russia's international broadcaster, RT, links an attack on pro-Russian separatist fighters in Eastern Ukraine to the far-right political party Right Sector.

As recently as November 2014, the Rossiia television channel was reporting on meetings at which all elements of the Russian political mainstream recalled the shared memories of the victory against Hitler and united against the threat of Ukrainian Nazism. On 4 November, it broadcast a story about a political rally organised to coincide with Russia's 'Day of National Unity' and attended by the Communist Party, the Kremlin-aligned United Russia Party, Zhirinovskii's Liberal Democratic Party, and the social democratic Just Russia Party. All four leaders were reported to have condemned fascist extremism at the heart of the new Ukraine (Zhirinovsky, Ziuganov, and Mironov, 2014).

Finally, however, the anti-fascist agenda coexists in an uneasy relationship with the links that the Kremlin has been forging with far-right forces throughout Europe (and indeed the USA) as part of its efforts to promote Russia as the world leader of 'traditional, conservative values'. Russia's endorsement of the nuclear family and the Orthodox Church, its antagonism to non-standard sexualities, and its scorn for 'politically correct', liberal tolerance of difference have resonated with the likes of Marine Le Pen in France, Tea Party supporter Pat Buchanan in the US, and Nigel Farage's UKIP in Britain. The visceral opposition of many of these groups to the EU, and to the entire 'European project', helps explain the support they have expressed for the Russian position on Ukraine and official Russian media outlets have not been slow to capitalise on this. Nigel Farage has appeared 17 times on Russia's international television channel, RT (Russia Today), since December 2010, and his relationship with it has come under scrutiny in the UK press. But as *The Guardian* points out, sympathy for Russia is not limited to the margins of British politics:

> Farage's views on the EU's role in the Ukraine are shared by some Tory Eurosceptic MPs. In a Bruges Group film on how the EU has blundered in the Ukraine, John Redwood says: "The EU seems to be flexing its words in a way that Russia finds worrying and provokes Russia into flexing its military muscles". (Wintour and Mason, 2014)

What might seem the most paradoxical and counter-intuitive of allegiances is, in fact, just one illustration of the multiple ideological reversals and realignments that are the continuing aftermath of the collapse of communism and the ending of the Cold War.

Conclusions

One conclusion we might draw from our survey of the Russian media response to the Ukraine crisis is that Russian tactics in what some have called the 'New Cold War' should not be attributed to a purely cynical eclecticism (exploiting whichever political and ideological currents and trends that serve current needs, no matter what their provenance). Although such eclecticism is apparent, we should not ignore the (so far unsuccessful) efforts to knit the dominant narratives, despite all their many contradictions, into an ideological fabric capable of providing the basis for a coherent worldview and a stable sense of national identity. Nor should the notion of an all-out 'information war' between Russia and the West, and the way it is used to justify any manner of distortion by omission, exaggeration, or sometimes downright untruth, be seen outside the context of the residual influence of the Leninist approach to media objectivity as a 'bourgeois construct', or of a reaction against established values of impartiality and objectivity that extends well beyond Russia (Wintour and Mason, 2014).

However, and in a further challenge to received wisdom on Russian media coverage of Ukraine, the development of the post-Ukraine Russian world view is not an entirely top-down process and betrays the influence of powerful sub-official and popular discourses, which must be alternatively appropriated, moderated, and reconciled with one another, and with the official line. Rather than a passive tool in the Kremlin's hands, the state-aligned media are at times serving as an active agent in managing this process.

It would be wrong, too, to explain Russia's actions and their mediation by pro-Kremlin press and broadcasting outlets as those of an aggressive, expansionist nation determined to extend its sphere of influence into new areas. Rather, they reflect the perception of a threat to what Russia sees as its rightful status as a great power, and to its current regional interests (however distorted and misplaced we may believe those interests to be). Finally, the visceral anti-western rhetoric that dominates Russia's public sphere to its inevitable detriment is not as undifferentiated as is often suggested; ultimately, Russia continues to harbour the desire to be seen as a European nation and as part of a continental bulwark against untrammelled American hegemony.

The correctives we propose to more reductive accounts of Russian media coverage of Ukraine do not diminish the reprehensibility of Russia's apparent willingness to flout both international law and basic standards of objectivity in news reporting. Nonetheless, the roots of the current crisis over Ukraine cannot be fully understood without appreciating the nuances, origins, and complexities of the media narratives by which Russia attempts to legitimate its behaviour.

References

Barry, E. (2014) 'Foes of America in Russia Crave Rupture in Ties,' *New York Times*, 15 March. Available at: http://www.nytimes.com/2014/03/16/world/europe/foes-of-america-in-russia-crave-rupture-in-ties.html?smid=tw-share&_r=0.

Channel 1 (2014) television programme, 'Novosti,' 5 March. Available at: http://www.1tv.ru/news/social/253539.

Dugin, A. (2014) 'Pozner,' *Channel 1,* 21 April. Available at: https://www.youtube.com/watch?v=XEwSPzOJvaI.

Interfax-Ukraine (2014) 1330 gmt, translated by BBC Monitoring, 6 December.

Kiselev, D. (2014) video, 'Voskresnyi vecher' *Rossiya 1*, 21 March. Available at: http://vk.com/video_ext.php?oid=-41821502&id=167928365&hash=1c09b7acecc4b5a2&hd=1.

Lavrov, S. (2014) television programme, 'Vystupleniye ministra inostrannykh del Rossii S. V. Lavrova na vstreche s chlenami Rossiyskogo soveta po mezhdunarodnym delam,' 4 June.

Miskimmon, A., O'Loughlin, B. and Roselle, L. (2013) *Strategic narratives: Communication power and the new world order*. New York; London: Routledge, p. 5.

Putin V. (2014) radio interview, 'Intervyu Vladimira Putina radio 'Yevropa-1' i telekanalu TF1,' *Kremlin.ru,* 4 June. Available at: http://kremlin.ru/transcripts/45832.

Putin, V. (2014a) 'Soveshchaniye poslov i postoyannykh predstaviteley Rossii,' *Kremlin.ru,* 1 July. Available at: http://kremlin.ru/transcripts/46131.

Putin, V. (2014b) video, 'Obrashchenie Prezidenta RF Vladimira Putina (polnaia versiia),' *Channel 1*. Available at: http://www.1tv.ru/news/social/254389.

Rossiya 1 (2014) video, 'Vesti nedeli,' *Rossiya 1*, 29 June. Available at: www.youtube.com/watch?v=SC0tsb4MRX4.

Rossiya 1 (2014a) video, 'Vesti nedeli,' *Rossiya 1*, 8 June. Available at: www.youtube.com/watch?v=QFZBCeaaoB0.

Rossiya 1 (2014b) video, 'Vesti nedeli,' *Rossiya 1*, 1 June. Available at: www.youtube.com/watch?v=48ud1pQqDWE.

Rossiya 1 (2014c) video,'Vesti nedeli,' *Rossiya 1*, 15 June. Available at: www.youtube.com/watch?v=cY3DCjK_rdU.

Rossiya 1 (2014d) video, 'Vesti nedeli,' *Rossiya 1*, 20 July. Available at: www.youtube.com/watch?v=_rLZaciNrQs.

Rossiya 1 (2014e) video, 'Vesti nedeli,' *Rossiya 1*, 8 June. Available at: www.youtube.com/watch?v=QFZBCeaaoB0.

Rossiya 1 (2014f) video, 'Vesti nedeli,' *Rossiya 1*, 29 June. Available at: www.youtube.com/watch?v=SC0tsb4MRX4.

Rossiya 1 (2014h) video, 'Vesti nedeli,' *Rossiya 1*, 16 March. Available at: https://www.youtube.com/watch?v=utgVhoLVxsg.

Russian Foreign Ministry (2013) *Kontseptsiya vneshney politiki Rossiyskoy Federatsii,* 12 February. Available at: http://www.mid.ru/brp_4.nsf/0/6D84DDEDEDBF7DA644257B160051BF7F.

Smyth, R, and Soboleva, I. (2014) 'Looking beyond the economy: Pussy Riot and the Kremlin's voting coalition,' *Post-Soviet Affairs*, 30(4), pp. 257-275.

Wintour, P. and Mason, R. (2014) 'Nigel Farage's Relationship with Russian Media Comes Under Scrutiny,' *The Guardian*, 31 March. Available at: http://www.theguardian.com/politics/2014/mar/31/nigel-farage-relationship-russian-media-scrutiny.

Yablokov, I. (2014) 'Pussy Riot as agent provocateur: conspiracy theories and the media construction of nation in Putin's Russia,' *Nationalities Papers*, 42(4), pp. 622-636.

Ziuganov, Z. and Mironov, S. (2014) video, 'Unite Against Ukrainian Nazism,' Vesti, *Rossiia 1*, 4 November. Available at: http://www.vesti.ru/doc.html?id=2098145.

17

The Ukraine Story in Western Media

MARTA DYCZOK
WESTERN UNIVERSITY

Introduction

Ukraine was all over the international headlines from the end of 2013 through summer 2014. The fast changing, complex story was usually narrated through rather simple frames and the greatest attention was devoted to issues with international significance. As the war in eastern Ukraine became protracted and Russia showed no signs of reversing its annexation of Crimea, the story began slipping from the international news.

When looking at how events in Ukraine were reported by western media, it is important to keep a few questions in mind. How was information collected and disseminated? How were media messages framed and by whom? What was the audience reaction and the impact on public opinion? Media studies scholars have long noted that while media is often perceived as a powerful tool in shaping public opinion, audiences are active and respond to media messages in different ways based on their beliefs and underlying value systems (Hall, 1980). At the time of this writing, winter of 2014-2015, it seems that international public opinion remains divided over the causes and consequences of events, the character of the Euromaidan protests, Putin's sending Russian troops into Crimea, and the nature of the military conflict in eastern areas of Ukraine. This is partly due to the fact that a variety of representations were visible in media reports.

The diverse reporting on Ukraine reflects the nature of how global media organisations function. They operate in a 24/7 environment, are subject to budgetary pressures, and few have permanent correspondents in Ukraine.

Also, they need to balance between attracting audiences, upholding the normative goal of objective reporting, presenting two sides of the story, and describing the news in simple, comprehensible narratives. As a producer explained to me just before I was going live on national Canadian television when the protests in Ukraine were beginning, 'Remember, you'll have 3 minutes to explain things to an audience that knows very little about Ukraine. Keep it clear and easily understandable.'

Equally important was the initial effectiveness of Russia's information machine. The Kremlin showed itself to be very skilled at quickly providing materials to international media outlets in the forms of press releases and statements by key Russian actors when news was breaking about Ukraine. Therefore, the framing and terminology used in international media reports was often shaped by these Russian sources. Russia directly reached out to western audiences with their English language TV Channel *Russia Today,* and paid major international newspapers, such as *The New York Times*, *The Wall Street Journal*, *The Daily Telegraph*, *Le Figaro*, *El Pais*, and others, to run their supplement, *Russia Beyond the Headlines* (Halby, 2014).[15]

Also, the messages coming out of Ukraine were sometimes mixed, or belated. When protests erupted in Ukraine, the then-government did its best to portray the protesters as rabble-rousing, fringe, fascist elements which were aiming to destabilise the country. The protesters were not a unified, cohesive group, and while many did attempt to get their message out to the international media, they were not always successful in doing so. The interim government did not do a very good job in presenting information to either Ukrainian or international media when they came to power in February, when Russian forces took control over Crimea, and when violence began in eastern Ukraine. This started to improve after Petro Poroshenko was elected president in May, but confusion remained. Ukraine officially continued to label its efforts in the Donbass as an 'Anti-Terrorist Operation' while repeatedly reporting on Russian military hardware and troops on its territory.

Competing Narratives

As already mentioned, there were variations among western media reports. Information and presentation is shaped by country of origin, the editorial policies of the media outlet, the form of ownership of the media outlet (public, private, independent), and type of medium (television, radio, newspapers, internet, social media). That being said, a number of general trends were

---

[15] This information was confirmed by a member of the editorial staff of one of these newspapers in a private exchange with the author. He explained that this was done for revenue purposes.

visible, which I noticed while monitoring the news and in my own 104 media appearances in Canada, the US, Britain, Italy, Ukraine, Japan, Hong Kong, and Australia, to media outlets of all genres and formats, from national corporately-owned television to public broadcasters, small independent newspapers, and blogs.

Euromaidan Protests

Western media reports and images about Ukraine during the Euromaidan protests often focused on the dramatic: clashes between protesters and riot police, attacks on journalists, deaths of protesters, high-level meetings and announcements by politicians, President Yanukovych travelling to Moscow, Prime Minister Azarov resigning, Canada introducing visa restrictions for key government officials responsible for violence, or the 1 February Munich Summit on Ukraine. Narratives were usually framed in rather simple terms. A struggle between Russia and Europe, East and West Ukraine, police versus protesters.

Two main representations dominated the reporting and analysis during this period. One was that Ukrainians were making a pro-European choice, were prepared to brave the cold and face riot police to stand up for their European values in central Kiev. Reports using this frame focused on the size, creativity, and endurance of the protests, showing the music, EU flags, statements of support by European and North American officials. The other common frame was that Ukraine was divided between those in the west who wanted to be seen as part of Europe, and those in the east who preferred to remain closer to Russia. In these reports, attention was given to the pro-Yanukovych supporters who assembled in their own camps, and the nationalist symbols and chants used by some of the pro-European protesters.

Most media made efforts to use expert commentary and voices from Ukraine (National Public Radio, 2014). Yet much of the coverage did not clearly explain that the protests were coming from various parts of the country and sectors of society that transcended the simple East/West divide. For example, few reports noted that many protesters were chanting pro-European slogans in Russian. Or that public opinion polls showed widespread dissatisfaction with the Yanukovych ruling elite nationwide, including in Crimea, Donetsk, and Luhansk.

Perhaps the greatest shortcoming in international reporting was that the causes of violence were not adequately explored. Dramatic images of clashes were widely circulated, and made it onto many top-photos-of-2014 lists. However, the overwhelming majority of protesters were peaceful, creative, and only a small extreme element advocated violent methods. The radicals caught the attention of the cameras, as did their slogans and nationalist insignia. But few reports were asking the question: who instigated the violence?

Unexpected Regime Change, Interim Government, and Russia's Annexation of Crimea

In the end, the protests succeeded in ousting Victor Yanukovych – he fled the country and turned up in Russia a few days later. But the unexpected and fast-moving events from late February through early March 2014 created a rather sensational and sometimes confused picture in many international media reports at the time. 'Ukraine Protesters Seize Kiev as President Flees,' was *Time* magazine's headline on 22 February, with the sub-heading 'President Yanukovych escapes to eastern power base of Kharkiv and refuses to resign' (Frizell, 2014). In fact, when Yanukovych disappeared, parliament called an emergency session and, running a bit roughshod over the rules, hastily elected Oleksandr Turchynov as interim president and Arseniy Yatseniuk as acting Prime Minister. The way this occurred raised the question of legitimacy. Legitimacy remained a recurrent theme in many international reports until Poroshenko was elected president in late May, as did the question of whether the far right was on the rise in Ukraine.

This also permeated into the reporting on Russia's annexation of Crimea which followed shortly. Overall reporting on Crimea at the time events were unfolding caused much misunderstanding for months to come. To be fair, it was a difficult story to report on. It was fast-moving, Russia was deliberately clouding the issues with its actions and statements, Ukraine was reeling from the power struggle that Yanukovych's flight caused, and western journalists who arrived on site were intimidated, sometimes prevented from filming (Ormiston, 2014). The result was that many mixed messages reached audiences.

From initial reports, it was not entirely clear what was happening. Two days after the invasion began, on 3 March 2014, AP reported, 'Ukraine's mission to the United Nations is claiming that 16,000 Russian troops have been deployed in the strategic Crimea region, while Russia's UN ambassador told the council that Ukraine's fugitive president requested troops.' That same day, in a live broadcast, CNN anchor Wolf Blitzer repeated a claim by Russia's United Nations Ambassador, Vitaly Churkin, that Nazi sympathisers had taken power in Western Ukraine. His colleague, CNN International correspondent Christiane Amanpour, jumped in and said, 'You've got to be really careful putting that across as a fact. Are you saying that the entire pro-European

Ukrainians are anti-Semites? That's what the Russians are saying, and that's what Professor Cohen is saying' (CNN, 2014). Confusing things further was the fact that the masked, heavily armed troops entering Crimea were not wearing any insignia and refused to identify themselves as Russian forces. So western reporters did not name them as Russians, and Ukrainians began calling them 'little green men.'

Dramatic images once again dominated reporting of the Crimea crisis, such as the standoff between unarmed Ukrainian forces carrying a flag and singing while facing masked men pointed machine guns at them and shot into the air (BBC, 2014). And the framing of the story lacked clarity. To an uninformed audience, it was not evident whether Russia was protecting ethnic Russians from an illegitimate fascist, right-wing government in Kiev, or whether Russia was invading a neighbouring country. The fact that Crimea's legitimately elected government was deposed at gunpoint was not highlighted, yet plenty of attention was devoted to the event called a referendum a few weeks later. Many media outlets ran headlines similar to that by CTV on 16 March, 'Crimea referendum results show more than 95% of voters seek to join Russia' (CTV, 2014), while few cited public opinion polls from a few weeks before showed that support for union with Russia was around 41% (Kyiv International Institute of Sociology, 2014). Many reports included the fact that Crimea had been transferred to Ukraine by Russia in 1954, far fewer noted that the peninsula was the Crimean Tatar homeland conquered by the Russian Empire in the 18th century.

The choice of images, terminology, information presented or omitted in many international media reports is one reason that the entire issue of what happened in Crimea, how, why, and the results, are still subject to debate.

War in Eastern Ukraine

The same is largely true about what was/is happening in eastern Ukraine, in the oblasts of Donetsk and Luhansk. The beginning of the story was originally overshadowed by events in Crimea. Heavily armed, masked men began storming and taking over government buildings in Donetsk at the same time as the 'little green men' were taking over in Crimea. The OSCE Mission was issuing reports on the violence as early as mid-March. However, the story did not really start hitting the international headlines until April, when pro-Russian forces announced that they wanted a referendum like the one that was held in Crimea, and Ukraine began pushing back in what it labelled an Anti-Terrorist Operation.

It was around this time that the phrase 'information war' began appearing regularly in the reporting and discussions about Ukraine. From April onwards, two distinct frames were visible. One was that pro-Russian separatists opposed the new government in Kiev, wanted to break away from Ukraine, and were prepared to use force to accomplish their goal. The other was that Russia was pursuing a hybrid war against Ukraine by sending in arms, funds, and personnel to fan the flames of separatism with the aim of de-stabilising the country and re-exerting control over it.

From April onward, reporting from the ground became difficult because journalists started being kidnapped by the heavily armed masked men (Dyczok, 2014).[16] This became evident to global audiences when Malaysia Airlines flight MH17 was shot down over Donetsk on 17 July. The international press corps rushed to the scene of the crash site, only to be denied access or given limited access, while being bombarded with contradictory versions of where the threat to safety was coming from and who shot the plane down.

Many reports presented the conflicting statements by Russian and Ukrainian sources. For example, the BBC reported that 'foreign volunteers, including Russians, have been fighting in Ukraine. Russia denies sending regular troops there. The Ukrainian government and the West say that Russia has sent heavy weapons and well-trained troops to help the separatists in eastern Ukraine' (Peter, 2015).

Fewer delved deeper into the underlying issues, questions, and evidence that might help shed light on the story. Pro-Russian separatist sentiment was widely written about, but rarely explained that although it existed since the country became independent in 1991, it hovered around 33-35% in Donetsk and 25% in Luhansk (KIIS, 2014). Few posed the question of timing – why did violence break out when it did? And the 20 November admission by Igor Girkin 'Strelkov', key organiser of the 'Donetsk People's Republic', that he served in the Russian Secret Service until 2013 and deliberately started armed conflict in Donetsk did not make it into many international reports (Prokhanov, 2014).

As the conflict dragged on, ceasefires and negotiations failed to produce results while numbers of casualties and internally displaced people grew, the story began to lose its immediacy and drama. It appeared in international headlines less frequently. Gradually there was more acknowledgement that some Russians were involved in what was still largely labelled 'the Ukraine Crisis.' Reports about right-wing resurgence dissipated after two elections

---

[16] In the first three weeks of April, at least 18 journalists were kidnapped.

(Presidential 25 May, and Parliamentary 26 October) showed that Ukrainians were not voting for right-wing candidates and parties. But the term 'Ukrainian civil war' continued to be regularly used.

Conclusion

Overall, it is difficult to assess what impact international reporting on the Ukraine story has had on public opinion worldwide. Some have argued that the normative rules of objective reporting – presenting all sides of the story, presenting only information that can be indisputably verified – have worked against the larger goal of providing an accurate picture of what is really going on in a situation where information is being used as a weapon (Lane, 2014; The Insider, 2014; Alex Shprintsen, CBC TV producer, in a series of conversations with the author).

Communication studies show us that one function of the media is agenda setting: not telling people what to think, but rather what to think about (McCombs, 2004). So when words and phrases like 'persecution of ethnic Russians,' 'referendum,' or 'illegitimate, right wing government' appear in reports, they remain in audiences' minds. That said, they likely evoke a variety of responses because each person interprets media messages through her/his own value system.

Another role media plays is that it frames news into narratives that use familiar reference points to help audiences make sense of information in ways that are familiar (Entman, 1993, pp. 51-58). Often the Ukraine story was reported in easily recognisable portrayals of protesters vs. police, East vs. West, a new Cold War. Over time, this led to Ukraine increasingly being represented as an object of a power struggle between Russia and the US/EU, rather than an independent subject of international affairs. But, as historian Ivan Lysiak-Rudnytskyi showed, Ukrainians have a way of turning things on their head and shifting the balance of power that can affect the course of history (Lysiak-Rudytskyi, 1981).

References

Dyczok, M. (2014) 'Masked Men vs Journalists,' *The Wall Street Journal*, 22 April. Available at: http://www.wsj.com/articles/SB10001424052702304393704579528101344061812.

Hall, S. (1980) 'Encoding/Decoding' in Hall, S., Hobson, D., Lowe A. and Willis, P. (eds) *Culture, Media, Language*. London: Hutchinson, 1980.

Halby, D. (2014) 'RBTH, Sputnik: The Old and New Russian Propaganda News Machine,' *No Mistral for Putin,* 12 July. Available at: http://nomistralsforputin.com/drupal/?q=RussianPropaganda.

Frizell, S. (2014) 'Ukraine Protesters Seize Kiev as President Flees. President Yanukovych escapes to eastern power base of Kharkiv and refuses to resign,' *Time,* 22 February. Available at: http://world.time.com/2014/02/22/ukraines-president-flees-protestors-capture-kiev/.

Ormiston, S. (2014) Interview, *CBC TV* Senior Reporter, 15 December, Toronto.

Ormiston, S. (2014) CBS player video, 'The danger of covering the Ukrainian Revolution,' *The National,* 28 December. Available at: http://www.cbc.ca/player/Kids/Parents/ID/2643700268/.

CNN (2014) *The Situation Room,* 3 March. Available at: http://www.mediaite.com/tv/cnns-amanpour-lashes-professor-for-repeating-russian-claims-about-ukrainian-opposition/.

BBC World Report (2014) 'Ukraine crisis: Armed stand-off at Crimean airbase', 4 March. Available at: http://www.bbc.com/news/world-europe-26429687.

CTV News (2014) 'Crimea referendum results show more than 95% of voters seek to join Russia,' 16 March. Available at: http://www.ctvnews.ca/world/crimea-referendum-results-show-more-than-95-of-voters-seek-to-join-russia-1.1731310#ixzz3NtlhQPKj.

Kyiv International Institute of Sociology (2014) *How relations between ukraine and russia should look like? Public opinion polls' results,* 8-18 February. Available at: http://www.kiis.com.ua/?lang=eng&cat=reports&id=236&page=1.

Lawrence P. (2015) 'Russia to hire more foreign troops in forces shake up,' *BBC World News,* 5 January. Available at: http://www.bbc.com/news/world-europe-30682465.

Prokhanov, A. (2014) 'Kto tyi Strelok,' *Zavtra,* 20 November. Available at: http://zavtra.ru/content/view/kto-tyi-strelok/.

Lane, H. (2014) 'Ukraine, the Media, and the Truth,' *Logos. A journal of modern society & culture,* 13(3-4). Available at: http://logosjournal.com/2014/lane/.

'Anatomy of Propaganda' (2014) *The Insider*, 26 December. Available at: http://theins.ru/politika/2320/.

McCombs, M.E. (2004) *Setting The Agenda: The Mass Media And Public Opinion*. Cambridge: Polity Press.

Plokhii, S., Kulykov, A. and Dyczok, M. (2014) radio programme, *The Takeaway,* National Public Radio, 20 and 21 February. Available at: http://www.thetakeaway.org/story/unrest-continues-ukraine/, http://www.thetakeaway.org/story/kiev-long-besieged-city/.

Entman, R.M. (1993) 'Framing: toward clarification of a fractured paradigm,' *Journal of Communications,* 43(4), pp. 51-58.

Lysiak-Rudnytskyi, I. (1981) *Rethinking Ukrainian History*. Edmonton: Canadian Institute of Ukrainian Studies Press.

18

Russia as Ukraine's 'Other': Identity and Geopolitics

MIKHAIL A. MOLCHANOV
ST. THOMAS UNIVERSITY

Russia's annexation of the Crimean Autonomous Republic and the barely hidden fomenting of the separatist movement in eastern Ukraine have brought the country to the edge of a new cold war with the West. Western media has depicted Putin's government as an antipode of all that is good and normal in international relations, as having been 'evil enough' (Motyl, 2014) to merit comparisons with neo-Nazis and the Ku Klux Klan. German Chancellor Merkel led an attack on Russia's president personally, starting with accusations of him living 'in another world' (Baker, 2014) and ending with a homegrown psychoanalysis of 'he acts the way he does to "prove he's a man"' (Ernst, 2014).

Ukraine, being in a de facto state of war with Russia's proxies in Donbas, has not fallen short of related rhetoric and sought to outdo its western sponsors in vilifying Russia and the Russians. A typical set of clichés includes 'a country of the insane' (Shchetkina, 2014) – although the WHO (2011) statistics show the actual burden of mental health disorders in Russia to be one half of the western average – 'a fake, phantom country... biggest madhouse on Earth' (Kostyk, 2014), 'a large gas pump with atomic missiles' (Lutsenko, 2014), 'a special operation writ large' (Golovakha, 2014), and, of course, a 'Mordor' (Presa Ukraïny, 2014).

Both the 'Mordor' and the 'madhouse' designations crept into official and semi-official pronouncements of Ukraine's political elite: ministers, spokespersons for the government, and the like. An advisor to Ukraine's Minister of Defence, Oleksandr Danyliuk, vows to engage the relatives of the Russian army volunteers fighting on the separatist side in Donbas 'so that they would become the principal anti-war activists in Mordor' (Vidomosti, 2014). The Minister of Interior answers the question on chances for Russia's invasion by qualifying it as 'a type of question of when the madman will have his next bout' (The Insider, 2014). The deputy governor of the Dnipropetrovsk region Borys Filatov calls Russian politicians 'the Kremlin bastards' (Kostyk, 2014). All of this gets sympathetic press in the West, which, in turn, reinforces the vilification zeal back in Ukraine. As the title of a recent Bloomberg View article goes, 'Putin's Russia, Tolkien's Mordor: What's the difference?' (Bershidsky, 2014).

Clearly, such portrayal, if anything, reinforces the besieged fortress mentality that keeps Putin's regime going. Vilification of the opponent does not help to solve either international or inter-ethnic conflicts, just the opposite. And yet, the situation of a de facto breach of Ukraine's sovereignty and territorial integrity, which the unlawful annexation of the Crimea represents, seemingly justifies the hostile rhetoric on Kiev's part. Equally, Russia's support of the separatist movement in Donbas cannot but trigger Ukraine's worst suspicions of a neighbouring country's desire to dismantle Ukraine by force. It appears natural, in such a situation, that Russia's image would get a serious beating in the eyes of the Ukrainian public. However, is it true that the current round of badmouthing Russia and the Russians is a purely situational development, a predictable reaction to the unfriendly actions of a neighbouring power? Or does it reveal something more profound than that, something perhaps indicative of not only the present state, but also the historic evolution of the Ukrainian national identity as such? Is Russia really a Ukraine's 'other,' and if it is, what are the factors that explain this distancing? Is Russia truly, as a Ukrainian philosopher recently observed, a 'Europe perverted, like Conchita Wurst, more or less' (Yermolenko, 2014)? Both framing and answering of the 'othering' question may be of direct importance to the resolution of the ongoing conflict.

The Origins of Alienation

Ukrainian identity was shaped through the centuries of counter-position to external overlordship. First, Mongol, then Lithuanian, Polish, and finally Muscovite incursions hardened the perception of separateness that descendants of the western branch of a once unified Kievan Rus' people felt toward their closest ethnic relatives to the North and North-East. Ukraine's ethnogenesis had been largely completed under the conditions of foreign domination of the erstwhile Kievan Rus' western lands. By the time it was over, the luckier eastern Rus'ians had managed to establish a new state of their own, resurrecting the tradition of the Kievan statehood in the Great Princedom of Muscovy. Ukraine stayed under foreign domination until the

Liberation War of 1648-1654 and the conclusion of the Pereyaslav Agreement with the Russian tsar Alexis. The essence of the agreement, which brought Ukraine's Cossack Hetmanate and the lands it controlled under the protection of the Russian tsar in a rather typical vassalage relationship of the time, is still hotly debated in both countries. While Russians have perceived it as an act of reunification, Ukrainian nationalist historians see Pereyaslav as the beginning of 350 years of Russia's colonial domination, which trampled underfoot the early sprouts of liberty and self-rule – the sprouts that could presumably blossom into a European-type of independent Ukrainian statehood, were it not for the Muscovite treachery and bad faith.

The perceptions of Russia's 'betrayal' of Ukraine at the birth of the Ukrainian national sovereignty have led to the development of what John Morrison (1993, pp. 679-680) describes as a 'permanent inferiority complex and a lack of confidence in negotiating with Moscow' on the part of the Ukrainian political elite who cannot stop fearing 'that any deal with Russia is a potential trap, however favourable to Ukraine its terms might appear.' Hence, Ukrainian elites were among the first to reject the terms of the Novo-Ogarevo agreement that Mikhail Gorbachev hoped would modernise and replace the old Soviet Union treaty. Ukraine's president Kravchuk torpedoed a quasi-federal version of the agreement on the establishment of the Commonwealth of Independent States (CIS), following which, a rather insubstantial accord of loose regional affiliation was signed by Russia, Ukraine, and Belarus. Finally, Russia's attempts to lure Ukraine into the Customs Union were met with a sense of distrust and apprehension: if Moscow was willing to cough up $15 billion in loans and lock-in its gas prices at a level 30 percent below the European average, there must have been a catch of some sort. That was a typical perception among the Maidan activists, who saw Russia's offer, which came concurrently with a technical delay in negotiations with the EU, as clear evidence of a plot to undermine the country's sovereignty and freedom of international association.

Had a similar offer come from any other country, it would, in all probability, be accepted with great enthusiasm. However, Russia's case is different. First of all, the Russian Empire and its successor state, the USSR, had been the two states most actively involved in shaping the Ukrainian national identity over the last 350 years. Second, the Russian imperial government had restricted the use of the Ukrainian language in printed media, on stage and in education on more than few occasions. Third, the Soviet regime was responsible for the worst tragedy in modern Ukraine's history – the great famine of 1933 ('Holodomor'). Against such a background, Ukrainian nationalists learned to perceive Russia as Ukraine's true Other, i.e. a nation as close to being Ukraine's opposite as could be reasonably imagined. In demonising Russia, they were much helped by a long shadow of history.

The Shadow of History

The would-be Ukraine experienced centuries of foreign domination: by Mongols, Lithuanians, Poles, and, in various parts of its future territory, Austrians, Hungarians, Romanians, Crimean Tatars, and Turks. However, it was Russia and the Russians that were destined to become the dreaded and hated Other in the eyes of the Ukrainian nationalist intellectuals from the early nineteenth century on. The paradox of the situation lies in the fact that, for the Russians themselves, Ukrainians have never been perceived as foreigners, but rather as a branch of the greater Russian tree, a marginally different part of the same 'all-Russian' ethnos. The protectorate that Alexis extended to the Cossacks and the subsequent annexation of a nucleus would-be Ukraine by Catherine the Great[17] were, to the Russian mind, as distant from the occupation of a foreign land as legal claiming of one's own inheritance could be from a highway robbery.

Russia's 'otherness' for Ukraine can be explained precisely by the degree of ethnic closeness and the soundness of the Muscovites' claim on the Kievan princes' patrimony. At the start of the Ukrainian nationalist mobilisation, its standard-bearers encountered a rather difficult dilemma of a disinterested 'Little Russian' population that seemed content with its 'ruski' identity – and the de facto subaltern status of the Ukrainian pen elite. After Ivan Kotliarevskyi's *Aeneid* (1798), there was no denial that the separate, even if closely related to the dominant language of the Russian empire, Ukrainian vernacular actually existed. Hence, a separate Ukrainian identity, still called the Russian ('ruski') in Galicia and other eastern regions of the Habsburg Empire, had entered the stage circa 1830s, and with it, a question: what to do with this separateness, once discovered?[18] The answer was easy in Ukraine's western lands, dominated by the non-Slavic ethnicities and the traditionally Ukrainophobic Polish *szlachta*. Ukrainians had to fight for their cultural and national self-determination. But what about the country's core, now safely within the dominion of Ukraine's ethnic and religious brethren – the Russians?

Having Ukrainian identity evolve so close to the Russian one and within the envelope of Russian state institutions presented Ukrainian elites with a choice between assimilation and revolt. Assimilation into the 'Little Russian' and, eventually, 'Great Russian' identity was not without its rewards, and became a

---
[17] See maps on the historic evolution of Ukrainian borders in Nicolai Petro's chapter in this volume.
[18] It must be added that many Galician intellectuals at the time kept craving unity, rather than separateness from Russia, pledging, in Markian Shashkevych's (n.d.) words, eternal bonds to their 'Russian hearts and the Russian faith.'

path that Ukrainian aristocrats, clergymen, and pen elites treaded for centuries. No less figures than Nikolai Gogol, the writer, and Hryhorii Skovoroda, an eighteenth-century wandering philosopher, a 'Russian Socrates,' spring to mind.

The revolt started with Taras Shevchenko and continued with a host of intellectuals whose attitude to Russia is best described as Russophobic in a literal sense, or full of existential fear and loathing of *moskali* (a pejorative for Russians), who were blamed for all real and alleged misfortunes of the Ukrainian people. However, this anti-Russian nationalism faced two problems that had to be explained away: one of successful cooptation of the Ukrainian elites into the institutions of the Russian state, and another of intense cross-fertilisation and fusion of the two cultures. While the first could be presented as manifestation of a devious assimilationist plan, the second has been decried as a result of the colonial Russian influences on the Ukrainian mind. In both cases, 'alien' influences had to be rejected and reversed to avail 'purification' of the national spirit – a must-do prerequisite for a political autonomy.

Myth-Making as Geopolitics

Ukraine's nationalists fought off, and defeated, more Russophile members of the movement who, like Mykhailo Drahomanov, rejected the idea of political separation from Russia as preposterous. Instead, they chose to advance the negative identity of Ukraine as a 'non-Russia' *par excellence*. This was no small feat, which required a good deal of rewriting of history in combination with geopolitical revisionism.

The historical construction focused on denying Russia's statehood its Kievan roots. The idea that Ukraine is part of Europe, while the 'Eurasian' Russia is not, can be found right at the beginning of a long tradition of Russophobic scholarship. An extreme version of this argument, originally advanced by an early champion of racial exclusivity, Franciszek Duchiński, in the mid-nineteenth century, has been recently reanimated in the Ukrainian political discourse (Molchanov, 2002, pp. 169, 222-227). Duchiński went to great lengths to underscore the 'Asianness' of the Russians, which in the Eurocentric universe of the time was tantamount to barbarism and accounted, in his view, for both the despotic and subservient propensities of the Russian psyche. To sever the Ukrainians from the Russians, he concocted a quasi-scientific explanation of ethnic differences between the two nationalities, imagining their descent from different and completely unrelated tribes: the 'Aryans' in the case of Ukraine, and the 'Turanians' in the case of Russia:

The Muscovites are neither Slavs nor Christians in the spirit of the [true] Slavs and other Indo-European Christians. They are nomads until this day, and will remain nomads forever. (cit. in Rudnytsky, 1987, p. 189)

The myth of the non-Slavic origin of Russians was enthusiastically embraced by the Ukrainian radical nationalists, and has had a certain impact on Western academia (cf. Paszkiewicz, 1983). It denies Russians not only the state and dynastic links to the Kievan Rus, but even a degree of ethnic kinship to the 'true' Eastern Slavs, presenting Russian origins as a result of interbreeding between Mongol invaders and local 'Finno-Ugric' tribes of the Volga basin. An underlying, though rarely stated, premise of this argument is racist: the truly 'Aryan' Ukrainians are not only sharply differentiated from but are presumed to be genetically and culturally superior to the 'Eurasian' Russians.

Fully in line with pseudohistorical musings a la Duchiński, Ukrainian writers today deny the Russians their Slavic origins, arguing that 'in truth, they are the people that descended from the Finno-Ugric tribes' (Ukrinform.ua, 2014). Respected Ukrainian scholars, though not going that far, concur in arguing for Ukrainian primordial uniqueness and early separation from other Eastern Slavs. Academician Yaroslav Isaievych (1996) advanced the idea that ethnic differences between future Russians, Ukrainians, and Belarusians can be traced back to the times of Scythians and Sarmatians. A standard university textbook asserts that 'the origins of the Ukrainian culture are lost in the hoary antiquity,' that 'Ukraine is the ancestral home of the Indo-European peoples,' and that 'the main population of Ukraine has not changed since the stone age' (Ryabchenko et al., 2014, pp. 13, 33, 48). A pseudo-scholar opinion popularised in mass media and repeated in a high school textbook maintains that 'in the 5th millennium BCE ancient Ukrainians invented the wheel and the plough… domesticated the horse' (Serediuk, 2007; Krivich and Surgai, 2009, p. 81). Meanwhile, Russia is seen as an anti-civilisation, 'the Moscow *ulus* based on the traditions of the Golden Horde,' as 'the Asian (Russian, Russian Orthodox) civilisation' that 'has no future' (Hryniv, 2014).

The Uses of Othering

After the start of a war against the pro-Russian separatists in Donbas by the Poroshenko government, the 'othering' of Russia has been elevated to new heights. Russophobic and not infrequently racist pronouncements typically characterise in-house speeches and propaganda of the right-wing nationalist groups, such as the proto-fascist Svoboda ('Freedom') party, the former strike force of the Maidan – the Right Sector, the Patriot of Ukraine, the Ukrainian National Assembly-Ukrainian National Self Defence (UNA-UNSO), the Stepan

Bandera 'Trident' ('Tryzub'), and others. Leader of Ukraine's Radical Party and the second runner-up in the 2014 presidential elections Oleh Lyashko demanded that the 'Moscow invaders and their accomplices' be executed by hanging (Baltija.eu, 2014; Lozovy, 2014). The website of the 'Tryzub' carries an appeal to 'dam the Kryvyi Rih quarries with corpses of the *moskali*' (Banderivec n.d.), while the website of the UNA-UNSO promises to dump the bodies of dead Russians into the Kerch Strait until such time when they form a bridge to 'reunite Kuban with Ukraine' (UNA-UNSO n.d.).

The nationalist volunteer militias, e.g. the Azov battalion, whose members also brandish the Nazi and SS insignia, have been at the forefront of Ukraine's civil war with pro-Russian separatists. The war, which they presumably fight to bring Ukraine closer to Europe, for many of them, including the Azov commander, Verkhovna Rada MP Andriy Biletskiy, is nothing else than implementation of the 'Ukrainian racial social-nationalism,' which, among other things, demands 'the racial cleansing of the nation' (Biletskiy n.d.). How so? The thing is, the Ukrainians, according to Mr. Biletskiy, form 'one of the biggest and one of the very best parts of the 'European White Race – the Creator of a great civilisation and the highest human achievements.' The 'historical mission' of the Ukrainian nation, he says, is 'to lead the White Peoples of the world in a final crusade for their survival – a crusade against the Semite-led subhumanity' (Biletskiy n.d.). As commentaries in Ukraine's social media attest, a sizeable portion of the country's 'netizens' would not be averse to the idea of consigning anyone suspected of pro-Russian sympathies to the ranks of thusly defined 'subhumanity'. The Azov's recent transformation into a special regiment of the National Guard of Ukraine, and Biletskiy's promotion to the rank of Lieutenant Colonel, both show that the government opted to turn a blind eye even to the most unpalatable declarations of its armed supporters.

The othering of Russia and the Russians produces surprising echoes of Biletskiy's pronouncements in speeches of Ukraine's top politicians and statesmen. The June 2014 speech by Prime Minister Yatsenyuk referred to the Donbas separatists as 'subhumans' and 'filth' (Uriadovyi portal, 2014), later replaced with 'inhumans' and 'evil' in the official English translation (Embassy of Ukraine in the United States of America, 2014). Presidential candidate Poroshenko had vilified the anti-government protesters in Donbas as 'terrorists, criminals and non-humans' that ought to be 'destroyed' as early as April 2014, and repeatedly designated armed opposition to his regime as 'non-humans' (Lb.ua, 2014; President of Ukraine, 2014a-b). A senior adviser to the Minister of the Interior indicated that his department was preparing suggestions on the curtailment of democratic rights and freedoms for the pro-Russian activists in Donbas: 'if a citizen wants to live in Russia, be my guest: Suitcase – station – Russia!' (Interfax-Ukraine, 2014).

The othering of the autonomisation movement in Donbas before the very first shot in the conflict was fired helped transform what started like civil disobedience protests into a full-blown separatist guerrilla. Systematic abasement of the Donbas defenders in the Ukrainian press as 'subhumans,' 'bastards,' 'imbeciles,' 'potato beetles,' 'cockroaches,' and the like cannot but foment their desire to continue resistance. Parallel to that, the othering of Russia as a 'country that supports and finances terrorism' (Shulha, 2014), the Russian President as a 'd---head' (Culzac, 2014), and the Russians as 'not a people, but a rabble' (Gazeta.ua, 2014) both justifies Kiev's actions in the civil war in the East and encourages its further escalation.

The othering of the opponent understandably serves as a potent instrument of war-mongering on both sides. It boosts patriotic credentials of the elected politicians; entrenches new, post-Maidan elites; propels journalistic, academic, and artistic careers; and helps transform yesterday's thugs into tomorrow's statesmen. Unfortunately for the majority of the population, it also prolongs the war and suffering. The ethno-nationalist mobilisation, achieved by means of othering of the ethnic outgroup members, builds politicians' power bases and generates resources for political action in the situation where other resources are lacking or are sorely inadequate. Additionally, nationalist othering helps to disguise the struggles whose real objects are money, power, status, and property by representing them, deceptively, as mere identity fights (Molchanov, 2000).

Geopolitical uses of othering are equally important. Russophobia plays well with the established western tradition of treating Russia as 'Europe's other,' a 'barbarian at Europe's gate,' a constant historical 'irregularity' (Neumann, 1999, pp. 103, 110). Ukraine's influential allies in the West, starting with the right-wing Ukrainian diaspora organisations, 'have considered Russia, both tsarist and communist, their historical enemy because it had been the prime oppressor of Ukraine's freedom' (Ukrainian Canadian Congress n.d., *Community profile*). Interestingly, some of the most authoritative for today's nationalist champions of the Ukrainian cause are found among the Nazi collaborators that fought the Soviet Union in World War II. These 'long-dead Ukrainian fascists' (Snyder, 2010) are still being worshipped today by the most active fighters against the pro-Russian rebels in Donbas. Fully in line with racialised views of their interwar predecessors, some of the modern Ukraine's radical nationalists are, once again, seeing their main enemy as the 'Muscovite-Jewish mafia,' and, should such views become widespread, it must bode ill for the country's Russian and Jewish minorities (Padden, 2014).

While Ukrainian neo-fascism is less than welcome in the West, Ukrainian Russophobia might well be. Just as Russia has been Europe's Other for centuries, it has been constructed as the American 'other' by a group of professional cold warriors, such as Zbigniew Brzezinski, Dick Cheney, and John McCain. As noted by Andrei Tsygankov (2009, pp. 105-106), one of the long-standing ideas of anti-Russian lobby in the US foreign policy establishment has been the one of breaking the Russia-Ukraine connection and tying Ukraine unconditionally (and at Russia's expense) to the West. Hence, Ukrainian politicians' moves to ostracise Russia strike a chord with an influential group of western elites that include advocates of the Euro-Atlantic hegemony, the liberal hawks, and the militant western values promoters, as well as historically Russophobic Eastern European nationalists (Tsygankov, 2009, pp. 13-14).

Finally, the othering of Russia and the Russian activists in Ukraine justifies the new elite's grab of power and property. The current government in Kiev is as oligarchic as ever, yet signifies an important change in the relative weight of different business clans that control the country's economy: the beginning of the demise of the Donetsk clan. Instead, the Dnipropetrovsk faction under the leadership of the billionaire-governor Ihor Kolomoisky is back, and ready to expand into the Donbas region (Prostakov, 2014). Supporters of the victorious faction have to be rewarded, and are being rewarded – by political appointments, concessions, and new acquisitions blessed by the state. Nationalisation of the titanium mining and processing plants previously controlled by Dmytro Firtash, and their de facto transfer to Kolomoisky, portends a new round of property redistribution (Boiko, 2014). In this battle, everyone designated as 'Moscow's agent' stands to lose, while primitive corporate raidership by victorious oligarchic groups gets glorified as defence of national interests.[19]

Conclusion

The seeming intractability of the conflict in east Ukraine can be explained by more than one factor. The explanation prevailing in the West is that of a 'bad' Russia pressuring Ukraine to abandon its European dream and consistently undermining the very sovereignty of the Ukrainian state. The 'bad Putin' theme is a variation on the topic. More perceptive analysts remind the readers of the NATO expansion to the East and argue that the West provoked Moscow into action (Mearsheimer, 2014). 'Nationalising policies' in Ukraine

---

[19] The importance of 'the shield of nationality' for protection of foreigners against corporate raidership has been noted in Wellhausen (2015). As a corollary to this proposition, we should not be surprised to find out that a symbolic stripping of nationality in the act of othering paves the road for dispossession of rival groups within the same society.

and the plight of the Russian-speaking minorities have also been invoked on more than one occasion (e.g. Molchanov, 2014; Petro, 2014). Regional alienation and de facto exclusion from the political process in Kiev played a large part. Had it not been for the Maidan activists twice – in 2004 and 2014 – overturning the results of what people in Donbas saw as a legitimate presidential election, the rebellion perhaps would not have started. Had it not been for killing of the pro-Russian demonstrators in Odessa on 2 May 2014, and the shelling and bombing of the Donbas cities during the 'anti-terrorist operation' by the Ukrainian army, the protest would not, perhaps, have morphed into a civil war.

This war is much helped by demonisation of the opponent, which goes on all sides of the conflict, inside and outside Ukraine itself. Moreover, ethnicisation of the essentially political and economic differences between Ukraine's regions makes compromise more difficult to reach. The invocation by the Ukrainian politicians and diplomats of the identity markers of a savage, beastly outgroup, a 'scum' (Portnikov, 2014), 'subhumans,' 'bastards,' when referring to separatists in Donbas, cannot but confirm the worst worries of those who might still be leaning to the idea of devolution and power sharing. The threats of legal punishment and political marginalisation propel continued resistance.

As the late Samuel Huntington argued, identity is a given that cannot be changed. An attempt to build a new Ukrainian nation by othering its Russophone components is doomed to backfire. By the same token, political mobilisation against the 'Russian aggressor' can be, at best, a temporary solution to the problem of civic unity. Russia may eventually close its borders with Ukraine, just as Kiev desires, and stop supporting the self-proclaimed *Novorossiya republics*. Kiev may eventually succeed in bringing the embattled region to heel. But will it succeed in reintegrating Donbas after the devastation caused by the war? Will Donbasites agree to be the second-class citizens in the ethno-nationally streamlined, Russophobic society? At the moment of this writing, it seems impossible to envision such an outcome. Perhaps the war against Donbas separatists has solidified Ukraine's political nation; yet it has also made it abundantly clear that the pro-Russian activists do not fit in there. It is entirely possible that Ukraine's ethno-regional split can still be healed. However, to make it happen, authorities in Kiev need to change their attitude to Russia and the Russians. Chanting 'Suitcase – station – Russia!' will not help.

References

Baltija.eu (2014) 'Deputat VRU prizval veshat' 'moskovskikh okkupantov' i ikh posobnikov [A deputy of the Verkhovna Rada of Ukraine called to hang 'Moscow invaders' and their accomplices],' *Baltija.eu*, 3 August. Available at: http://baltija.eu/news/read/39454.

Baker, P. (2014) 'Pressure rising as Obama works to rein in Russia,' *The New York Times*, 2 March. Available at: http://www.nytimes.com/2014/03/03/world/europe/pressure-rising-as-obama-works-to-rein-in-russia.html?_r=2.

Banderivec (n.d.) 'Sluzhbe bezopasnosti Ukraïny adresuetsia [To the State Security Service of Ukraine],' *Bandarivec*. Available at: http://banderivec.org.ua/index.php?page=pages/zmista/zmista309.

Bershidsky, L. (2014) 'Putin's Russia, Tolkien's Mordor: What's the difference?' *Bloomberg View*, 11 December. Available at: http://www.bloombergview.com/articles/2014-12-11/putins-russia-tolkiens-mordor-whats-the-difference.

Biletskiy, A. (n.d.) 'Ukraïns'kyi rasovyi sotsial-natsionalizm – ideologiia Organizatsiï 'Patriot Ukraïny' [The Ukrainian racial social-nationalism – An ideology of the Organization 'The Patriot of Ukraine'],' *Slovo Oriïv*, 35. Available at: http://www.slovoor.info/SO35/St35Vid.htm.

Boiko, D. (2014) 'Koalitsiia i interesy oligarkhov [The coalition and the oligarchs' interests],' *Ekonomicheskaia Pravda*, 3 November. Available at: http://www.epravda.com.ua/rus/publications/2014/11/3/502604/.

Culzac, N. (2014) 'Putin is a d**khead' says Ukrainian foreign minister Andrii Deshchytsia,' *The Independent*, 16 June. Available at: http://www.independent.co.uk/news/world/europe/ukrainian-foreign-minister-calls-putin-a-dhead-at-public-protest-9540454.html.

Embassy of Ukraine in the United States of America (2014) 'Ukraine's Prime Minister Yatsenyuk: We will commemorate the heroes by cleaning our land from the evil,' 15 June. Available at: http://usa.mfa.gov.ua/en/press-center/news/24185-mi-uvichnimo-pamjaty-gerojiv-ochistivshi-nashu-zemlyu-vid-nechistiarsenij-jacenyuk-u-spivchutti-ridnim-i-blizykim-zagiblih-vojiniv-u-lugansyku [cf. a screenshot of the original version at http://ukraineantifascistsolidarity.wordpress.com/2014/06/20/they-lost-thei/].

Ernst, D. (2014) 'Merkel on Putin: He acts the way he does to 'prove he's a man,' *The Washington Times*, 9 December. Available at: http://www.washingtontimes.com/news/2014/dec/9/angela-merkel-vladimir-putin-he-acts-way-he-does-p/.

Gazeta.ua (2014) 'Rosiiany – tse ne narod, a nabrid' – Top-10 tsytat Gebbelsa ['Russians are not a people but a rabble' – Goebbels's top-10 quotes],' 16 July. Available at: http://gazeta.ua/articles/history/_rosiyani-ce-ne-narod-a-nabrid-top10-citat-gebbelsa/570126.

Golovakha, Ie. (2014) Interview, 'Krym – tse nasha nepomirna tsina…[Crimea is our immeasurable price…],' by Yakhno, O., *Den*, 27 March. Available at: http://m.day.kiev.ua/uk/article/podrobici/ievgen-golovaha-krim-ce-nasha-nepomirna-cina.

Hryniv, O. (2014) 'Vtorgnennia varvariv: Moskovs'kyi ulus proty zakhidnoï tzyvilizatsiï [An invasion by barbarians: The Moscow ulus against the Western civilization],' *Rukh*, 5 May. Available at: http://www.nru.org.ua/news/aktualno/756-profesor-oleh-hryniv-vtorhnennya-varvariv-moskovskyi-ulus-proty-zakhidnoi-tsyvilizatsii.

Interfax-Ukraine (2014) 'MVD vystupaet za ogranichenie prav separatistov izbirat' i byt' izbrannymi [The Ministry of the Internal Affairs is for limitation of the separatists' rights to elect and get elected],' 9 July. Available at: http://interfax.com.ua/news/general/212760.html.

Isaievych, Y. (1996) *Ukraina davnia i nova: narod, relihiia, kul'tura* [*Ukraine ancient and modern: The people, religion, culture*]. L'viv: In-t ukrainoznavstva im. I. Kryp'iakevycha.

Kostyk, V. (2014) 'Rosiia – tse kraïna-fantom, kraïna-fake, kraïna-iliuzia' – Filatov [Russia is a phantom country, fake country, a country-illusion' – Filatov],' *Presa Ukraïny*, 1 October. Available at: http://uapress.info/uk/news/show/41340.

Krivich, I. and Surgai, L. (2009) *Ukraïnska mova. 9 klas: Plany-konspekty urokiv* [*The Ukrainian language. 9th grade: Lessons' summaries*]. Kharkiv: Ranok.

Lb.ua (2014) 'Terorystiv na Skhodi Ukraïny potribno sudyty abo znyshchuvaty – Poroshenko [The terrorists in the East of Ukraine must be prosecuted or destroyed – Poroshenko],' *Lb.ua*, 30 April. Available at: http://ukr.lb.ua/news/2014/04/30/265016_terroristov_vostoke_ukraini_nuzhno.html.

Lozovy, A. (2014) 'VK Wall posts,' 2 August. Available at: https://vk.com/wall139835612_57612?reply=57614.

Lutsenko, Yu. (2014) 'Lutsenko: Rosiia – tse velyka benzokolonka z atomnymy raketamy [Lutsenko: Russia is a big gas pump with atomic missiles],' *ICTV*, 20 October. Available at: http://fakty.ictv.ua/ua/index/view-media/id/71627.

Mearsheimer, J. (2014) 'Why the Ukraine crisis is the West's fault: The liberal delusions that provoked Putin,' *Foreign Affairs*, September/October, 1(12).

Molchanov, M. (2000) 'Postcommunist nationalism as a power resource,' *Nationalities Paper,* 28 (2), pp. 263-288.

Molchanov, M. (2002) *Political culture and national identity in Russian-Ukrainian relations*. College Station, TX: Texas A&M University Press.

Molchanov, M. (2014) 'What does it take to save Ukraine?' *Open Democracy*, 27 May. Available at: https://www.opendemocracy.net/od-russia/mikhail-molchanov/what-does-it-take-to-save-ukraine.

Morrison, J. (1993) 'Pereyaslav and after: The Russian-Ukrainian relationship,' *International Affairs* 69(4), pp. 677-703.

Motyl, A. (2014) 'Putin, just evil enough,' *CNN Opinion*, 25 July. Available at: http://www.cnn.com/2014/07/25/opinion/motyl-putin-is-evil/.

Neumann, I. (1999) *Uses of the Other: 'The East' in European identity formation*. Minneapolis: University of Minnesota Press.

Padden, B. (2014) 'Ukraine's far right candidate reflects mainstream nationalist views,' *Voice of America*, 16 May. Available at: http://www.voanews.com/content/ukraines-far-right-candidate-reflects-mainstream-nationalist-views/1916403.html.

Paszkiewicz, H. (1983) *The rise of Moscow's power*. Trans. P.S. Falla. Boulder, CO: East European Monographs.

Petro, N. (2014) 'The real war in Ukraine: The battle over Ukrainian identity,' *The National Interest,* 4 December. Available at: http://nationalinterest.org/feature/the-real-war-ukraine-the-battle-over-ukrainian-identity-11782.

Portnikov, V. (2014) 'Putin poslav na smert na Donbas nebezpechnu dlia nioho 'navoloch' – Veselovsky [Putin has sent the 'scum' that was dangerous to him to die in Donbas – Veselovsky],' *Radio Svoboda*, 17 October. Available at: http://www.radiosvoboda.org/articleprintview/26642708.html.

Presa Ukraïny (2014) 'Novyny z Mordoru [News from Mordor],' 1 October. Available at: http://uapress.info/uk/news/show/41325.

President of Ukraine (2014a) 'President's commentary on liberation of Sloviansk from militants [In Ukrainian],' *Press Service of the President of Ukraine*, 5 July. Available at: http://www.president.gov.ua/news/30676.html.

President of Ukraine (2014b) '17 hostages were released from militants - Petro Poroshenko [In Ukrainian],' *Press Service of the President of Ukraine*, 29 July. Available at: http://www.president.gov.ua/news/30878.html.

Prostakov, G. (2014) 'Kod dostupa k Vostoku [The access code to the East]. *Vesti. Reporter*, 19(37),' 6-12 June. Available at: http://reporter.vesti-ukr.com/art/y2014/n19/8982-kod-dostupa-k-vostoku.html.

Ryabchenko, O., Belikov, Yu., Burmaka, V. et al. (2014) *Istoriia ukraïns'koï kul'tury* [*The history of the Ukrainian culture*]. Kharkiv: KhNUMG.

Rudnytsky, I. L. (1987) *Essays in modern Ukrainian history*. Cambridge, MA: Harvard University Press.

Serediuk, O. (2007) 'Treba buty golovoiu, a ne khvostom [One ought to be a head, not a tail],' *Volyns'ka pravda*, 31 October. Available at: http://www.pravda.lutsk.ua/ukr/news/105/.

Shashkevych, M. (n.d.) 'Iz psalmiv Ruslanovykh [From Ruslan's psalms],' *Izbornyk*. Available at: http://litopys.org.ua/zahpysm/zah04.htm.

Shchetkina, E. (2014) 'Rosiia – tse kraïna bozhevil'nykh? [Russia – a country of the insane?],' *dsnews.ua*, 8 October. Available at: http://www.dsnews.ua/society/chomu-rosiya---tse-krayina-bozhevilnih-08102014182100.

Shulha, Ye. (2014) 'Rechi svoïmi imenamy. [Call things with their own names],' *Ukraïna Moloda*, 30 September. Available at: http://www.umoloda.kiev.ua/number/2535/283/89624/.

Snyder, T. (2010) 'A fascist hero in democratic Kiev,' *The New York Review of Books*, 24 February. Available at: http://www.nybooks.com/blogs/nyrblog/2010/feb/24/a-fascist-hero-in-democratic-kiev/.

Tsygankov, A. (2009) *Russophobia: Anti-Russian lobby and American foreign policy*. New York: Palgrave Macmillan.

The Insider (2014) 'Arsen Avakov: U premiera dolzhny byt' MVD, Minyust i Minfin. Eto minimum [Arsen Avakov: The Premier must have the Ministry of Interior, Ministry of Justice and Ministry of Finance. This is a minimum],' 17 November. Available at: http://www.theinsider.ua/politics/5468dc0a6d2cd/.

Ukrainian Canadian Congress (n.d) *Community profile*. Available at: http://www.ucc.ca/ukrainians-in-canada/community-profile/.

Ukrinform.ua (2014) 'Oleksandr Paliy: Ukraïna zavzhdy bula i bude na svoïkh zemlyakh [Oleksandr Paliy: Ukraine has always been and will always be on its lands],' *Ukrinform*, 7 May. Available at: http://www.ukrinform.ua/ukr/news/oleksandr_paliy_ukraiina_zavgdi_bula_i_bude_na_svoiih_zemlyah_1936240.

UNA-UNSO (n.d.) 'Zaiava UNA-UNSO z pryvodu podii bilia ostroba Tuzla [The UNA-UNSO statement regarding events around Tuzla Island].' Available at: http://una-unso.info/article/artid-2/lang-ukr/index.html.

Uriadovyi portal (2014) 'Arseniy Yatsenyuk vyslovyv spivchuttia ridnym i blyz'kym zagyblykh u Luhans'ku voïniv [Arseniy Yatsenyuk expressed condolences to the families and friends of the military men killed near Luhansk],' *Uriadovyi portal*, 14 June. Available at: http://www.kmu.gov.ua/control/uk/publish/article?art_id=247389338&cat_id=244276429.

Vidomosti (2014) 'Vnaslidok vtorhnennia v Ukraïnu zahynuly shchonaimenshe 2 tysiachi rosiis'kykh viis'kovykh [At least 2 thousand Russian servicemen died as a result of their invasion of Ukraine],' *Vidomosti-UA.com*, 2 September. Available at: http://vidomosti-ua.com/news/94285.

Wellhousen, R. (2015) *The shield of nationality: When governments break contracts with foreign firms*. New York, NY: Cambridge University Press.

World Health Organisation (2011) *Mental Health Atlas 2011*. Available at: http://www.who.int/mental_health/evidence/atlas/profiles/en/#S.

Yermolenko, V (2014) 'Rosiia – tse chasto Yevropa navyvorit. Yak Konchita Vurst, pryblyzno [Russia is oftentimes Europe perverted, like Conchita Wurst, more or less],' *UAINFO*, 19 May. Available at: http://uainfo.org/blognews/324168-rosya-ce-chasto-yevropa-navivort.-yak-konchta-vurst-priblizno.html.

Part Four

PERSPECTIVES

19

Western Economic Sanctions and Russia's Place in the Global Economy

RICHARD CONNOLLY
UNIVERSITY OF BIRMINGHAM

The Ukraine crisis and the imposition of economic sanctions by Western powers and their allies have the potential to cause a radical shift in economic policy in Russia, with important implications for Russia's future place in the global economy. This is because Western economic sanctions and Russia's response to those sanctions have set Russia on a course towards greater isolation from the Western parts of the global economy, and towards greater state control of economic activity at home. This chapter considers the effects that Western sanctions have had to date, and what they might mean for the future of the Russian economy. The first section provides a brief description of the sanctions regimes put in place by Western powers and Russia over the course of 2014. A second section considers the immediate impact that these sanctions have had upon the Russian economy. A third section explores some of the possible effects that sanctions may have upon domestic political economy in Russia. A fourth and final section considers the possibility of a Russian economic 'pivot' to Asia.

Economic Statecraft by Russia and the West

Economic statecraft refers here to the economic measures employed by Western powers, their allies, and Russia as instruments of foreign policy, especially in relation to Russia's role in the conflict in Ukraine (Baldwin, 1985; Hanson, 1988). In addition to measures targeted at individuals, Western countries imposed a range of so-called sectoral sanctions. They include: the suspension of preferential economic development loans to Russia by the

European Bank for Reconstruction and Development (EBRD); a ban on trading bonds and equity and related brokering services for products whose maturity period exceeds 30 days with some of Russia's largest state-controlled banks (including Sberbank and Gazprombank), three Russian energy companies (including Rosneft, Transneft, and Gazprom Neft, although not Gazprom, which has been subject to US sanctions), and three Russian defence companies (OPK Oboronprom, United Aircraft Corporation, Uralvagonzavod); a ban on loans to five major Russian state-owned banks: Sberbank, VTB, Gazprom Bank, Vneshekonombank (VEB), and Rosselkhozbank; an embargo on arms trade between EU members and Russia; a ban on exports of so-called dual-use items, i.e. civilian industrial goods that can be used as (or to produce) weaponry or for other military purposes; and a ban on exporting certain energy equipment and providing specific energy-related services to Russia's most technology-intensive oil exploration and extraction projects (e.g. Arctic deep-water exploration and onshore tight oil).

In response, Russia imposed its own counter-sanctions. While a range of different counter-sanctions were applied by Russia from March 2014 onwards, the most economically significant sanctions were applied in August 2014, with the one-year ban on imports of fruit, vegetables, meat, fish, milk, and dairy from all EU countries, as well as additional Western countries, including the USA, Norway, Australia, and Japan.

Immediate Effects of Economic Sanctions

Western governments targeted three sectors with the sectoral sanctions regime devised in the summer of 2014: the defence industry, the oil industry, and the financial sector. Thus far, the effects have not been uniform, with only the financial sector experiencing any significant effects to date.

Output in the defence industry rose in 2014, despite sanctions, due to growing demand from abroad (in 2014, Russia was the world's second largest exporter of armaments) and from at home (i.e. due to the rise in procurement that was planned as part of the State Armaments Programme to 2020 [*GPV-2020*]) (Rosstat, 2014). Although Russia had some important defence ties with some Western countries, the vast majority of its exports go to countries in Asia, Africa, and Latin America. Consequently, such sanctions should only have an impact over a longer period if military-use technology transfers from the West to Russia are suppressed, and if this then results in a degradation of the Russian armaments industry.

Sanctions have not affected production levels in the oil industry, either.

Instead, output has continued to rise, reaching a post-Soviet record of over 10.6 million barrels a day in November. This is because Western sanctions are not designed to affect production levels in the immediate future. Rather, they are designed to affect future production in Russia's newer, harder-to-reach deposits in the Arctic, off-shore and in Russia's Bazhenov tight oil deposit.

Sanctions on the financial sector have exerted a more immediate impact on the Russian economy. Access to Western capital markets is now largely closed to most Russian corporations, forcing many Russian firms to repay their external debt ahead of schedule due to the impossibility of refinancing or 'rolling over' their credit lines. Total non-financial corporate (which includes many large state enterprises, such as Rosneft and Gazprom) and financial sector external debt amounted to around $610 billion in September 2014 (CBR, 2014). At the prevailing exchange rates in December 2014, this amounted to over 60 per cent of GDP. Of this, nearly $130 billion is scheduled for repayment before the end of 2015, raising the prospect of Russian firms scrambling to secure scarce dollars to service their external debt (CBR, 2014). While this is causing some discomfort for many firms, it is also true that most of the firms with foreign currency-denominated external debt are natural resource exporters who also generate substantial foreign currency revenues, which should enable them to service their debt obligations.

Russia's own counter-sanctions have yet to have any observably positive effects in the form of a significant increase in output in the agricultural sector. This is probably because producers in those sectors that Western producers were most active, such as pork, beef, and dairy products, as well as specific categories of fruit and vegetables, have traditionally been inefficient. Indeed, it was precisely these sub-sectors that proved resistant to accession to the World Trade Organisation in 2012 due to fears that they would not be able to compete with foreign producers (Connolly and Hanson, 2012). This has meant that domestic production has not risen dramatically, as some initially hoped. Instead, exporters from countries that have not participated in the Western sanctions regime, such as Argentina, Brazil, China, Chile, and Turkey, have all benefited by increasing their share of the Russian food market. The prospects for food production in the affected sectors may be brighter: government policies to promote the development of domestic producers through a state-led import substitution strategy are being devised, and may involve an expansion of subsidies and other forms of state support.

The costs associated with the imposition of the agricultural counter-sanctions are borne by Russian consumers. The cost of food forms a large proportion of the typical household budget. As a result, any price rises caused by the food embargo are bound to have an immediate effect on Russian consumers. To date, food prices have risen, nudging Russia's end-of-year consumer price index (CPI) towards double-digit levels, with the price of banned products rising considerably faster than average (Rosstat, 2014). However, the embargo appears to be hitting middle-class, urban consumers more than most due to their propensity to consume imported food products to a greater extent than poorer sections of the population.

Finally, the fact that the Russian economy appears to be slowing down at the same time that sanctions have been applied has created the impression that sanctions are *causing* growth to slow. The rapid depreciation of the rouble in late 2014 reinforced this perception. However, such an interpretation conflates correlation with causation. The Russian economy was already in the midst of a protracted reduction in the average annual rate of GDP growth before the Ukraine crisis. Western economic sanctions may have exacerbated a pre-existing trend, but the effect has been modest. Instead, the appreciation of the dollar against all major currencies and, more importantly, the precipitous decline in oil prices over the course of the second half of 2014 provide a more accurate explanation for the depreciation of the rouble and the deterioration in business confidence that was evident towards the end of the year (Connolly, 2015).

To sum up so far, the economic effects of the economic statecraft that has accompanied the Ukraine crisis have so far been relatively modest. This is to be expected. After all, official statements from Western governments do not indicate that sanctions are intended to cause a slowdown in overall Russian economic performance. It is important, however, to try, insofar as is possible, to separate the effects of sanctions from the effects of pre-existing ailments afflicting the Russian economy. Without making this distinction, it is possible to fall into the trap of asserting that Western powers are responsible for any deterioration in Russian economic performance, an argument that is increasingly and misleadingly deployed by both the authorities in Russia and by some commentators in the West.

Longer-Term Effects of Sanctions

If the economic effects of economic statecraft are relatively modest, the long-term effect on the trajectory of political economy in Russia could well be more profound. Assuming that the sanctions regimes stay in place for a period of years rather than months, it is useful to consider how this might shape the model of political economy in Russia.

The longer sanctions persist, the more the market-oriented (i.e. liberal) policy elite – hitherto well entrenched in Russia's key economic policy positions in the Ministry of Finance and Ministry of Economic Development, as well as the Central Bank of Russia – is likely to be marginalised. This appears to be the case thus far. Economic statecraft has meant that economic policies that are consistent with a more *dirigiste* and introverted economic policy are becoming increasingly popular. Already, import substitution is being promoted across different sectors of the economy, most notably in defence, energy, manufacturing, and agriculture – the key sectors of the Russian economy. 'Soft' capital controls are in place to regulate the sale of foreign currency from Russia's largest enterprises, and the state is intervening in the financial sector to maintain financial sector stability (Finmarket.ru, 2014). Under such conditions, sections within the Russian elite in favour of even greater military spending and state-led modernisation will likely become emboldened at the expense of the more liberal, 'economic' bloc within the elite. Over time, this may result in the state using its dominant position in Russia's 'commanding heights' to raise the rate of investment in the economy through the use of state-directed lending to selected 'strategic' enterprises.

Sanctions may thus serve to entrench the current system of governance rather than weaken elite support for Putin. This could happen because sanctions have specific distributional effects in oligarchic societies like Russia, and can serve to bolster the state and enrich politically important individuals and organisations (Brooks, 2002). The leadership may use the opportunity presented by the deterioration in relations with the West to transfer economic resources to key political allies.

To illustrate this point, consider how Russia is currently responding to the embargo on the sale of Western defence or dual-use technology to Russia, and to the severance of trade relations with Ukrainian defence enterprises. While supply chains have been interrupted, this has offered the leadership the chance to shift more resources to develop the domestic defence industry instead. Already, programmes to produce substitutes for items previously imported from Ukraine and the West are being drawn up that will require the allocation of significant state resources.

Such import substitution strategies are unlikely to be efficient from an economic point of view, as it is unlikely that Russia will produce goods as efficiently or to the same standard as Western firms any time soon. But from a political perspective, the diversion of extra resources to the domestic defence industry would create a constituency that benefits from sanctions. In the context of Russia's ongoing rearmament programme, this outcome could further increase defence industry support for the current leadership.

Similar effects are likely to be observed in the energy industry. It is widely acknowledged that Russia will require access to foreign technology and know-how in the future if it is to exploit the geologically harder to reach oil and gas deposits in the Arctic and the Far East. But because the existing sanctions regime is designed to deny Russia the tools to do this, the government might opt to expand direct state ownership of the industry, and form partnerships with state-owned companies from friendlier countries (China, for instance) to develop indigenous industrial capabilities to replace Western technologies.

Again, such a solution would not be as economically efficient as current arrangements to access technology and know-how through joint ventures with the likes of BP and Exxon-Mobil. But those charged with managing an energy industry dominated even more by the state than it is now would arguably become even more powerful, not less. As with the defence industry, such import substitution policies are likely to be politically efficient, if not economically efficient.

Taken together, the trajectory of Russia's reactions to economic sanctions only briefly outlined here are pushing it away from the path of reintegration with the global economy that she has undergone over the course of the last twenty years. Instead, a self-sufficient, quasi-autarkic relationship with the global economy may emerge. Although Russia would remain far more open than it was during the Soviet era, it would be a deeply worrying step backwards for those hoping the country would become an open and active part of the global economy. Domestically, the creeping accumulation of measures that expand the role of the state in the economy – from 'soft' capital controls to the wide range of import substitution policies that include financial support and measures to suppress competition – threatens to create a more overtly *dirigiste* system of political economy that exists at present.

A Pivot to the East?

The final element of Russia's reaction to Western economic statecraft is its stated aim of intensifying its economic and political relations with Asia, especially China. Even before the Ukraine crisis, Putin, apparently taking a leaf out of US President Barack Obama's book, announced a new 'pivot to Asia' strategy, in the hope that Russia will be able to leverage the perceived economic dynamism of countries like China and South Korea to its advantage (Lo and Hill, 2013). Many within the Russian elite feel that Asia, and especially China, is a more dynamic economic region than the West, and one that comes with less political baggage.

An Asian pivot has other advantages. In particular, it is viewed as providing a rationale to boost the development of Russia's Far East. Although the region is full of valuable natural resources, it suffers from a sparse and declining population and a neglected economy. Developing the region would, like it did under Soviet rule in the 1960s and 1970s, require considerable state involvement. Again, powerful constituencies from within the Russian elite would likely benefit from any state-led development project in the Far East.

Therefore, any moves towards greater integration with the Asia-Pacific economy should be viewed as connected to wider tendencies towards greater state involvement in the economy. Indeed, the agreements on greater cooperation between Russia and China signed in recent years, and including the much-celebrated gas deal apparently formulated in May 2014, are typically agreements between state and quasi-state entities on both sides. This pattern of state-centric relations is surely more appealing to the Russian leadership than the more market-based relationships required for closer relations with Western economies.

However, there are some important obstacles to any planned Asian pivot. On the one hand, Russia's trade relations with Asian countries, and especially China, have grown rapidly in recent years. In 2000, the northeast Asian trio of China, South Korea, and Japan accounted for just 5.5 per cent of total Russian imports (UN Comtrade, 2014). By 2012, this figure had grown to 25 per cent. Russian exports to the region also grew, albeit at a slower rate. In 2000, the three Asian countries accounted for 7.5 per cent of total Russian exports; by 2012, this had grown to 12.5 per cent.

On the other hand, the paltry level of Asian investment in Russia also reveals serious gaps in economic integration. Even after a number of high profile energy and infrastructure deals, China, South Korea, and Japan collectively account for just over one per cent of foreign direct investment in Russia. So while Russia may be importing a growing volume of goods from Asia, it still turns overwhelmingly to Europe for capital.

Second, Russia needs to invest in costly infrastructure in its Far East (roads, railways, pipelines, and so on) if it is to fully engage with Asia's growing economy. Any such spending will require massive private and public investment, and it is far from clear whether such spending will materialise. If it does, it is likely that resources will come from the Russian state, adding yet more substance to the reassertion of the state in the Russian economy.

Third, the growing asymmetry between Russia and China may be even more important. Quite simply, the Russian economy is dwarfed by China's and the gap between them is growing. While the prospect of closer ties with its largest neighbour offers a tantalising prospect – an economic and political counterbalance to the West at a time when relations with the US and Western Europe are at a 20 year low – the Chinese are not under any such pressure. Russia is a relatively minor trade partner, accounting for just over 2 per cent of China's total trade. With Russia's relations with the West deteriorating, it is more likely China will exploit Russia's relative isolation and secure more favourable terms in any deals.

Overall, while pivoting to Asia might be desirable in principle to Russia's ruling elite, the reality of the situation is that Europe will continue to be Russia's main source of trade and capital, as well as technology and know-how, for the foreseeable future. Moreover, should the Russian state intensify efforts to accelerate the strengthening of economic ties with Asian economies, it is likely that centralised economic development of Russia's Far East will be the order of the day, rather than any natural, market-based switch. As a result, expansion of trade with Asia is likely to be built on state-to-state relations with China and India in the areas of energy and defence.

Conclusion

As should now be clear, Western economic sanctions are moving Russia away from a model of economic development approximating the Western model, i.e. based on the primacy of the market and openness to the global economy, or at least the Western-dominated parts of the global economy. In its place, policy-makers are slowly constructing a system that eschews market-based solutions to economic development problems, and which favours selective integration with the global economy, with a preference for other state-driven political economies. The leadership in Russia is, in line with many previous Russian governments throughout history, using the presence of an external threat to justify centralisation of the model of political economy at home. This model is beginning to take shape, and involves the suppression of economic competition, state control over the 'commanding heights' of the economy, especially finance, energy, and defence, and the deterioration of the business environment for the market-based portions of the Russian economy. In short, such a model threatens to roll back many of the more positive elements of Russian economic transformation that have taken place since 1991.

References

Baldwin, D.A. (1985) *Economic Statecraft*. Princeton University Press.

Brooks, R. (2002) 'Sanctions and Regime Type: What Works, and When?' *Security Studies*, 11(4), pp. 1-50.

Central Bank of Russia (2014) *Monetary Policy Report December 2014*. Moscow: Bank of Russia.

Connolly, R. and Hanson, P. (2012) 'Russia's Accession to the World Trade Organisation: Commitments, Processes,' *Eurasian Geography and Economics*.

Connolly, R. (2015, forthcoming) 'Troubled Times: Stagnation, Sanctions and the Prospects for Economic Reform in Russia,' *Chatham House Russia and Eurasia Programme Research Paper*, London: Chatham House.

Hanson, P. (1988) *Western Economic Statecraft in East-West Relations*. London: Royal Institute of International Affairs/Routledge.

Finmarket (2014) 'Goskompanii obyazhut prodavat' po $1 mlrd v den' dlya stabilizatsii situatsii na valyutnom rynke,' [State-owned companies obliged to sell $1 billion per day to stabilise foreign exchange market], *Finmarket.ru*. Available at: http://www.finmarket.ru/main/article/3899135 (Accessed 23 December 2014).

Lo, B. and Hill, F. (2013) 'Putin's Pivot: Why Russia is Looking East,' *Foreign Affairs,* 31.

Rosstat (2014). Available at: rosstat.ru (Accessed 6 January 2015).

United Nations (2014) *Comtrade Trade Database*. Geneva: United Nations.

20

Democracy and Geopolitics: Understanding Ukraine's Threat to Russia

PAUL D'ANIERI
UNIVERSITY OF CALIFORNIA, RIVERSIDE

Russian leaders and western analysts have advanced a number of arguments justifying or explaining Russia's 2014 invasions of Ukraine. Understanding the motivations for Russia's actions is important in the short term because efforts to anticipate the course of the conflict depend on understanding Russia's goals. In the long term, however, finding a durable settlement will depend on understanding what Russia hopes to gain. Moreover, strategy for many states in the region, for the US, and for NATO depends on understanding the scope of Russian ambitions.

Much of the discussion in the west has centred on the question of whether Russia's actions should be thought of as aggressive or defensive. Both of those views see the motivation as primarily geopolitical. In contrast, this chapter focuses on sources of the invasion that are both domestic and transnational: Russia invaded in Ukraine, at least in part, to prevent the transnational spread of revolution from Ukraine to Russia. For post-revolution Ukraine to succeed as a stable, prosperous, liberal democracy tied closely to Europe would fundamentally undermine the claim that Russia cannot succeed as a liberal democracy. Putin's legitimacy rests largely on that claim. If Ukraine could succeed as a democracy, Russians might logically ask themselves why Russia could not do the same. Moreover, the success of the 'revolution of dignity' would demonstrate a method for bringing such change to Russia.

This explanation does not directly contradict geopolitical perspectives, but to the extent that the motivations concerned Ukraine's effect on Russian domestic politics, the implications for future Russian behaviour are different. Either geopolitical explanation would lead us to expect that Russia will seek to stabilise some revised status quo. The domestic explanation leads us to believe that Russia will seek to prevent any level of stability that enables a territorially truncated Ukraine to proceed with domestic reform and closer ties with Europe.

Geopolitical Explanations

The aggressive or opportunistic view sees Russia as having seized upon instability in Ukraine to seize territory that it has long coveted.

> The ultimate goal, which has motivated and guided [Vladimir Putin] since he took over the presidency 14 years ago and which he has pursued with remarkable consistency and persistence, is to recover most, if not all, key assets – political, economic and geostrategic – lost in the collapse of the Soviet state (Aron, 2014).

The defensive view sees Russia, alarmed by the eastward expansion of the European Union and NATO, as reacting to the threat that Ukraine's revolution would lead to the expansion of hostile European powers into territory that had traditionally belonged to Russia, and through which Russia has repeatedly been invaded: 'The United States and its European allies share most of the responsibility for the crisis. The taproot of the trouble is NATO enlargement, the central element of a larger strategy to move Ukraine out of Russia's orbit and integrate it into the West' (Mearsheimer, 2014). 'Twenty years of NATO's eastward expansion has caused Russia to feel cornered… the Ukraine crisis was instigated by the West's attempt, last November, to smuggle the former Soviet republic into NATO' (van den Heuvel and Cohen, 2014).

This debate between offensive and defensive, which echoes the debate between 'traditional' and 'revisionist' explanations of the Cold War, is based on an underlying agreement that the conflict is essentially about geopolitics – about whether Ukraine will be part of the East or West, about whether Russia will accept or reject the borders it was left with after the dissolution of the Soviet Union, and about whether we are entering a new cold war. In contrast, much of the western literature in recent years has viewed the spread of democracy via popular revolutions without much reference to geopolitics – democratisation simply represented the spread of a universally recognised value.

The Transnational Spread of Democracy and Autocracy

The 'third wave of democratisation' has spawned a large literature on the transnational diffusion of democracy. Much of this literature focused on the role of the EU in promoting democracy in post-communist Eastern Europe. Following the 'coloured revolutions' in Serbia, Georgia, Ukraine, and Kyrgyzstan, many analysed the diffusion of revolutionary tactics. In its most simplistic form, it seemed that there was a recipe for overthrowing the corrupt hybrid regimes of the region.

At least since the 2004 Orange Revolution, we have seen a concerted response by Russia and other autocratic regimes. Domestically, autocratic governments, not only in Russia but in Central Asia and Latin America as well, put pressure on NGOs and opposition politicians and created pro-government groups, such as Russia's Nashi, that could be called upon to counter protestors in the street. Moreover, these governments have collaborated to combat the transnational spread of democracy. Autocracy as well as democracy can diffuse, and Russia among others has increasingly sought to promote it (D'Anieri, 2014). By watching each other's examples, they copy successful domestic tactics. By invoking the rhetoric of pluralism, they have sought to counter the notion that one social system is best. By creating their own monitoring groups, they have provided international legitimacy to elections that other groups would not approve.

From this perspective, the lines between domestic, transnational, and international/geopolitical blur. Because changes in regime type can have enormous geopolitical impacts, the spread of particular regime types, or the resistance to them, becomes a geopolitical tactic. If the West, in viewing democracy as a universal value, underestimates this, Russia clearly does not. Putin sees the spread of promotion of democracy as aimed against Russia's interests. Thus, Putin has pointed to what he sees as the hypocrisy of the US position on Crimea. In the case of Kosovo, Putin argues, the US stated that the secession of a territory could be legal even against the opposition of the state from which it was seceding (Putin, 2014a). By alleging a double standard, Putin hopes to demonstrate that US talk of international law and democracy is a geopolitical weapon, not an actual principle.

Sources of Putin's Legitimacy

Vladimir Putin has based his legitimacy on several claims. Not least of these is the argument that he has been constitutionally and democratically elected. That he sees value in this source of legitimacy is shown by the fact that he took the trouble of passing the presidency to Dmitri Medvedev for a term.

Clearly, however, he understands that his claim to democratic legitimacy differs from that made in western democracies, because he and his team have constructed an alternative conception of democracy, which they have called 'managed democracy' or 'sovereign democracy,' similar to what Guillermo O'Donnell has called 'delegative democracy' (O'Donnell, 1994; Kubicek, 1994).

'Managed democracy' consisted of three pillars: control of other political institutions by a powerful presidency, control over mass media, and control over elections (Petrov, 2005). While the first of these was put in place, at least on paper, by Boris Yeltsin as early as 1993, the latter two were initiated during the early years of Putin's rule. Important early steps included the takeover of much of Russia's independent media and the abolition of elections for regional governors. The key was the weakening of institutions with sources of legitimacy independent of the presidency.

The term 'sovereign democracy' was elaborated upon by Vladislav Surkov, an advisor who has held senior positions in both Putin and Medvedev governments (Sakwa, 2011). While there was never any precise definition of 'sovereign democracy,' or more specifically of how 'sovereign' democracy differed from other forms, it appears that the word 'sovereign' in this formulation had both domestic and international connotations. Domestically, the state was to be dominant, and thus relatively autonomous from society. In contrast to the western notion of 'popular sovereignty,' 'sovereign democracy' assumed that the state leads the people, rather than the other way around. Internationally, the term appears to mean that Russia's notion of democracy is to be defined solely on Russian terms, and that international or transnational claims on what democracy should mean in Russia are rejected as interferences in Russia's internal affairs. To simplify, Putin's autocracy is legitimate because it is necessary: it has created and maintained internal order in a Russia that had nearly collapsed under a regime based more on western notions of democracy. It has also protected Russia against a hostile West that has used democracy promotion as a tool to weaken it. In sum, while 'sovereign democracy' sounds like a theoretical construct or an ideology, in practice it turned out to be a very particular proposition: that only Vladimir Putin could maintain Russia's internal stability and prevent its humiliation by hostile external forces.

A second source of legitimacy, in the eyes of many analysts, is the growth of Russia's economy. Growth in the Russian economy under Putin, in contrast with the collapse of the 1990s, justifies Putin's methods of rule. More broadly, the performance of autocratic regimes like Russia and China contrasts with stagnation in the US and Western Europe. It also contrasts with poor performance in Ukraine.

How Ukraine Threatens Putin's Legitimacy

Ukraine threatens Putin's claim that western style democracy is inappropriate for Russia. In this respect, the widespread Russian view that Ukraine is 'really' part of Russia is particularly dangerous. If Ukraine is indistinguishable from Russia, and Ukraine can establish a European style democracy – and even aspire, however unrealistically, to EU membership – why could not Russia?

When a pro-western and anti-Russian Viktor Yushchenko looked likely to win the 2004 Ukrainian presidential election, Russia threw considerable weight behind the campaign of Viktor Yanukovych. The subsequent Orange Revolution demonstrated Russia's fears: in Ukraine, a pro-reform and anti-Russian government came to power in place of a pro-Russian one. In Russia, people angered over cuts in social benefits took to streets. While Putin's government was able to resist these protests, they led to several new steps, including the formation of the new Nashi pro-government youth organisation and the doctrine of 'sovereign democracy.'

However, when Putin oversaw the falsification of the 2011 parliamentary election, protests re-emerged on a much larger scale. In having Dmitry Medvedev step aside in 2012, so that Putin could resume the presidency, Putin left no doubt as to who was in charge, regardless of who held which office. The point was not just about the sovereignty of the state, but about Putin's leading role in it. In both instances, it appeared as though Putin understood that unless his dominance was widely understood, there was a danger that some elites might challenge his role (see Hale, 2014).

However, falsifying the 2011 elections brought its own problems, namely protests in the streets that resembled the protests that had set off the Orange Revolution in Ukraine and the Rose revolution in Georgia. These protests, welcomed and encouraged by the United States, represented a genuine challenge to Putin's power, and while he was able to beat them back, it appears that he continues to perceive such a threat.

The events in Ukraine in 2013-2014 reinforced that threat. It is unclear whether Putin really believes what he says about the role of the EU and US in fomenting the overthrow of Viktor Yanukovych (2014b) – though the presence of Senator John McCain and Assistant Secretary of State Victoria Nuland on the Maidan made the accusation more plausible. The prospect was that Ukraine would, with the aid of the EU, begin turning itself around. If so, it could become an attractive model for Russians, and a very different model than the one Putin has been insisting is the only one available. Putin expressed this candidly in November 2014, stating,

> In the modern world extremism is being used as a geopolitical instrument and for remaking spheres of influence. We see what tragic consequences the wave of so-called colour revolutions led to. For us this is a lesson and a warning. We should do everything necessary so that nothing similar ever happens in Russia (quoted in Korsunskaya, 2014).

Implications

To the extent that Russia's invasion of Ukraine was driven by the fear of 'contagion' of popular revolution, what impact does it have on the future of the conflict? In contrast to a solely geopolitical understanding of the conflict, this view would lead us to focus less on either the territorial questions or on the relationship with Europe and the US, and more on the situation within Ukraine.

If we focus primarily on territory, whether we see Russia's motivations as aggressive or defensive, then the logical goal is the establishment of some new territorial status quo in Europe. Whether that means consolidating the gains of 2014, or expanding further, the goal would be to obtain eventual acceptance of the new boundaries. With Crimea, that already may have been achieved. Even a defensive interpretation might expect Russia to seize a land corridor linking Crimea to Russia, or even to go all the way to Transnistria, seizing Odessa along the way, and cutting off Ukraine from the Black Sea. Any territorial expansion beyond the immediate neighbourhood of the September 2014 ceasefire line would be to further challenge Europe, and possibly to demonstrate how little it could do to prevent Russia from pursuing its objectives. A more limited solution would be a quid pro quo in which Russia agreed to maintain the new status quo in return for Europe keeping Ukraine at a distance. Something similar to this has been proposed by two prominent American strategists, Michael O'Hanlon and Jeremy Shapiro (O'Hanlon and Shapiro, 2014).

If Russia's actions in Ukraine have been motivated more by fear of revolutionary contagion, as hypothesised here, then Russia's strategy going forward might look very different. It will not be enough to hold Crimea and Donbas if what is left of Ukraine becomes a functioning democracy. Russia does not necessarily need to seize more territory, but it does need to prevent Ukraine from stabilising. By freezing the conflict – but maintaining the potential for it to reignite quickly – Russia can ensure that investors shun Ukraine, that the government is distracted from other endeavours, and that self-organised military forces retain their strength at the expense of the Ukrainian state.

Mearsheimer (2014) advocates some form of neutralisation of Ukraine – citing the model of Austria in the Cold War. If the conflict is entirely geopolitical, that might work. But if it is also about Ukraine's domestic politics and their implications for Russia, such a result would likely be unacceptable to Russia. A deeper problem with neutrality is that it is much harder to do in the post-Cold War world than in the Cold War world. Building a functioning liberal democracy in Ukraine almost certainly depends on close ties with the European Union – both for support of reform, and for strictly economic reasons as well. Competing in Europe on uneven terms with members of the EU, Ukraine's economy would almost certainly stagnate – forcing it to cut a deal with Russia.

The overlap of domestic, transnational, and geopolitical factors will make the conflict extremely difficult to resolve. For Russia to feel secure with regard to Ukraine, Ukraine needs not only to be territorially truncated or geopolitically neutralised; it needs either to be controlled by Russia – and autocratic – or to be dysfunctional. If neutralisation is not a viable strategy, then renewed stability would depend either on the West acquiescing in renewed Russian control of Ukraine, or on Russia accepting the loss of Ukraine (minus Crimea and the Donbas). It is more likely that a non-cooperative result will emerge, in which Russia may limit its military activity, but will continue to ensure that Ukraine cannot do what is needed to prosper or join Europe.

References

Aron, L. (2014) 'What makes Putin tick? A primer for presidential candidates,' *Los Angeles Times,* 3 December.

Cohen, S.F. (2012) 'America's Failed (Bi-Partisan) Russia Policy,' *Huffington Post*, 28 February. Available at: http://www.huffingtonpost.com/stephen-f-cohen/us-russia-policy_b_1307727.html.

Hale, H. (2014) *Patronal Politics: Eurasian Regime Dynamics in Comparative Perspective*. Cambridge: Cambridge University Press.

Korsunskaya, D. (2014) 'Putin says Russia must prevent 'color revolution',' *Reuters*, 11 November. Available at: http://www.reuters.com/article/2014/11/20/us-russia-putin-security-idUSKCN0J41J620141120.

Kubicek, P. (1994) 'Delegative Democracy in Russia and Ukraine,' *Communist and Post-Communist Studies,* 27(4), pp. 423-441.

Mearsheimer, J. (2014) 'Why the Ukraine Crisis Is the West's Fault: The Liberal Delusions That Provoked Putin,' *Foreign Affairs*, September/October, Available at: http://www.foreignaffairs.com/articles/141769/john-j-mearsheimer/why-the-ukraine-crisis-is-the-wests-fault.

O'Donnell, G. (1994) 'Delegative Democracy,' *Journal of Democracy,* 5(1), pp. 55-69.

O'Hanlon, M. and Shapiro, J. (2014) 'Crafting a win-win-win for Russia, Ukraine and the West' *Washington Post*, 7 December. Available at: http://www.washingtonpost.com/opinions/crafting-a-win-win-win-for-russia-ukraine-and-the-west/2014/12/05/727d6c92-7be1-11e4-9a27-6fdbc612bff8_story.html.

Petrov, N. (2005) 'From Managed Democracy to Sovereign Democracy: Putin's Regime Evolution in 2005,' PONARS Policy Memo No. 396.

Putin, V. (2014a) 'Address by the President of the Russian Federation,' 18 March. Available at: http://eng.kremlin.ru/news/6889.

Putin, V. (2014b) 'Meeting of the Valdai International Club [transcript of Putin's remarks],' 24 October. Available at: http://eng.kremlin.ru/news/23137.

Sakwa, R. (2011) 'Surkov: dark prince of the Kremlin', *Open Democracy*, 7 April. Available at: https://www.opendemocracy.net/od-russia/richard-sakwa/surkov-dark-prince-of-kremlin.

van den Heuvel, K. and Cohen, S.F. (2014) 'Cold War Against Russia—Without Debate', *The Nation*, 19 May.

21

Perspectives for Russia's Future: The Case for Narrative Analysis

EDWIN BACON
BIRKBECK, UNIVERSITY OF LONDON

Any observer looking at Russian politics at the end of 2014 cannot fail to be struck by the magnitude of change over the course of that year. 2014 saw Russia expand its territory by the absorption of Crimea, taking to itself the land of a neighbouring state against the wishes of that state's government. It saw Russians fighting in a conflict against the Ukrainian armed forces on the territory of Ukraine. It saw Russia's relatively stable, albeit fractious, relationship with the western powers dramatically worsen, with sanctions imposed by the US and the EU on many of those close to President Putin. It saw economic decline, as the rouble and oil prices fell dramatically and official Russian forecasts posited recession in 2015.

Few, if any, analysts predicted these developments. A year earlier, in December 2013, the headlines from Russia were different. An official amnesty in December 2013 mandated the release of the highest profile prisoners in Russia – oligarch Mikhail Khodorkovsky and Pussy Riot members Nadezhda Tolokonnikova and Maria Alekhina – all of whom had been the subjects of sustained campaigns for their freedom in the West. A few months earlier, in September 2013, leading opposition figure Aleksei Navalny performed strongly in Moscow's mayoral election, as other opposition candidates across the country gained a handful of seats and mayoralties, including that of Russia's fourth largest city, Yekaterinburg. Even in early 2014, Russia's global image was burnished by a successful Winter Olympics in Sochi.

The ominous turn of events in 2014 reveals the complexities of forecasting

Russia's path of development. A tendency to polarisation and preconception can lead to insufficient attention to nuance and competing voices within Russia. My recent research has focused on two particular approaches to assessing political developments within Russia, namely political narratives and political forecasting (Bacon, 2012a; Bacon, 2012b). This article sets out how narrative analysis helps us to discern Russia's key interests from the perspective of the ruling regime, and then draws on these findings to consider the complexities of scenario building as Russia moves into the second half of this century's second decade.

The Russian Narrative

In terms of public political narratives, at the methodological centre of narrative analysis lies the normative assertion that in order to better understand a political system, we should take seriously – and therefore pay close attention to – the stories that its political actors tell about themselves and their system. This is not a Russo-specific assertion. To understand the United States, we need to be cognisant of narratives representing the US as the leader of the free world and promoter of democracy. To understand the EU, we must acknowledge its developing story of ever-closer union. These narratives are repeated, believed, and enacted. They highlight factors that matter within a political system. They reveal self-conceptualisations that play into policy development. US Secretary of State John Kerry acknowledged the ubiquity of systemic narratives after meeting with Russian Foreign Minister Sergei Lavrov in March 2014, noting that they 'talked for a good six hours and… really dug into all of Russia's perceptions, their narrative, our narrative, our perceptions, and the differences between us' (Kerry, 2014).

To assert that narratives matter and that we should take seriously what political actors say about themselves and their systems is not, of course, to accept the content of these narratives as true and right. Public political narratives are artificial constructs, making selective use of different elements to create a desirable account. In analysis of public political narratives, these elements – or 'narrative parts' – are identified and interrogated. Choices made in terms of inclusions and omissions serve to reveal the central concerns of political actor-narrators. The narrative parts include temporalities and agents, symbols and motifs, plots and sub-plots. Analysis of narrative parts highlights the choices made in terms of when stories begin and end, who are the heroes and villains, what are the most significant themes, and how the story might develop. Applying the narrative analysis approach to Russia's stance on Ukraine in 2014 facilitates clarification of those elements which particularly motivate Russian action. I have developed such an analysis in detail elsewhere (Bacon, 2015), and summarise it here before turning to the application of that analysis in developing future scenarios.

Official Russia has built a narrative around events in Ukraine, which, in terms of temporalities, looks back further than the narrative of the Putin regime has habitually done. This is not just a matter of the narrative's unexpected emphasis on the pre-modern period – as exemplified by President Putin's dwelling on the 10th century baptism of Grand Prince Vladimir in his annual address to parliament in December 2014 (Putin, 2014c) – but of the temporal pivot around which Russia's national narrative now revolves, namely the end of the Cold War. For most of the Putin era (from 2000 onwards), his regime defined itself and its actions as post-Yeltsin, with the turn of the millennium being the decisive moment. The symbols of the Putin narrative (for example, the introduction of the National Unity Day holiday and the establishment of the United Russia party) developed the story of President Putin bringing unity and stability to a country riven with political, socio-economic, and ethno-national fissures during the 'time of troubles' of the 1990s. From early in Putin's third term, and particularly in 2014, the narrative's temporality has decisively shifted. The key moment now is the Soviet collapse, after which – so Russia's narrative now relentlessly reminds us – Russia 'found itself in such a difficult situation that realistically it was simply incapable of protecting its interests'. But today, that narrative asserts, the time has come 'to refute the rhetoric of the Cold War' since a strong and independent Russia with national interests which demand respect is back on the scene (Putin, 2014a). In 2014, this insistence on respect for national interests was, according to President Putin, a key factor which led to the absorption of Crimea and Sevastopol into the Russian Federation.

Analysing narrative parts facilitates our awareness of where the Kremlin believes the events of 2014 in Ukraine stem from in temporal terms. The narrative analysis approach also enhances awareness of whom Russia perceives as ally or opponent. In the story told by President Putin – most notably in his speech on the acceptance of Crimea and Sevastopol into the Federation in March 2014 – two particular nuances stand out. First, the view widely held in the West of Russia and Ukraine as enemies does not match that held by Vladimir Putin. In his narrative, the 'fraternal Ukrainian people' are part of the 'we' on whose behalf Russia is standing against potential western encroachment. Second, there remains a small degree of ambiguity in the way the West, and particularly the United States, is portrayed in the Putin narrative. Although the Russian narrative repeatedly portrays 'the United States or its allies' as the villains of the piece who use any excuse to contain Russia (Putin, 2014c), Russia's president also insists on using the words 'partners' and 'friends' in relation to them, as exemplified both in the Crimea Speech of March 2014 and in his address to parliament in December 2014. When questioned as to his use of the phrase 'our American friends' in a television interview in November 2014, President Putin responded, 'of course, they are all our friends' (Putin, 2014b).

The ambiguity in Putin's references to Western friends and partners reflects the important final aspect of narrative analysis in relation to Russia and Ukraine which this short article covers, that is, the existence of plot and sub-plot. It is perhaps beyond cliché to note the historical ambiguity and conflict within Russia in terms of relations with the West and whether Russia's path is as a unique civilisational exemplum or, as Putin himself once put it, part of the 'mainstream of civilisation' (Putin, 1999). The contemporary version of this debate spans questions of democratic development versus increased authoritarianism, and decisions over whether Russia's path in terms of economic, security, and diplomatic priorities should be predominantly internationalist or nationalist, European or Eurasian, ideological or interest-based. Narrative analysis distinguishes between plots and sub-plots in political narratives, with the latter providing flexibility and alternative policy options. The sub-plot within a political narrative does not represent an opposing view, since the narrative of opposition forces differs from that of the ruling regime, but rather a sub-plot presents another course of action within the overarching story. For most of the Putin years, since 2000, the regime's narrative plot has – whatever its relationship to reality – posited Russia as a reliable international partner, modernising and democratising in peaceable and non-ideological pragmatism within the framework of international law. The alternative path of nationalism, military power, and Great Power hegemony existed only as a sub-plot, to be hinted at as a potential turn to be taken, but for the most part serving as background. Events in Ukraine in 2014 saw the sub-plot become the main plot in Russia's political narrative. The pronouncements of Russia's political élite have followed this new line with ubiquitous ease and notable rapidity, as talk of historical vocation, military glory, and western malfeasance dominate where more sober, restrained, and diplomatic language had previously been the norm.

The changing influence of think tanks close to the regime illustrates well this shift. During the Medvedev presidency (2008-2012), the think tank closest to the regime was the Institute of Contemporary Development (INSOR), whose board of trustees is chaired by Medvedev and whose reports habitually sought to push policy in a more liberal and reformist direction. In the autumn of 2012, apparently with tacit government encouragement (Khamraev, Savenko, et al., 2012), a new ultra-conservative think tank, the Izborskii Club, was formed, bringing together the leading names in anti-western and Eurasianist thinking, such as Aleksandr Dugin, Aleksandr Prokhanov, and President Putin's advisor on Eurasian integration, Sergei Glazyev. Their early reports seemed somewhat fantastical and detached from the real world, being replete with vague notions of Orthodox 'spirituality', militarism, and nostalgia for a non-existent Red-White amalgam of the Soviet Union and Imperial Russia (Delyagin, Glazyev, et al., 2012; Izborskii Club, 2012; Dugin, 2013). As noted in this article's opening paragraph, the changes, which 2014 wrought in official Russia's narrative, are such that these ideas now appear close to the official line. When the United States imposed its first round of sanctions on named Russian individuals, Sergei Glazyev was on its list. If INSOR seeks to push Russia in a more reformist direction, the Izborskii Club pushes for further steps along a reactionary path. The extent to which the discourse of official Russia has travelled along this path may perhaps be judged by German Chancellor Angela Merkel's reported assertion that President Putin has 'lost contact with reality' and is 'living in another world' (Baker, 2014). The world of Russian ultra-conservatism is a far cry from the norms of western diplomatic engagement.

Analysing the development of Russia's political narrative in 2014 brings to light the central concerns of the Putin regime in relation to events in Ukraine, revealing a nationalist revanchism which draws on notions of Russian power and destiny, and sees the West as an undesirable and hostile other. At the same time, however, the notion of sub-plot has significance as it keeps alive alternative approaches. President Putin still insists on referring to Western partners and American friends. Prime Minister Medvedev remains chair of the INSOR board of trustees. The current sub-plot of international law and Russia as a state willing 'to have as many equal partners as possible, both in the West and in the East' (Putin, 2014c) remains in play as a potential future scenario, albeit one that seems unlikely to come to the fore again in the short term.

Building Future Scenarios

When it comes to developing future scenarios for Russia following on from the tumultuous events of 2014, the place of narrative is pertinent. Since the end of the Cold War, the dominant methodology employed by analysts and academics seeking to anticipate potential futures for states and regions has been the scenario approach. The scenario methodology identifies key drivers and elaborates their effect in a series of divergent scenarios, for example, best case, worst case, and continuity (Bacon, 2012c). Narratives play a central role in scenario development, as they are used to draw disparate drivers into a coherent and feasible story of the future. In the case of Russia's post-2014 future, there has – at the time of writing – been no systematic scenario development process conducted and published in the light of the annexation of Crimea and the conflict in Ukraine. On the Russian side, the Kremlin's narrative has been notably lacking in terms of future vision. Whereas the political narrative of Putin and Medvedev in previous years presented a clear picture of a modern, law-based, and more democratic Russia to come at some undefined yet not-too-distant future point, in 2014, there was little focus on future vision. On the Western side, in contrast, there has been no shortage of forecasts, though these have tended to come from media and policy analysts, rather than academics, and have correspondingly lacked something in terms of methodological rigour.

The most common western forecast at the end of 2014 is that, faced with declining oil prices, a collapsing rouble, and western sanctions, Russia's economic difficulties will worsen to such an extent that political pressure on President Putin will see him removed from office (Bacon, 2014). The political scientist stands no more equipped than any knowledgeable Russia-watcher when it comes to certainty over whether such a scenario will come to pass or not. That said, the study of forecasting does provide the tools for a short and concluding critical analysis of this scenario based around two common hazards of forecasting, namely the temptation to shape forecasts around the forecaster's own preferences and prejudices, and the danger of positing an outcome without a preceding process.

In a paper at the Association for Slavic, East European, and Eurasian Studies Convention 2014, David Fogleson analysed portrayals of and predictions about the Putin regime in the *New York Times*. He noted the preponderance of negative articles about Russia in the past decade and drew particular attention to the persistent image of Russia as 'an unstable nation headed for a popular revolt against the Putin regime' (Fogleson, 2014). Critically analysing the repeated appearance of this forecast since 2005, Fogleson concludes that, given Putin's survival in power, the 'correspondents would be disappointed. But disappointments have not led *The Times*' editors to rein in prophets of Putin's demise in the last year… One could go on citing examples of how wishful thinking on *The Times*' editorial pages ran counter to the rising Russian patriotic support for Putin, whose approval rating climbed to over 80% according to public opinion surveys' (Fogleson, 2014). Shearer and Stark go so far as to argue that the 'predilection among reporters for looking at events through the prism of their own expectations and beliefs' is 'especially noticeable among Moscow correspondents' (Shearer and Starr, 1996, p. 37).

The phenomenon of wishful forecasting has a strong tradition in relation to Russia. Although it is widely accepted that remarkably few analysts in the 1980s predicted the collapse of the Soviet Union (Seliktar, 2004), such was not the case almost two decades before the Soviet collapse, when Dziewanowski was able to assert that 'predicting the downfall of the Soviet regime has been a favourite academic pastime in the West for well over half a century. Probably no other regime has ever survived so many prophecies of inevitable catastrophe' (Dziewanowski, 1972, p. 367). Dziewanowski's prophets were in the end correct, since the Soviet Union collapsed, but few would see the repeated and temporally inaccurate prediction of that collapse as effective scenario development.

The same might be said about constant assertions of the coming collapse of the Putin regime. The notion that such a collapse might come about through economic pressure appears at first glance to provide a certain explanatory rigour to the scenario. However, what is lacking here is process. The jump is made from the likely behaviour of a key driver – Russia's economy – to a single political outcome. More rigorous scenario development would explore a range of potential political responses to economic decline, from regime collapse to regime strengthening enhanced by factors such as anti-western feeling or a more authoritarian turn by a defensive élite. Furthermore, the need for process to proceed outcome in scenario development insists, too, on providing an account of *how* Putin's removal from power might come about. Absent revolution, there are a limited number of ways in which a Russian president can leave office, and those who assert Putin's coming downfall need to consider the process by which economic difficulty might lead to a change of the entrenched political leader or regime, particularly given that that there are numerous examples of severe economic problems in Russia without such a change. As I have noted elsewhere (Bacon, 2014), the scenario of authoritarian stability and global power alongside economic decline and consumer dissatisfaction ought at least to be considered, given that it kept the Brezhnev regime in power for decades. After all, the purpose of scenario development is not to predict, but to anticipate possible futures.

References

Bacon, E. (2012a) 'Public Political Narratives: Developing a Neglected Source through the Exploratory Case of Russia in the Putin-Medvedev Era,' *Political Studies*, 60(4), pp. 768-786.

Bacon, E. (2012b) 'Writing Russia's Future: Paradigms, Drivers, and Scenarios,' *Europe Asia Studies*, 64(7), pp. 1165-1189.

Bacon, E. (2012c) 'Comparing Political Futures: The Rise and Use of Scenarios in Future-Oriented Analysis,' *Contemporary Politics,* 18(3), pp. 270-285.

Bacon, E. (2014) 'Russia's Ominous 2014, and What Comes Next,' *10 Gower Street: The Birkbeck Politics Department Blog*. Available at: http://10-gower-street.com/2014/10/28/russias-ominous-2014-and-what-comes-next/ (Accessed 17 December 2014).

Bacon, E. (2015 forthcoming) 'Putin's Crimea Speech, 18 March 2014,' *Journal of Soviet and Post-Soviet Politics and Society*, 1(1).

Baker, P. (2014) 'Pressure Rising as Obama Works to Rein In Russia,' *New York Times*, 3 March.

Delyagin, M., Glaz'ev S., et al. (2012) 'Strategiya 'Bol'shogo ryvka,' *Izborskii klub: russkie strategii,* 1(1), pp. 46-73.

Dugin, A. (2013) 'Aleksandr Dugin: Russkii otvet na vyzov zapada,' *Izborskii klub: russkie strategii,* 1(1), pp. 74-79.

Dziewanowski, M. K. (1972) 'Death of the Soviet Regime: A Study in American Sovietology by a Historian,' *Studies in Soviet Thought,* 12(4), pp. 367-379.

Fogleson, D. (2014) 'Dark Pictures are Easy to Paint: Journalists and American Images of post-Soviet Russia in Historical Perspective,' *Association for Slavic, East European, and Eurasian Studies Convention*, San Antonio, Texas.

Izborskii Club (2012) 'Rozhdenie Izborskogo Kluba,' *Izborskii klub: russkie strategii,* 1(1), pp. 2-11.

Kerry, J. (2014) 'Remarks by Secretary Kerry: March 2014,' Available at: http://www.state.gov/secretary/remarks/2014/03/223523.htm (Accessed 17 December 2014).

Khamraev, V., Savenko A., et al. (10 September 2012) 'Antivaldai'skaia vozvyshennost,' *Kommersant*.

Putin, V. (1999) 'Rossiya na rubezhe tysyacheletiy (Russia at the turn of the millennium),' *Nezavisimaya gazeta,* 30 December.

Putin, V. (2014a) 'Obrashchenie prezidenta Rossiiskoi Federatsii,' *Rossiiskaya gazeta*, 19 March.

Putin, V. (2014b). 'Intervyu informatsionnomu agentstvu TASS,' Available at: http://kremlin.ru/news/47054 (Accessed 17 December 2014).

Putin, V. (2014c) 'Poslanie Prezidenta Federal'nomu Sobraniyu,' Available at: http://news.kremlin.ru/transcripts/47173 (Accessed 17 December 2014).

Seliktar, O. (2004) *Politics, paradigms, and intelligence failures : why so few predicted the collapse of the Soviet Union*. Armonk, N.Y: M.E. Sharpe.

Shearer, E. and Starr, F. (1996) 'Through a Prism Darkly,' *American Journalism Review*, 18(7), pp. 36-40.

22

Diversity Policy in Ukraine and Its Neighbours: Running on the Spot Again?

ALEXANDER OSIPOV
EUROPEAN CENTRE FOR MINORITY ISSUES

What role may 'diversity policies' in Ukraine and beyond play in further national developments? My major points here are that Ukraine and all three neighbouring post-Soviet countries are implementing basically the same model inherited from the communist past, that it turns to be viable in a long run, and in the long run it is likely to keep contributing to political stability.

Certainly, such a notion as 'diversity policy' in the sense of a coherent strategy and institutional setting is questionable. Nevertheless, one may conditionally regard 'state responses to ethnic diversity' or the 'totality of national policies aiming at the accommodation of ethnic heterogeneity' (Rechel, 2009, p. 8) as a single policy area deserving analysis as such, although it may be unpredictably broad and have no clear and fixed boundaries.

Macro-political differences between the post-Soviet countries also beg questioning cross-national comparisons as such. Indeed, Ukraine is a country with a pluralist electoral democracy, having opted for European integration and the respective reforms, and Moldova is similar; by contrast, Russia and Belarus are authoritarian systems. From another perspective, Ukraine at least symbolically positions itself as a 'nationalising state' (Brubaker, 1996) supposed to serve primarily the needs of its core ethnicity – the Ukrainians. On the contrary, Russia remains a 'multinational federation' and avoids explicit references to any founding ethno-nation; the latter (with some reservations) takes place also in Belarus.

One may agree, however, that most post-Soviet countries essentially still have a lot in common – they share such features as symbiosis of formal and informal institutions, and affiliation of businesses with governmental offices and respectively capturing of the state apparatus by private groups of interests (Ryabov, 2011). The commonalities are most striking in ethnic policies and their underpinning institutional settings (Biaspamiatnykh et al., 2014), and in this context, the legislation on minorities or nationalities issues and the existence of specialised executive bodies are not important as such. The special laws on minorities (such as in Ukraine, Belarus, and Moldova) or ethnicity-related issues are broad in scope, declarative, and contain vaguely defined provisions, while the special governmental bodies are powerless and serve merely as supervisory organs, coordinators of individual cultural programmes, and channels of communication between minority NGOs and the government. More important is the coherence in general principles, discursive and practical patterns demonstrated by public authorities and their civil society counterparts in the ways they frame and discursively reproduce ethnic heterogeneity in their countries.

In brief, the main features of the model appear as (1) reconciliation of conflicting claims through 'systemic hypocrisy' (Brunsson, 1989); (2) 'symbolic production' (Bourdeu, 1993, pp. 29-73) of social reality as a substitute for instrumental policies; and (3) co-optation, control, and marginalisation of potentially troublemaking public activists and activities through neo-patrimonial institutional settings. A significant feature of these policies is that they are a continuation of Soviet policy-making in the ethno-national sphere as it was formed in late 1980s prior to the USSR's breakdown.

It is already a common wisdom that ethno-nationalism was ideologically and institutionally embedded in the Soviet system of government. While the USSR was officially referred to as a non-ethnic or, more precisely, a supra-ethnic formation, its first-level constituent entities (union republics) and a number of second-tier building blocks (such as autonomous republics, provinces, and districts) were considered as ethnicity-based units (Martin, 2001; Slezkine, 1994). In symbolic and institutional sense, such recognitions generated certain problems: ethnic fundamentals of the Soviet republics and autonomies in combination with ethnic heterogeneity of their populaces by definition meant the emergence of first- and second-class citizens; the Soviet policies of social and cultural unification could not but be at odds with the institutionalisation of ethnicity. The solution found is an eclectic combination of different and contradictory statements; bracketing out and hushing up controversial issues; and systemic discrepancies between talks, decisions, and actions ('systemic hypocrisy', according to Brunsson (1989)).

One may say that these patterns are still reproducing themselves in official rhetoric and patterns of governance of most post-Soviet countries (Hughes and Sasse, 2002). Rhetoric and practices of 'nationalisation' in Ukraine and its post-Soviet neighbours as a rule are not coherent and consistent (Kulyk, 2001; Kuzio, 2001), and even in terms of symbolic representation, most of these countries are 'hybrid forms' combining the vocabularies of civic and ethnic nationalisms (Brubaker, 1996, p. 105). Practices are often at odds with declarations; the latter are obscure and open to interpretation, while the former are often pursued regardless of normative frameworks. The post-Soviet governments are sending mixed messages to their populaces, and all segments of their citizenry – those seeking affirmation of the new ethno-national profile of their countries and those who wish to maintain the Soviet ethno-linguistic status-quo – can find some discursive and organisational niches for themselves within the system. One can talk about an equilibrium between activities aiming at different constituencies (roughly speaking, pro-nationalist and pro-status-quo). This balance shifts over time and does not necessarily satisfy all the target audiences, but in general it has turned out to be workable.

The ethnic fundamentals of Ukraine are reflected in the 1996 Constitution and several pieces of legislation. The 'Ukrainian nation' is pointed out as the basis of the state as opposed to the 'Ukrainian people', in the meaning of the entire citizenry, but numerous constitutional and legal provisions on equality of all citizens serve as a counterbalance. Over the 23 years of independence, the Ukrainian population received contradictory messages from the government and the elites. Endless complaints of the last two decades about both 'Ukrainisation' and 'anti-national policies aiming at freezing the Soviet realities' can be easily grounded with empiric evidence taken from language, mass-media, educational, and cultural policies (see Malgin, 2005; Ryabcuk, 2011).

Notably, according to the Soviet tradition, languages are referred to in legislation and practical policies as attributes of ethnicities. The status of the Ukrainian language as the sole state language of Ukraine corresponds with the symbolic ethno-national underpinning of the Ukrainian state. In practice, the government and policy-makers cannot but recognise the realities – that Russian remains the lingua franca while clear boundaries between linguistic communities are lacking and language is decoupled from the ethnicity of its bearers. This generates a combination of official nationwide mono-lingualism with limited attempts to introduce it in practice, and with the de facto toleration of bi-lingualism in the public sphere (Kulyk, 2006; Bowring, 2014).

Ukraine is not unique, since numerous post-Soviet laws on languages lack clarity, and the status of languages remains not clearly defined. As a result, the authorities enjoy a great deal of flexibility in the implementation (or non-implementation) and further justifications of their activity and inactivity. The formula used before the Soviet Union's demise (state language plus Russian as the language of interethnic communication, plus optional protective treatment of individual minority languages), although transformed in different directions, has survived to date in Belarus, Moldova, and Ukraine. In fact, the law-makers symbolically strike a balance between speakers of different languages while practice is regulated by ad hoc political considerations and flexible informal rules.

Last but not least is that all potential dissident or protestant voices are, as a rule, incorporated into the system of government and stick to the agendas the governments impose. Discursively, as a rule, most ethnic activists have nothing against the very concept of ethno-national statehood; they as well as the government manifest their eagerness to prevent hate speech and ethnic conflicts, and they are against the 'politicisation of ethnicity' (and therefore ready to limit their activities to narrowly interpreted 'culture'). In institutional terms, ethnicity-based organisations opt for activities acceptable to the official authorities and performed in the framework proposed by official bodies (usually these are consultative bodies for minorities) or mainstream political parties. This phenomenon has little to do with direct administrative pressure; rather, it is an outcome of the general perception that private activities can be successful if and only if they are incorporated into governmental patronage.

Surprisingly enough, the Russian Federation demonstrates similar features. The Russian Constitution and legislation do not single out Russians as the founding ethno-nation; nevertheless, numerous official statements explicitly emphasise the leading role of ethnic Russians in the current polity, the national history, and international relations (the 'Russian World'), or the need to protect the 'disadvantaged' ethnic core of the state (Rutland, 2010, pp. 123-129). Besides, the entire discourse of the country's integrity and the need to secure equal rights of all citizens justifies centralisation and homogenising policies in all spheres of public life (Prina, 2011).

The Russian regional laws on languages adopted in the 1990s declared 'titular' languages as state languages of the republics on a par with Russian. In fact, the implementing mechanisms are lacking, and these laws play a symbolic role unless a regional government has the resources and political will to go further in their implementation in education and media. The latter is achieved again to a large extent through informal or nebulously formulated rules, or by discretion of the officials in charge (Zamyatin, 2014). Accordingly, ethnic activism acts as an agent of the state. This begs no questions in the current circumstances of authoritarian rule and militant nationalism, but in the 1990s, ethnic activists and leaders of the ethnic republics demonstrated the same mode of behaviour.

Was this model a result of some sophisticated planning? There is no evidence of this; rather, it looks like inertia of the Soviet period coupled with the lack of governmental resources either to introduce a complex system of power-sharing and positive action or to suppress groups not fitting into the ideal of homogeneous nation-state. A deep transformation of the linguistic and cultural characteristics of the society (either 'nationalisation' or further Russification) would bear risks and require unaffordable resources. Instead, the elites opted for symbolic production at the same time 'nationalising' and 'multi-national' statehoods rather than clear institutional changes. Different views on the historic past of the newly independent states (or sub-state units in Russia) and their desired ethno-cultural and linguistic profile in most cases cannot be reconciled discursively and institutionally; therefore, the elites have to stick to eclectic rhetoric and address different audiences with different and even incompatible messages. Besides, maintenance of the state apparatus as a device for the distribution of material and non-material benefits through the web of clienteles and patronage relations create incentives for people and organisations who can speak on behalf of non-dominant groups to become part of the system and follow the mainstream rules of the game and protocols of communication. In the cases of Russia and Belarus, one should bear in mind the repressive capacities of the governments.

Can one say that this development is a success story? The given model cannot be deemed ideal; in certain cases, it generated and perpetrated, rather than mitigated, tensions. For example, the 'nationalising' rhetoric of the Ukrainian authorities and cultural elites too often provoked negative reactions in the general public in predominantly Russian-speaking regions (Malgin, 2005), although barely had a really negative impact on people's daily lives. However, the 2014 crisis demonstrates that the threat to the country's stability and integrity came from the outside; a part of the popular opposition to the Ukrainian state played a significant role in some peripheral areas while the country at large withstood both the domestic unrest and the external intervention. In a broader scale, neither Russia nor Moldova and Belarus have demonstrated any clearly articulated and organised domestic opposition on ethno-national or linguistic grounds to the mainstream perspective, in part because the latter is too eclectic, and almost each of the potential majority and minority spokesperson can find his or her place within the established system.

Can one say that the 'revolution of dignity' and other recent changes in

Ukraine mean a cardinal shift in the country's diversity policies? An obvious change is the increased amount of official and non-official talks about the birth of 'political' or 'civic' nation in Ukraine. One can definitely agree that the second Maidan and the conflict with Russia have psychologically consolidated the population of Ukraine regardless of ethnicity, and the presidential and parliamentary elections demonstrate that the previous negative expectations of further deepening cleavages and/or electoral support to radical nationalists have not come true. Apparently, the previously hot topics such as language legislation and its implementation have been put aside. However, one should mention that the topic of 'civic' nation is not a new one for Ukraine; a similar rhetoric is in wide official use in Belarus and Russia. Civic nationalism can be interpreted in multiple ways and can be easily employed for the justification of homogenisation or marginalisation of minorities. Besides, it is often mechanically combined with talks or actions specific for ethnic nationalisms.

There are no guarantees that the further distancing of the Ukrainian political class and the general public from Russia may not lead to subsequent linguistic and cultural Ukrainisation, and then a new round of domestic tensions, and then a new search for balance. The post-Maidan legislative initiatives, such as the ones aimed at abandoning the 2012 law on language policies or at penalising the *Holodomor* denial, are in this vein. The official recognition of Crimean Tatars as an indigenous group in Crimea may be interpreted as a clear signal that the Ukrainian government will provide for the preferential treatment of the 'indigenous' population to the detriment of the 'non-indigenous'. In sum, this means that the mainstream eclectic ideological framework remains untouched; the contradictions will be resolved through balancing between different demands and preferences.

In terms of organisational settings, there is also no evidence that the legislative or executive branches will form new agencies, which would be capable of re-shaping and clarifying diversity policies. The mandate and competences of the commissioner on ethno-national affairs appointed in June 2014 are limited and vaguely defined, and the state is doing very little to establish new mechanisms for dialogue with minority organisations and experts. The perspectives for administrative decentralisation and the effects it may generate for diversity management are still far from being clear.

Ironically, similar questions and expectations apply to Ukraine's antipode – Russia. The rise of anti-Western and anti-Ukrainian sentiments has not affected so far the rhetoric of 'multinational people' and of the need to consolidate the Russian 'civic nation'. On the other hand, the talk about Russia's cultural plurality and the federal structure do not stop unification in education, language policies, and mass media, as well as the ambivalent relations of the government with radical Russian nationalists. The 'nationalities policy' remains in the domain of symbolic representations and is backed by a weak organisational underpinning. Ethnic spokespersons and organisations so far are incorporated into the stable system of communication with official authorities and demonstrate full loyalty.

In sum, 'diversity policy' in Ukraine, Russia, as well as Moldova and Belarus, bears basically the same features. The said policy is mainly about creating and disseminating a narrative about the country as a multi-ethnic collectivity with certain ethnic or cultural core and thus a hierarchy – explicit or implicit – of ethnicities and languages. To be conciliatory rather than conflict-generating, this narrative needs to be eclectic and thus to certain degree satisfactory to all segments of the population. Differences between 'civic' and 'ethnic' nationalism do not matter, because all top-down messages can be formulated and delivered either way. The system demonstrates flexibility in the sense that the emphasis is shifting over time because of the political context; it has survived through more than two decades of independence and can survive longer.

References

Biaspamiatnykh, M. et al. (2014) *Politika upravleniya ethnoculturanym raznoobraziem v Belarusi, Moldove i Ukraine* [Policies of Ethno-cultural Diversity Management in Belarus, Moldova and Ukraine]. Vilnius: EHU.

Bourdieu, P. (1993) *The Field of Cultural Production: Essays on Art and Literature*. London: Polity Press.

Bowring, B. (2014) 'The Russian language in Ukraine: complicit in genocide, or victim of state-building?' in Ryazanova-Clarke, L. (ed.) *The Russian Language Outside the Nation. Speakers and Identities.* Edinburgh: Edinburgh University Press, pp. 56-78.

Brubaker, R. (1996) *Nationalism Reframed. Nationhood and the National Question in the New Europe*. Cambridge: Cambridge University Press.

Brunsson, N. (1989) *The Organization of Hypocrisy. Talk, decisions and actions in organizations*. Chinchester, New York: John Wiley & Sons.

Hughes, J. and Sasse, G. (2002) 'Conflict and accommodation in the former Soviet Union: the role of institutions and regimes,' in: Hughes, J. and Sasse, G. (eds) *Ethnicity and Territory in the Former Soviet Union: Regions in Conflict*. London: Frank Cass, pp. 220-240.

Kulyk, V. (2006) 'Constructing common sense: Language and ethnicity in Ukrainian public discourse,' *Ethnic and Racial Studies*, 29 (2), pp. 281-314.

Kulyk, V. (2001) 'The Politics of Ethnicity in Post-Soviet Ukraine: Beyond Brubaker,' *Journal of Ukrainian Studies*, 26 (1-2), pp. 197-221.

Kuzio, T. (2001) 'Nationalising states' or nation-building: a critical review of the theoretical literature and empirical evidence,' *Nations and Nationalism*, 7(2), pp. 135-154.

Malgin, A.V. (2005) *Ukraina. Sobornost i Regionalism* [Ukraine. Sobornost and regionalism]. Simferopol: Sonata.

Martin, T. (2001) *The Affirmative Action Empire: Nations and Nationalism in the Soviet Union, 1923-1939*. Ithaca, New York: Cornell University Press.

Prina, F. (2011) 'Homogenisation and the 'New Russian Citizen': A Road to Stability or Ethnic Tension?,' *Journal on Ethnopolitics and Minority Issues in Europe,* 10(1), pp. 59-93.

Rechel, B. (2009) 'Introduction' in: Rechel, B. (ed.) *Minority Rights in Central and Eastern Europe*. London: Routledge, pp. 3-16.

Rutland, P. (2010) 'The Presence of Absence: Ethnicity Policy in Russia' in: Newton, J. and Tompson, W. (eds) *Institutions, Ideas and Leadership in Russian Politics*. Basingstoke: Palgrave Macmillan, pp. 116-136.

Ryabchuk, M. (2011) *Postkolonialny syndrom. Sposterezhennia* [Post-colonial syndrome. Observations]. Kyiv: "K.I.S."

Ryabov, A. (2011) *No Institutions. In: 20 Years Without the Berlin Wall: a Breakthrough to Freedom*. Moscow: Carnegie Moscow Center, pp. 14-20.

Slezkine, Y. (1994) 'The USSR as a Communal Apartment, or How a Socialist State Promoted Ethnic Particularism,' *Slavic Review*, 53(2), pp. 414-452.

Zamyatin, K. (2014) *An Official Status for Minority Languages? A Study of State Languages in Russia's Finno-Ugric Republics.* Helsinki: University of Helsinki.

Conclusion

Monism vs. Pluralism

RICHARD SAKWA
UNIVERSITY OF KENT

The focus of this collection has been on the dynamics of developments in Ukraine in the context of Russo-Ukrainian relations, with analysis of internal developments in both countries. A number of intersecting crises have been identified, each of which exacerbates the others while their interactions only intensify the contradictions that provoked the crises in the first place. The first crisis is the one within Ukraine itself, which can be identified as the *Ukrainian* crisis, while the second is the extreme turbulence in international affairs and in particular in the system of European security, which is conventionally labelled the *Ukraine* crisis. This is accompanied by a potential crisis in the Russian developmental model, exacerbated by events in Ukraine since late 2013 and the new era of contentious politics. These three crises feed on each other, but each has distinctive roots. Clearly, there can be no sustainable solution to the challenges of Ukrainian and Russian national development unless the broader crisis in international affairs is also resolved. However, at present there is little prospect of the latter, hence the former are likely to continue for some time.

European Monism

The articles presented in this collection clearly indicate a crisis in European development. The Ukraine crisis demonstrated the triumph of a monist vision of Europe, one in which the European Union (EU) would be the main representative of what it means to be European in the context of the Euro-Atlantic alliance system. On the other side, although the Russian power system is profoundly monistic, in terms of European politics as a whole, the country stands for pluralism in the international system. This paradox is not yet reconciled, and endows the whole subject of study with numerous false windows and contradictory perceptions. The crisis is precisely a struggle over who will get to decide the fate of Europe, accompanied by rhetorical, discursive, and practical struggles over the national and political identity of Russia and Ukraine.

As far as Europe is concerned, two models are on offer, although with different inflections they do not necessarily have to be in conflict. Since the end of the Cold War, the idea of *Wider Europe* has become the predominant one in the West. This is the project of a continent centred on the EU, with European space represented as Brussels-focused, with concentric rings emanating from the centre, although with weakening force as they reach the periphery. The six founding members of the European Economic Community created in 1957 have now been joined to encompass 28 members, with the latest entrants coming from the former communist part of the continent. The Central and East European countries sought liberal democracy, market reform, and, above all, the 'return to Europe', and this has been achieved with significant results. A remarkable public consensus prevailed in these countries, and in an astonishingly short period they joined the expanded Atlantic community. This was an exemplary manifestation of the 'Wider Europe' model of development, and it has undoubtedly delivered substantial (although not always uncontested) benefits to the countries concerned.

It is these benefits that Georgia, Moldova, and Ukraine now seek, although in these contested 'lands in between' there is no longer the same coincidence of domestic aspirations and geopolitical orientations. The 'European choice' is, paradoxically, precisely not European – it is Atlanticist, which is not the same thing at all. Atlanticism entails a combination of the EU's focus on normative, developmental, and governance issues with the hard security concerns of the NATO alliance and issues of Washington's leadership. Thus, the 'European choice' has lost much of its European character, and as far as Russia is concerned, has become far more contentious.

It is no accident that the Ukraine crisis was precipitated by the Association Agreement with the EU. Although negotiations had begun in 2007, before the Eastern Partnership had taken shape (EaP was formally launched in May 2009), the confrontation over the AA and its associated Deep and Comprehensive Free Trade Agreement (DCFTA) ultimately represented a spectacular failure to establish a framework for inter-regional cooperation and engagement. This is very different from what had taken place in other spheres. Agreements with North African countries and much of Central Europe effectively took place in a regional vacuum. No one questioned the right of Poland and the Czech Republic, or even Slovenia and Croatia, to achieve their 'return to Europe', especially since in most of these countries there was a demonstrable popular consensus in favour. There was no such consensus in Ukraine, and despite the virulence of the monist Ukrainian nationalist assertions in favour of the 'European choice', a significant part of the population sought to retain historic links with Russia. The issue here is not Ukraine's sovereign choice to decide, but recognition that, when it came to the EU, and even more over NATO membership aspirations, society was divided. Equally, the issue is not so much the mere fact of the EU advancing to the East, but the now recognised failure to negotiate the terms of this advance into what is obviously a contested neighbourhood. Several articles in this collection give details of these divisions and different views on integration.

This is where the second model of European development becomes operative. The idea of a *Greater Europe* has long been advanced as the framework to overcome the division of the continent. One of the most eloquent and resonant visions of such a Europe was the one outlined by Mikhail Gorbachev, in the final period of the Soviet Union. Gorbachev issued the manifesto for this model of Europe when he spoke of the Common European Home in his speech to the Council of Europe in Strasbourg on 6 July 1989. He outlined a vision of a Europe comprising different social systems (Soviet socialism still existed), but united through respect for sovereignty and political pluralism (Gorbachev, 1989). This would be a continent united in its diversity, since when Gorbachev first advanced the concept he believed that the Soviet Union would develop on the basis of a 'humane, democratic socialism'. Instead of concentric rings emanating from Brussels, weakening at the edges but nevertheless focusing on a single centre, the idea of Greater Europe posits a multipolar vision of Europe, with more than one centre and without a single ideological flavour. Gorbachev's dream of a 'Common European Home' transcending the bloc politics of the Cold War era has resonance to this day, and has recently been the subject of a major study by the Institute of Europe in Moscow (Gromyko (ed.) 2014).

For the partisans of the wider European agenda, however, Russia's advocacy of a greater European agenda taints the whole idea. Even though Gaullist ideas of a broader common European space from the Atlantic to the Pacific have often been addressed, notably in Nicholas Sarkozy's idea of pan-Europa (Sarkozy, 2009), it is Russia which is identified with the greater European project. Among the Greater Europe plans was the idea of a new European Security Treaty, mooted by Medvedev in a speech in Berlin on 5 June 2008, which called for the creation of a genuinely inclusive new security system to ensure that new dividing lines were not drawn across the continent. The initiative was greeted with polite contempt by the Western powers, although the 'Corfu process' was established to assess the proposal. In keeping with his original strong European leanings, in a speech in Berlin on 26 November 2010, Putin called for the geopolitical unification of all of 'Greater Europe' from Lisbon to Vladivostok to create a genuine 'strategic partnership (Putin, 2010). As late as January 2014 in Brussels, in what turned out to be the last routine EU-Russia summit, Putin once again referred to the idea of creating a free-trade zone from the Atlantic to the Pacific (Putin, 2014).

The greater European agenda has failed to gain traction, and is now considered as little more than an attempt by Russia to drive a wedge between the two wings of the Atlantic alliance, the EU and the US. In other words, a monist vision of European security identity prevails, and alternative models of European architecture delegitimised. My fundamental argument in this chapter is that this European monism not only found a ready reception among Ukrainians, but in fact helped sustain a narrow vision of European national identity. Equally, it has only reinforced the monism of the Russian political order, lacking a benign geopolitical environment to advance a more pluralistic domestic managerial system.

Ukraine between Monism and Pluralism

Narrow representations of Europe found natural allies among the monist nationalists in Ukraine, provoking the greatest threat to European peace since 1945. This is not the place for an extended analysis of the tensions within the Ukrainian state-building project since 1991, nor for a full discussion of the events since 2013 (for a more detailed analysis, see Sakwa 2015, from which this article draws). However, for the purposes of the broader argument, it is necessary to outline the monism within Ukraine that is the counterpart of the monism that has become predominant in Atlantic Europe. Although it is now customary to laud the 'pro-European' choice of the Ukrainian electorate evidenced in the May 2014 presidential and the October 2014 parliamentary elections, the tensions between contrasting Ukrainian state-building models have not disappeared (as several chapters in this collection demonstrate), and will undoubtedly resurface to poison European international relations in years to come.

On the one hand, there is the 'Ukrainising' position that posits a monist vision of the Ukrainian nation, stretching back to the historical break with the Kievan tradition wrought by the Mongol invasions from the thirteenth century. This is the view that instead of a single East Slavic community, the Ukrainian nation evolved separately from its Russian and Belarusian confrères. In the post-communist era, this monism is reinforced by post-colonial ideas about the need to extirpate the baleful consequences of Russian imperial domination. From this perspective, it is quite unacceptable to grant Russian equality as a state language, since this would occlude the natural pre-eminence of the Ukrainian language and inhibit hegemonic interpretations of Ukrainian traditions. Thus, the heart of this model of state building is separation from Russia politically, and intense efforts to build up an alternative cultural foundation to the polity. Any engagement with Russia from this perspective was contingent and forced, until the country could achieve its 'natural' orientation to Europe. It is this monist version that is now supported uncritically by the partisans of wider Europe and the Atlantic powers in general, even though its 'restitutive' assumptions (that there is some primordial Ukrainian nationhood that needs to be recovered and purged of unnatural accretions) are inevitably challenged by other narratives.

On the other hand, the more pluralistic reading of Ukrainian history is advanced by parts of the Russophone population, and endorsed by Vladimir Putin and a large part of the Russian elite. This is the view that Ukraine is a fundamentally pluralistic community, not in the multicultural sense of adapting to the arrival of different nations, but in the fundamental sense that the country, like Russia, is pluricultural, comprising a number of autochthonous communities. Thus, Valentin Yakushik (2005) argues that Ukraine is bicivilisational, with Ukrainians and Russians as co-equals in the state, together with a rich variety of other peoples, notably Ruthenians, Gagauze, Hungarians, Jews, Romanians, and Crimean Tatars. Nicolai Petro in this collection refers to the Russophone population as 'the Other Ukraine', and stresses that the current tension goes back generations. Mikhail Pogrebinskii and his colleagues have explored the features of Ukraine's inherent pluralism (see, in particular, Pogrebinskii et al. and Kiryukhin in Pogrebinskii and Tolpygo (eds), 2013). From this perspective, it is the failure to give constitutional expression to this pluralism that provoked the crisis of 2014.

The debate focuses on who has the right to decide what it means to be Ukrainian. Both monists and pluralists united in the early stages of the 'revolution of dignity' from November 2013 in their condemnation of the corruption and degradation of Viktor Yanukovych's presidency, but they differed in the model of the Ukrainian state that they wished to see emerge from the crisis. The restitutive model, when applied in Estonia and Latvia, provoked endless tensions which are still not resolved, despite the two countries being members of the EU, but when applied in Ukraine, it has deeply polarising consequences. Numerous surveys demonstrated that secessionism hardly figured in the early ambitions of the pluralists, yet with the victory of a particularly narrow and aggressive form of monist nationalism in the February Revolution of 2014, it is hardly surprising that there was a counter-mobilisation in favour of pluralism and insistence that the 'other Ukraine' was a legitimate partner in rebuilding the Ukrainian state. Instead, this voice is now harried and persecuted.

The Ukraine Crisis: Geopolitics at Home and Abroad

The divisions within Ukrainian state building have now become internationalised. On the one side, the Atlantic community has lined up with the Ukrainian monists, while Russia supports the pluralists. Even though the idea of 'federalisation' within Ukraine elicits a sharply negative reaction among the Ukrainian monists, the necessity of some sort of substantive decentralisation of authority and responsibility to the regions commands a great deal of support. Just as the idea of greater Europe is tainted by its association with Russia, so too is the idea of Ukrainian federalism, for the same reason. Elements of the European bipolarity of the Cold War years has been restored, with Russia now once again ranged against the rest, although now lacking the bloc of allegedly friendly states in Eastern Europe. This in part helps explain why Russia has been so keen to recreate the functional substitute for the old Comecon states in the form of the Eurasian Economic Union.

The Ukraine crisis is ultimately only a symptom of a much deeper failure to establish an equitable and inclusive post-Cold War international order. In the absence of peace conference, an asymmetrical peace was imposed in Europe. Both NATO and the EU expended considerable effort to mitigate Russia's alienation. Russia joined NATO's Partnership for Peace (PfP) in 1994; in 1997, the Founding Act on Mutual Relations, Co-operation and Security was signed, which created a NATO-Russia Permanent Joint Council (PJC); and in 2002, a new NATO-Russia Council (NRC) with greater authority replaced the PJC. However, regular political and military dialogue between the partners at times of crisis, as in 2008 during the Russo-Georgian war, were suspended, only highlighting that these bodies were indeed mitigatory rather than substantive. From the Atlanticist point of view, this was only natural: Russia was only half the former Soviet Union, and in certain respects a failed economy and polity, so why should it be treated as an equal in geopolitical terms? At the same time, it was only natural that the perceived security vacuum in Central and Eastern Europe should be filled by a defensive alliance, which, by reducing insecurity and risks, would in the end enhance even Russia's security.

In the early years of his leadership, Putin was ready to accept these arguments, and worked hard to improve relations with both the EU and NATO, although he, no less than Boris Yeltsin, insisted on Russia's great power status. The puzzle to be explained, then, is why relations with both organisations deteriorated so spectacularly, to the point that today outright military conflict is not to be excluded. All sides undoubtedly bear their share of responsibility, but ultimately it was the failure to grasp the realities of the new geopolitics of Europe and the failure to imagine a different future for Europe that has created the new dividing lines.

In the end, NATO's existence became justified by the need to manage the security threats provoked by its own enlargement. At the Bucharest NATO

Summit in April 2008, Georgia and Ukraine were promised eventual membership, although Membership Action Plans (MAPs) were deferred because of German and French concerns that moving to Russia's borders and encircling the country could provoke a dangerous reaction. From Russia's perspective, there was no security vacuum that needed to be filled; from the West's perspective, who was to deny the 'sovereign choice' of the Central and Eastern European states if they wished to enter the world's most successful multilateral security body. The former Warsaw Pact and Baltic states joined NATO to enhance their security, but the very act of doing so created a security dilemma for Russia that undermined the security of all. This fateful geopolitical paradox – that NATO exists to manage the risks created by its existence – provoked a number of conflicts. The Russo-Georgian War of August 2008 acted as the forewarning tremor for the major earthquake that engulfed Europe over Ukraine in 2013-14.

Russia, Ukraine, and the Breakdown of European Order

One of the main narratives of the current crisis is that Russia has become a revisionist state. The takeover of Crimea in March 2014 can certainly be interpreted in this light (for example, Allison, 2014). However, the Putinite view is that Russia's actions were a response to the prior breakdown of the system of international law (notably in Western intervention in Iraq and recognition of Kosovo's independence in 2008), and then the breakdown of the Ukrainian state order. The associated debates are well covered in this collection. The key point is that the Ukraine crisis is both a symptom and the cause of the crisis in international politics. It is also an indication of the inability to establish what would pass for 'normal' relations between Russia and Ukraine in the post-Cold War period. Indeed, relations between the former Soviet republics throughout the Eurasian region are characterised by distrust and the failure to establish a genuinely new post-Soviet community based on sovereign equality and shared security institutions.

The Ukraine crisis and the drastic breakdown in relations between Russia and Ukraine are thus, in the old Marxist parlance, 'over-determined'. By this I mean that there are a multiplicity of causes, any one of which may well have been sufficient to provoke a crisis, but taken together a veritable 'perfect storm' has engulfed the two countries and Europe as a whole. It may be useful to summarise these factors, although no attempt will be made to examine them in depth here. I will start from the general and then move to the specific, recognising that each issue is highly controversial. Nevertheless, for clarification of the fundamental issues at stake, such an exercise is useful.

Above all, it is now clear that no effective system of European security and political order was established in the post-Cold War era. It is not helpful to look for people to blame for this lamentable state of affairs, but instead we should look to the structural causes. Undoubtedly, Putin has now challenged the established system, but it should be remembered that he came to power as one of the most committed Europeans that Russia has ever had as a leader. For a variety of reasons, his attempts to achieve the integration of Russia into European and Euro-Atlantic structures failed, and instead he became increasingly alienated from these institutions. Russia as always was facing fundamental domestic problems, including the second Chechen war, regional fragmentation, and much else. His responses were typically robust, and in many cases accompanied by egregious human rights violations, but overall they were legitimate, although perhaps disproportionate, responses to real challenges, and were recognised as such by the Russian population, as reflected in consistently high opinion poll ratings. These were not simply manufactured through media manipulation (although there was plenty of that as well), but reflected a deep current of popular support for his policies and achievements, which included until recently a spectacular rise in living standards.

Thus, the common trope of arguing that Putin's lack of connection with reality is to blame for the current crisis results too often in scapegoating, and excuses a more fundamental failure to examine the structural roots of the crisis. These lie in the asymmetrical end of the Cold War and the failure to create an inclusive and equitable system of European security, and this in turn arose from the inability to accept Russia as it is – a great power with legitimate interests in Europe and Eurasia, although accompanied by some profound governance problems. Recognition of this, of course, does not entail a repudiation of values or the occlusion of the sovereignty of neighbours, but it does suggest that a more realist and less ideological approach would have established an environment in which differences could have been resolved through dialogue and diplomacy. Instead, now the very notion of dialogue is discredited, while the practices of diplomacy have degenerated into name-calling and sanctions. All the European and Atlantic powers bear their share of responsibility for this.

Further, the breakdown in Russo-Ukrainian relations has long been in the making. On the one side, the consolidation of a distinctive type of Russian political economy and public sphere became increasingly incognisant of the interests and concerns of neighbours. In other words, the Russian power system itself in the Putin years moved away from the riotous, and in many ways damaging, pluralism of the Yeltsin years in the 1990s towards a far more monist system. There remains significant freedom of debate in the public sphere, but the political expression of pluralism is tightly controlled. In addition, it would be inaccurate to describe the Putin system as 'nationalist' in the classic sense, since Russia remains a deeply pluricultural society, in ethnic, religious, and indeed in political cultural terms, and any attempt excessively to privilege one community over the others would threaten the stability of the whole. This is why the Putin system has tried to remain so resolutely 'centrist', drawing on the power of all factions and communities, but not allowing any to predominate. Nevertheless, reflecting the alienation from the existing international order and the political struggles of the period of contentious politics in 2011-12 accompanying Putin's return to the presidency, the regime has become somewhat radicalised. This is a radical centrism that is ready to challenge the hegemonic powers abroad, to reshape the political relationships in Eurasia and Europe, and to advance a revivalist conservatism at home (Sakwa, 2014).

At the same time, the Ukrainian national project also became radicalised, as reflected in several of our contributions. Already, the Orange Revolution of Autumn 2004 had propelled a radical nationalist to power, and although the administration of Viktor Yushchenko was torn by factional conflicts with others from the Orange camp, notably Yulia Tymoshenko, his leadership represented a breakout from Kuchma-style multivectorism. The repressive and abusive presidency of Yanukovych served further to radicalise not only the Ukrainising tendency, but this was now complemented by the strengthening of the militant radicalism of the inter-war and wartime years. This was accompanied by a renewed emphasis on the 'European choice'. The Association Agreement offered by the EU in the framework of the Eastern Partnership proposed a lifeline to break out from the corruption and economic degradation in which Ukraine had been mired for so long. The original idealism of the Maidan protests was based on the profound repudiation of the failures of the past, but its idealism was not rooted in a substantive real political constituency. It was not able to sustain a political formation that could institutionalise its idealism. Instead, the protest movement became radicalised, and in conditions of external threat, it took extreme Ukrainian nationalist forms that was then instantiated in the power system created in the presidential and parliamentary elections of 2014. In short, the Ukrainian polity assumed extreme monist forms. This monism, as noted above, is reinforced by the monism of the Euro-Atlantic system.

How to escape from this cycle of intensifying monism, which has created a situation where a full-scale war in Europe is no longer inconceivable? The refusal of the Kiev authorities to negotiate, let alone recognise, the insurgent forces in the Donbass leaves only the military solution in play. The EU and the Atlantic community have failed to provide a framework for a negotiated settlement, although the brave and important work of certain institutions, above all the OSCE and the UN, should be recognised. The anti-Russian monism of the US Congress has long been acknowledged as a problem

(Tsygankov, 2009), and this certainly does not create a benign environment for a settlement of European problems. As for Russia, it is obvious that the Putin administration cannot abandon the insurgents. This would be considered a betrayal that would resonate down the ages. Russia was reluctantly drawn into the Donbass conflict, reflected in Putin's pleas not to stage the 11 May 2014 referendums in Donetsk and Lugansk, but it cannot now abandon the 'separatists' (although initially it was not separation from Ukraine that was sought, but only a more pluralistic form of Ukrainian state-building). The stalemate is complete. Only after the intensification of the multiple crises will the fever break, and the healing process begin – if there is anyone left to do the healing.

References

Allison, R (2014) 'Russian "Deniable" Intervention in Ukraine: How and Why Russia Broke the Rules', *International Affairs*, 90(6), pp. 1255-1297.

Gorbachev, M. (1989) '"Europe as a Common Home," Address given by Mikhail Gorbachev to the Council of Europe, Strasbourg, 6 July. Available at: http://polsci.colorado.edu/sites/default/files/1A_Gorbachev.pdf.

Gromyko, A. (ed.) (2014), *Bol'shaya Evropa*. Moscow: Institute of Europe.

Kiryukhin, D. (2013) 'Multikul'turalizm, natzionalizm i identichnost': Ukrainskii kontekst', in Pogrebinskii, M. B. and Tolpygo, A. K. (eds) *Krizis multikul'turalizma i problemy natsional'noi politiki*. Moscow: Ves' Mir, pp. 195-218.

Pogrebinskii, M., Popov, A. and Tolpygo, A. (2013) 'Formirovanie polikul'turnoi Ukrainy: Istoricheskii ocherk i sovremmenoe sostoyanie', in Pogrebinskii, M. B. and Tolpygo, A. K. (eds) *Krizis multikul'turalizma i problemy natsional'noi politiki*. Moscow: Ves' Mir, pp. 237-281.

Putin, V. (2010) Speech delivered to the Fourth Berlin Economic Leadership meeting, 'Von Lissabon bis Wladiwostok. Handelspakt zwischen Russland und Europa: Moskau will als Lehre aus der größten Krise der Weltwirtschaft seit acht Jahrzehnten wesentlich enger mit der Europäischen Union zusammenarbeiten', *Süddeutsche Zeitung,* 25 November 2010. Available at: www.sueddeutsche.de.

Putin, V. (2014) 'Russia-EU Summit', 28 January 2014. Available at: http://eng.kremlin.ru/transcripts/6575.

Sakwa, R. (2015) *Frontline Ukraine: Crisis in the Borderlands*. London: I. B. Tauris.

Sakwa, R. (2014). *Putin Redux: Power and Contradiction in Contemporary Russia*. London & New York: Routledge.

Sarkozy, N. (2009), 'Discours de M. le Président de la République', Nîmes, 5 May. Available at : http://www.elysee.fr/.

Tsygankov, A. P. (2009) *Russophobia: Anti-Russian Lobby and American Foreign Policy*. Basingstoke: Palgrave Macmillan.

Yakushik, V. (2005), 'Revolyutsiya, no ne oranzhevaya', *Den'*, No. 232, 15 December. Available at : http://www.day.kiev.ua/154501/.

Contributors

Edwin Bacon is Reader in Comparative Politics at Birkbeck, the University of London. He has published widely on Russian affairs, including books on the domestic politics of Putin (*Securitising Russia*, 2006), the Brezhnev years (*Brezhnev Reconsidered*, 2002), and forced labour in the Stalin era (*The Gulag at War*, 1994). He is also the author of *Contemporary Russia* (Palgrave, 2014), now in its third edition. He has served as a Specialist Adviser to the House of Common's Foreign Affairs Select Committee, and as a Senior Research Officer in the Foreign and Commonwealth Office. He has advised the Finnish parliament's Committee for the Future, and in Autumn 2014 was a Visiting Fellow at the Aleksanteri Institute, University of Helsinki.

Paul Chaisty is the University Lecturer in Russian Government and Director of the Russian and Eurasian Studies Centre at St. Antony's College, Oxford University. His publications include *Legislative Politics and Economic Power in Russia* (Palgrave, Basingstoke, 2006), as well as articles in journals such as *Europe-Asia Studies*, *Government and Opposition*, *The Journal of Legislative Studies*, *Legislative Studies Quarterly*, *Party Politics*, and *Post-Soviet Affairs*. Together with Stephen Whitefield, he is currently involved in research project titled 'Nationalism and State-Building at a Crucial Turning Point: Democracy, Authoritarianism and Political Mobilisation in Ukraine and Russia.' He is also writing a book which explores the phenomenon of coalitional presidentialism in the former Soviet Union, Africa and Latin America.

Elena Chebankova is a Senior Lecturer in Politics and International Relations at the University of Lincoln. She is the author of *Russia's Federal Relations: Putin's Reforms and Management of the Regions and Civil Society in Putin's Russia*. She is currently researching ideological landscape in contemporary Russia. She holds a PhD in Social and Political Sciences from King's College, Cambridge. She has previously held Research Fellowships at Wolfson College Cambridge and Linacre College, Oxford.

Richard Connolly is Senior Lecturer in Political Economy and Co-Director of the Centre for Russian, Eurasian and European Studies, University of Birmingham. He is also Visiting Professor on the Master of Global Public Policy program at the Russian Presidential Academy of National Economy and Public Administration. His research and teaching on the political economy of Russia focuses on industrial development and structural transformation, economic policy, trade and investment, and Russia's role in the wider global economy. He is the author of *Economic Structure and Social Order Development in Post-Socialist Eastern Europe* (Routledge, 2012) and a number of journal articles. He is currently working on a book exploring the relationship between Russia's role in the global economy and its system of domestic political economy.

Paul D'Anieri is Professor of Political Science, Provost and Executive Vice Chancellor at the University of California Riverside. His research focuses on Ukraine, Ukrainian-Russian relations, and hybrid regimes. His current work examines the global competition to define domestic and international standards of legitimacy. His most recent book is *The Contest for Social Mobilization in Ukraine* (Johns Hopkins University Press, 2009). He is also author of a textbook, *International Politics: Power and Purpose in Global Affairs*, currently in its third edition. His earlier books include *Economic Interdependence in Ukrainian-Russian Relations* (SUNY, 1999) and *Understanding Ukrainian Politics: Power, Politics, and Institutional Design* (M.E. Sharpe, 2007).

Marta Dyczok is Associate Professor at the Departments of History and Political Science, Western University, Fellow at the University of Toronto's Centre for European, Russian, and Eurasian Studies (CERES), Munk School of Global Affairs, Adjunct Professor at the National University of the Kyiv Mohyla Academy. She was a Shklar Research Fellow at the Harvard Ukrainian Research Institute (2011) and a Fellow at the Woodrow Wilson Center for International Scholars in Washington DC (2005-2006). She has published three books: *Media, Democracy and Freedom. The Post Communist Experience* (co-edited with Oxana Gaman-Golutvina, 2009), *The Grand Alliance and Ukrainian Refugees* (2000), and *Ukraine: Change Without Movement, Movement Without Change* (2000). Her doctorate is from Oxford University and she researches media, memory, migration, and history.

Mark Galeotti is Professor of Global Affairs at New York University's Center for Global Affairs. A specialist in modern Russian crime, intelligence, and security affairs, he was educated at Cambridge and the London School of Economics, has served as a special advisor to the British Foreign Office, and consults widely with commercial and government bodies around the world. He has 14 books to his name, the most recent being *Russia's Wars in Chechnya, 1994-2008* (Osprey, 2014), and is completing a history of Russian organised crime.

Stephen Hutchings is Professor of Russian Studies and Director of Research in the School of Arts, Languages and Cultures, University of Manchester. He is a Fellow of the Academy of Social Sciences. He arrived at the University of Manchester in 2006, having worked previously at the University of Surrey, and the University of Rochester, New York. He has published five monographs and five edited volumes on various aspects of contemporary Russian literary, film, and media studies with major publishers including Cambridge University Press, Routledge, and Palgrave. His most recent books include *Islam, Security and Television News* (co-authored with Christopher Flood et al; London: Palgrave 2012), and *Television and Culture in Putin's Russia* (co-authored with Natalia Rulyova; Abingdon: Routledge, 2009). He has held five large research grants with the Arts and Humanities Research Council since the year 2000. He was President of the British Association for Slavonic and East European Studies from 2010 to 2013 and is currently Associate Editor of the *Russian Journal of Communication*. He is a frequent contributor to the media, including Radio 4's *The Today Programme* and *BBC Breakfast*, and has advised BBC Monitoring and the Foreign and Commonwealth Office.

Ivan Katchanovski teaches at the School of Political Studies and the Department of Communication at the University of Ottawa. He was Visiting Scholar at the Davis Center for Russian and Eurasian Studies at Harvard University, Visiting Assistant Professor at the Department of Politics at the State University of New York at Potsdam, Post-Doctoral Fellow at the Department of Political Science at the University of Toronto, and Kluge Post-Doctoral Fellow at the Kluge Center at the Library of Congress. He is the author of *Cleft Countries: Regional Political Divisions and Cultures in Post-Soviet Ukraine and Moldova* and co-author of *Historical Dictionary of Ukraine* (2nd edition) and *The Paradox of American Unionism: Why Americans Like Unions More Than Canadians Do, But Join Much Less*.

Denys Kiryukhin is a research scholar at the Skovoroda's Institute of Philosophy, The National Academy of Sciences of Ukraine. His research focuses on theory of justice, social and political development of post-communist states, and history of philosophy. He is a co-author of *Ukraine without Kuchma* (Optima, 2007, in Russian) and *The Crises of Multiculturalism and Problems of National Politics* (Ves` mir, 2013, in Russian), and the author of *An Introduction to Hegel`s Philosophy of Religion: Philosophy as a Speculative Theology* (Parapan, 2007, in Ukrainian).

Taras Kuzio is a Research Associate at the Canadian Institute of Ukrainian Studies, University of Alberta, and a non-resident Fellow at the Center for Transatlantic Relations, School of Advanced International Studies (SAIS),

John Hopkins University. Previously, he was a Senior Visiting Fellow at the Slavic Research Center, Hokkaido University, Japan, and the School of Advanced International Studies, John Hopkins University; a Visiting Professor at the Institute for European, Russian and Eurasian Studies, Elliott School of International Affairs, George Washington University; and Senior Research Fellow in the Centre for Russian and East European Studies at the University of Birmingham, UK. He is the author and editor of fourteen books, including *Open Ukraine. Changing Course towards a European Future* (2011), *Democratic Revolution in Ukraine* (2011), *From Kuchmagate to Orange Revolution* (2009), *Theoretical and Comparative Perspectives on Nationalism* (2007), and *Ukraine-Crimea-Russia: Triangle of Conflict* (2007).

Marlene Laruelle is Research Professor of International Affairs at The Institute for European, Russian and Eurasian Studies (IERES), Elliott School of International Affairs, The George Washington University, Washington DC. She holds a PhD from the National Institute for Oriental Languages and Cultures in Paris. She has authored *Russian Eurasianism: An Ideology of Empire* (Johns Hopkins University Press, 2008), *In the Name of the Nation: Nationalism and Politics in Contemporary Russia* (Palgrave, 2009), and *Russia's Strategies in the Arctic and the Future of the Far North* (M.E. Sharpe, 2013). She currently works on Russia's identity politics and intellectual debates on national identity.

David R. Marples is Distinguished University Professor, Department of History & Classics, University of Alberta. He holds a PhD in Economic and Social History from the University of Sheffield (1985). At the University of Alberta, where he has been employed since 1991, he received a McCalla Professorship in 1998, the Faculty of Arts Prize for Full Professors in 1999, the J. Gordin Kaplan Award for Excellence in Research in 2003, a Killam Annual Professorship in 2005-06, and the University Cup, the university's highest honor, in 2008. He has held several major awards from the Social Sciences and Humanities Research Council of Canada (SSHRC), most recently for the topic 'History, Memory, and World War II in Belarus.' He is author of fifteen single-authored books and two edited books on topics ranging from 20th Century Russia, Stalinism, contemporary Belarus, contemporary Ukraine, and the Chernobyl disaster. His recent books include *Our Glorious Past: Lukashenka's Belarus and the Great Patriotic War* (Stuttgart: Ibidem Verlag, 2014), *Heroes and Villains: Creating National History in Contemporary Ukraine* (Budapest: Central European University Press, 2008), and *The Lukashenka Phenomenon* (Trondheim, 2007). He is also the co-editor of *Ukraine's Euromaidan: Analyses of a Civil Revolution* (Stuttgart: Ibidem Verlag, 2015).

Mikhail A. Molchanov is Professor of Political Science at St. Thomas University in Canada and foreign member of the National Academy of Pedagogical Sciences of Ukraine. His current research interests include Ukrainian-Russian relations, regionalism in Eurasia, and Russian foreign policy. He is co-editor and co-author of *The Ashgate Research Companion to Political Leadership* (Ashgate, 2009) and *Ukrainian Foreign and Security Policy: Theoretical and Comparative Perspectives* (Praeger, 2002). His *Political Culture and National Identity in Russian-Ukrainian Relations* (Texas A&M University Press, 2002) examines post-communist nationalism as a state-building resource strategically utilised by the elites. His articles have appeared in *Journal of European Integration*, *Nationalities Papers*, *Canadian Slavonic Papers*, *Perspectives on Global Development and Technology*, *Polis* (Russia), *Suchasnist* (Ukraine), and in other journals and books. Professor Molchanov's next book, *Eurasian Regionalisms and Russian Foreign Policy*, is to be published by Ashgate in 2015.

Olga Onuch is a Senior Lecturer in Politics at the University of Manchester and an Associate Fellow, at Nuffield College, at the University of Oxford. She specialises in the comparative study of protest politics and elections in democratising states in Latin American and Eastern Europe. Olga is an expert on protests and activism in Ukraine and is the principle investigator of the Ukrainian Protest Project and co-investigator of a 2014 NSF funded Ukrainian Electoral Survey (Henry Hale P-I). She is a member of the OSF-funded Strategic Advisory Group, tasked with advising the government and president of Ukraine. Her book *Mapping Mass Mobilizations* (2014) investigates mass-mobilisation in Ukraine and Argentina. Her research has also been highlighted on Al Jazeera English, BBC World Service, NPR, IBT and Radio Free Europe. Follow her on Twitter @oonuch.

Alexander Osipov is a Senior Research Associate of the European Centre for Minority Issues (Flensburg, Germany) from September 2010. He heads ECMI's Justice & Governance Cluster. Previously he was involved in a series of research and human rights advocacy projects related to some transnational minorities in the former Soviet Union and the issues of ethnic discrimination in the Russian Federation. Currently his research interests include ethnic and racial discrimination, non-territorial autonomy, and models of diversity policies. He is also researching post-communist transformation in Belarus, Ukraine, and Moldova. His publications include 'Non-territorial Autonomy and International Law' in *International Community Law Review* (2011), 13(4), 393-411, and 'Non-Territorial Autonomy as a Way to Frame Diversity Policies: The Case of Russia' in Ephraim Nimni, Alexander Osipov, David J. Smith (eds), *The Challenge of Non-Territorial Autonomy: Theory and Practice* (Peter Lang, Oxford and Bern, 2013), 133-148 (forthcoming).

Nicolai N. Petro is Professor of Political Science at the University of Rhode Island. He received his PhD in Foreign Affairs from the University of Virginia in 1984. During the collapse of the Soviet Union, he served as special assistant for policy in the US State Department. He is the author or editor of eight books and has written about Russia and Ukraine for many publications, including *The American Interest*, *Asia Times, Christian Science Monitor*, *The Nation*, *The National Interest*, and *The New York Times*. In 2013-2014, he was a Fulbright Research Scholar in Ukraine working on his latest book, *Blessed Is the Kingdom: The Orthodox Church and the Struggle for the Soul of Modern Russia*, which is under contract to Stanford University Press. His website is www.npetro.net.

Mikhail Pogrebinskiy is a political analyst and director of the Kiev Center of Political Research and Conflict Studies. His professional interests include analysis of the current political situation, formation of civil society institutions, Russian-Ukrainian relations, and election campaigns. At different times he was a deputy, member of Kiev city executive committee, and assistant to the deputy Chairman of the Verkhovna Rada of Ukraine. He also worked at the presidential administration. Since 1989, he has been taking part in election campaigns as a manager and adviser. A member of the Council of Experts on Internal Policy under the President, adviser to the Prime Minister (1998-2000), adviser to the Head of Presidential Administration (2002). Since 1993, he has been director of Kiev Center of Political Research and Conflict Study. In 2014, he issued a collection of his articles and publications titled *Political Adviser. Thoughts about Ukrainian Politics* (Folio). He is the co-author and editor of a number of books, including *The Orange Revolution* (Optima, 2004), *Ukraine without Kuchma* (Optima, 2007), *Russian Language in Ukraine* (HMPS, 2010), and *The Crises of Multiculturalism and Problems of National Politics* (Весь мир, 2013), among others.

Peter Rutland is a Professor of Government at Wesleyan University in Middletown, Connecticut. He holds a BA from Oxford and a Ph.D from the University of York. He is associate editor of *Russian Review* and editor-in-chief of *Nationalities Papers*, the journal of the Association for the Study of Nationalities. He blogs about nationalism at http://nationalismwatch.wordpress.com/. He is the author of *The Myth of the Plan* (1985) and *The Politics of Industrial Stagnation in the Soviet Union* (1991), and editor of *Business and State in Contemporary Russia* (2001). His current research topics include the state of R&D in Russia and the role of identity politics in the failure of democracy in Russia. His publications are available online at http://prutland.web.wesleyan.edu/research.htm. Recent publications include 'Petronation? Oil, gas and national identity in Russia,' *Post-Soviet Affairs* (2014); 'Explaining Pussy Riot,' *Nationalities Papers* (2014); and. 'Neoliberalism in Russia,'. *Review of International Political Economy* (2013).

Richard Sakwa is professor of Russian and European Politics at the University of Kent, an Associate Fellow of the Russia and Eurasia programme at Chatham House, and a Fellow of the Academy of Social Sciences. His main research interests are Russian domestic and international politics, European international relations, and comparative democratization. Recent books include *The Crisis of Russian Democracy: The Dual State, Factionalism, and the Medvedev Succession* (Cambridge University Press, 2011), *Putin and the Oligarch: The Khodorkovsky-Yukos Affair* (I. B. Tauris, 2014), *Putin Redux: Power and Contradiction in Contemporary Russia* (Routledge, 2014), and *Frontline Ukraine: Crisis in the Borderlands* (I. B. Tauris, 2015). He can be contacted at: R.Sakwa@kent.ac.uk.

Joanna Szostek is a postdoctoral fellow at the UCL School of Slavonic and East European Studies (SSEES). She received a DPhil in Politics from the University of Oxford in 2013. Her doctoral research shed light on the factors which shape news coverage of Russia in Ukraine and Belarus – this work has been published in *East European Politics and Societies* and is under review with other journals. For her postdoctoral project, she is investigating the reception of anti-Western narratives among university students in Moscow. Broadly speaking, her research interests centre on the role of the mass media in relations between states, with a particular focus on the post-Soviet region. Before entering academia, Joanna worked for several years as a senior monitoring journalist for the BBC.

Greta Uehling received her PhD in Cultural Anthropology from the University of Michigan, Ann Arbor in 2000. Her dissertation was based on ethnographic fieldwork carried out in Crimea beginning in 1995, and won a Distinguished Dissertation Award from the Michigan Society of Fellows. In 2004, she held a post-doctoral fellowship with the Solomon Asch Center for the Study of Ethnopolitical Conflict at the University of Pennsylvania. Her first book, *Beyond Memory: The Deportation and Return of the Crimean Tatars*, was published in 2004. She has worked with several international organizations on the issues confronting Crimea and Ukraine, including the United Nations High Commissioner for Refugees, the Organization for Security and Cooperation in Europe, and the UN High Commissioner for National Minorities. She currently teaches in the Programme on International and Comparative Studies at the University of Michigan. Most recently, she was awarded a Fulbright research grant.

Edward W. Walker is Associate Adjunct Professor in the Department of Political Science and Executive Director of the Berkeley Program in Eurasian and East European Studies at the University of California, Berkeley. His book *Dissolution: Sovereignty and the Breakup of the Soviet Union* (Rowman &

Littlefield, 2003) explains the breakup of the Soviet Union into fifteen successor states, emphasising the role of the institutions and the mythologies of Soviet federalism and nationality policy. He is also the editor of a posthumous volume of writings by Mark Saroyan, *Minorities, Mullahs, and Modernity: Reshaping Community in the Former Soviet Union* (1997), and he has written and taught on communist systems and post-communist politics, nationalism, ethno-politics, and ethnic conflict in the former Soviet Union; problems of federalism, secession, and nationalism; religion and the state; frozen conflicts in post-Soviet space; political Islam movements in the Soviet successor states; and geopolitics in Eurasia. A National Fellow at the Hoover Institute in 1998-1999, Walker received his PhD in Political Science from Columbia University in 1992; he has an MA from the Paul Nitze School of Advanced International Studies (1986) and a BA from Harvard (1977).

Andrew Wilson is Reader in Ukrainian Studies at University College London and a Senior Policy Fellow at the European Council on Foreign Relations, and therefore an advisor to many EU governments. His book *Ukraine Crisis: What It Means for the West* was published by Yale in 2014. He has worked extensively on the comparative politics of the post-Soviet states since 1990. His other books include *Belarus: The Last European Dictatorship* (2011), *The Ukrainians: Unexpected Nation* (3rd edition, 2009), *Ukraine's Orange Revolution* (2005), and *Virtual Politics: Faking Democracy in the Post-Soviet World* (2005). He can be contacted at: andrew.wilson@ecfr.eu

Stephen Whitefield is Professor of Politics in the Department of Politics and International Relations, and Fellow in Politics at Pembroke College, University of Oxford. He is the author of *Industrial Power and the Soviet State* (OUP, 1993) and, with Robert Rohrschneider (Kansas University), of *The Strain of Representation: How Parties Represent Diverse Voters in Western and Eastern Europe* (OUP, 2012), as well as many peer-reviewed articles on issues in social and political change and stability in post-Communist Europe. More recently, he has embarked on research on public opinion in Egypt and on the role of emotions in British politics. With Paul Chaisty, he is now working on a project on comparative nationalism in contemporary Russia and Ukraine.

Note on Indexing

E-IR's publications do not feature indexes due to the prohibitive costs of assembling them. However, if you are reading this book in paperback and want to find a particular word or phrase you can do so by downloading a free e-book version of this publication in PDF from the E-IR website.

When downloaded, open the PDF on your computer in any standard PDF reader such as Adobe Acrobat Reader (pc) or Preview (mac) and enter your search terms in the search box. You can then navigate through the search results and find what you are looking for. In practice, this method can prove much more targeted and effective than consulting an index.

If you are using apps such as iBooks or Kindle to read our e-books, you should also find word search functionality in those.

You can find all of our e-books at: http://www.e-ir.info/publications